Writing for Antiquity

*Damn the age; I will write
for Antiquity!*

CHARLES LAMB
IN 1829

GLYN DANIEL

Writing for Antiquity

AN ANTHOLOGY OF EDITORIALS
FROM *ANTIQUITY*

Introduction by
PHILIP HOWARD

With 28 illustrations

THAMES AND HUDSON

These editorials first appeared in the journal *Antiquity*,
published by Antiquity Publications Ltd © Ruth Daniel
1958, 1960, 1961, 1962, 1963, 1964, 1965, 1966,
1967, 1968, 1969, 1970, 1971, 1972, 1973, 1974, 1975,
1976, 1977, 1978, 1979, 1980, 1981, 1982, 1983, 1984,
1985, 1986.

This anthology © 1992 Thames and Hudson Ltd,
London

First published in the United States in 1992 by
Thames and Hudson Inc., 500 Fifth Avenue, New York,
New York 10110

Library of Congress Catalog Card Number 91-68526

Printed and bound in Yugoslavia

CONTENTS

PREFACE

'Ruth and I saw that the March 1958 number appeared on time: it was a major effort and I had to write an editorial.'

Thus – perhaps with unusual understatement – my husband Glyn Daniel recalled in his memoirs the first issue of *Antiquity* he edited: for O. G. S. Crawford, Editor for thirty years of the quarterly review of archaeology he had founded in 1927, had died suddenly at the end of November 1957, and Glyn was appointed to succeed him. Thereafter he contributed an editorial to every number up to and including September 1986, when the third and present Editor, Christopher Chippindale, took over.

I felt honoured when asked to make this selection of *Antiquity* leaders, as Philip Howard calls them in his generous Introduction; then quickly felt daunted when I realized the task would involve reducing a quarter of a million words by seventy-five per cent to a manageable 60,000. Happily Thomas Neurath – a former pupil of Glyn's and now Managing Director of Thames and Hudson – came to the rescue with a first culling, Paul Bahn cut further (and made the index), and Frank Collieson prepared copy, read proofs, and – with Charles Lamb's help – provided a title for the book. Their selection from Glyn's editorials accurately reflects the style and balance of the originals, the amount of space devoted to recurring themes, and above all the passions and prejudices of their author. I am enormously grateful to them.

The Flying Stag   RUTH DANIEL
Cambridge
November 1991

INTRODUCTION

Most journalism is ephemeral, here today, and lining for the budgerigar cage tomorrow. That is what the words journalism, ephemeral, and newspaper proclaim, with their meanings sticking up through their etymology like menhirs through the turf. Editorials or leaders, as we call them in the trade, are no different from the rest, except that, according to market research, for what it is worth (not a lot), they are read by only a small fraction of readers. The art of writing a good leader is to tell the reader what he thinks, not what you think. It is caviare to the general. Accordingly, a collection of leaders between hard covers might seem a contradiction in terms, or a category mistake, as hopeless a project as trying to catch a falling star, or telling me where all past years are. (In fact, if you had to find somebody to attempt such impossible feats, Glyn Daniel is the name that comes to mind.) But not all leaders are so short-lived. Some have brought down governments and shaken the pillars of the Establishment. The leaders collected here did something more useful and long-lasting than those worthy objects. They changed the way we look at the world, and added to the gaiety as well as the civility of nations. These are leaders made to last. It is an education as well as an entertainment to have them available on the shelf and bedside table, as well as in the archives.

They were written over nearly thirty years by one of the most influential men of our time. (Glyn would have smiled and made a deprecating mouth to read that.) He was also one of the most urbane and delightful of men. The leaders were written in the quarterly review of archaeology founded in 1927, called *Antiquity*, which Glyn edited from 1958 to 1986. This might sound as dry as Oxyrhynchus dust to ignorant outsiders or men from Mars, of interest to professional archaeologists maybe, but of little matter to that veteran man on the Clapham omnibus, whose origin in idiom is the kind of puzzle that would have amused our author. *Antiquity* and its leaders under Glyn Daniel helped to turn archaeology from a hobby for eccentrics and pirates into a great academic discipline and − through his television appearances as well − a mass popular enthusiasm. They formed our contemporary enthusiasm for our heritage and roots. They made archaeology a serious and almost embarrassingly popular subject for undergraduates to study at Cambridge and other universities. In the long eye of history, these tidal shifts in public sensibility are more important and interesting than the rise and fall of governments. When scholars come to write the cultural and intellectual history of our time, they will record the vast increase in our backward-looking sensibility about our past, and our roots, and our archaeology, and our environment. Glyn Daniel will be one of the great names in this tidal change, the imaginative academic and brilliant practitioner of what he called *haute vulgarisation*, the mixture of education and entertainment in his writing, and his television, and mass communication.

So there is a fair amount of archaeology in these leaders. There would be, wouldn't there, in a magazine called *Antiquity*? There is golden treasure about finds and digs, hypotheses and controversies, forgeries and fakes. Glyn was always fascinated by the wilder shores of his beloved subject, and as a serious as well as a humorous scholar, he was a hammer of the bogus and the fraudulent. He could be ferocious.

But he was the opposite of a narrow scholar who cannot see out of the walls of his little trench. So, as well as a witty running commentary and controversy on the archaeological issues since the Second World War, these leaders embrace and enjoy the other enthusiasms and quirks of this many-sided man: the French countryside, museums and government policy, five capital rules for lecturers (which I, a chaotic and incoherent lecturer, when forced to perform, keep trying to follow), bogus Druids at Stonehenge, the pleasures of receiving abusive letters addressed to the editor, rejection slips used by Chinese journals, the love of good food and drink and the good company that goes with them. He helped to have archaeology recognized as one of the important humanities, and he was the most humane of men. *Homo sum; humani nil a me alienum puto.* Although his speciality was the distant past, his eyes were also insatiably interested in the present. There was nothing and nobody he did not find interesting. That is why these leaders go into a division above everyday journalism. They are in the tradition of the old English literary form of the essay, scribbled out against a deadline by Sam Johnson and Charles Lamb and Chesterton for the delight of their contemporaries and us as well today. They mature with age, like Glyn's claret. If you enjoy reading a witty and wise mind at work (which is one of the chief pleasures of reading), you will enjoy these leaders, even if you cannot tell Carchemish from carbon dating. This is a wonderful collection in the best traditions of passionate essay-writing, the higher journalism as Glyn would say in his self-mocking way.

It is a perilous business to straddle the two worlds of scholarship and journalism. The journos think you must be tightly buttoned up in your boring pedantry. The academics look down their noses at you as having sold out to the yahoos. Both are secretly jealous of this Icarus of two worlds. And yet it is worthy work to transmit the latest thoughts of scholars to the mass public. Unless it is done, both public and scholars perish. There have always been good scholars and good popularizers. You can count those who can do both in a generation on the fingers of one hand. In these days, when scholarship and science have flown out into the stratosphere of specialization, far beyond the ken of ordinary people, the man who can straddle the two worlds without doing the splits is a prince. And he pays the price. When Glyn Daniel died too early in 1986, a notably mean and bitchy obituary was written about him by a former colleague in *The Times*, alas. He could not forgive Glyn for having been such a popular and honest celebrity. Of course, the bitching was at once corrected by the great and good archaeologists of the world. But it shocked me, because it showed the perils that a scholar runs when he tampers with the popular.

I had known about Glyn Daniel since I started to take an interest in the big world outside. *Animal, Vegetable, Mineral?* was my favourite television programme, as it was for millions of others in the 1950s. I admired the dapper and bespectacled chairman in his bow-tie, and looked forward to his passages of arms with the colder figure of Mortimer Wheeler. When I grew up, I wanted to be as nonchalantly learned, and witty, and at ease with life as he. (Failed again, Howard.) Later I had friends and acquaintances who were pupils of Glyn's, and was amazed and envious to hear them speak of him as a contemporary friend, who taught them about wine, and travel, and good manners, and how to cope with the little disturbances of life. He sounded the ideal tutor. He was clearly a great teacher.

I met him in person far too late at a dinner of the *Ad Eundem* club, to which I had just been elected, with some trepidation. The *Ad Eundem* (from *Ad Eundem Gradum* ... , used in the incorporation of Oxford/Cambridge degrees) was founded in the 1860s by reformist members of Oxford and Cambridge who wanted to throw their universities open to the nation irrespective of creed or race. This overdue reform was achieved by the Tests Act of 1871. Today the *Ad Eundem* consists of ten resident members of Oxford and ten of Cambridge, and ten graduates from each place who have gone out into the cold world outside. We dine once a term alternately in Oxford and Cambridge. There are no speeches, just good conversation. Today, *mirabile dictu*, we have women members, a revolution that was warmly supported by Glyn, though not by all the older members.

The resident members tend to be masters and mistresses, presidents and wardens of colleges. We work our way around the great houses of Oxbridge Academe, eating and drinking like sumo wrestlers, because each host or hostess in turn is using the occasion to show off the superior merits of her or his particular college. Glyn was the Cambridge secretary of the *Ad Eundem* for twenty years, as well as Steward of his beloved St John's from 1946 to 1955. This meant that the dinner of the *Ad Eundem* when it came round to St John's was something else (though I would not wound other members of the club by saying so in public). I arrived off the train in this alien university in a rush from the word laboratory, and found myself, imperfectly dressed in dinner jacket, with paper clips instead of the studs I had forgotten, in the combination room of St John's, a beautifully panelled Tudor gallery with long candle-lit table and impeccably (well, better than me) black-tied dons. Gulp. Then Glyn appeared and made me laugh and took charge and put me at ease. He liked people. We should have met earlier. And we had many rousing and hilarious *Ad Eundem* dinners after that, but (for Bacchus' sake don't tell the others) none as grand and as merry as those in St John's.

Glyn Daniel was born on 23 April 1914 in the schoolhouse of Lampeter Velfrey in what was then Pembrokeshire and is now part of Dyfed. His father was the village schoolmaster. He inherited the best kind of Welsh genes, including a love of learning for its own sake, eloquent loquacity, and a belief that a man's a man for a' that. His interest in archaeology and the backward-looking angle were kindled at Barry County School through an eccentric and brilliant headmaster. Always look for an unusual teacher in the childhood of a great man. He went on to University College, Cardiff, and then found his second home at St John's, Cambridge, where he was awarded first-class honours with distinction in archaeology and anthropology. He had just been elected a Fellow of John's and found his obvious niche as a baby don and the best kind of Cambridge academic, when the war shattered his career. Because of his service with the Cambridge OTC, he was offered a commission in the Green Howards. But it seemed a waste of his particular talents. So he went for a walk on the Backs, and then wrote a letter to the Air Ministry asking if they had any use for a person trained in geography and archaeology with reasonable competence in the interpretation of air photographs. A letter by return of post asked him to attend an interviewing board at the Air Ministry immediately. For once the services recognized a square peg for a square hole, and signed him up. He spent the war as an intelligence officer with the RAF. He was mentioned in despatches during a three-year stint in charge of photo-interpretation in India and South-East Asia, and rose to Wing Commander.

Glyn's war work interlocked with the new science of archaeology from the air by photography. But by far the most important thing that happened during the wasted war years was that he met and fell in love with and married Ruth Langhorne, a WAAF officer, daughter of another headmaster, and, of all things, an Oxford graduate. They were married, according to Glyn, 'to my eternal happiness and joy', and it is impossible to exaggerate the importance of Ruth in Glyn's subsequent career. They were a formidable and enchanting team. Behind every great man, look for the woman who does the editing, washes the socks, and whispers in his ear, like the slave in the chariot beside the Roman triumphing conqueror, 'don't take yourself too seriously'. Not that there was ever any danger of that with Glyn.

After the war, he and Ruth came home to Cambridge. Glyn was appointed a lecturer in archaeology, then Disney Professor, then Emeritus Professor. As well as being a fine teacher, he was also a prolific writer. His great academic interests were the mysterious megaliths of western Europe, and the history and development of archaeology as a serious discipline. In his brilliantly condensed *Short History of Archaeology* he showed how archaeology, which began as looting works of art, as Mummius did at Corinth, gradually changed to careful excavation and then to deliberately planned excavation to solve particular problems. Glyn wrote: 'It is the unfolding achievement of man, an achievement which is part of the patrimony of us all, that makes the study of the awareness of this past so interesting and so relevant.' He and Ruth turned *Antiquity* into a model for learned journals, punctilious about truth and facts, but taking the broad and humane view of history. He taught us that archaeology is not just another human science, but our family story to show how we became (fairly) civilized creatures. His work on television as the first television don was as important, in its own way, for bringing to the public the excitement of his subject, and the notion that the past is alive and relevant for all of us.

Give them a chance, and the English are frighteningly philistine and mercenary and snobbish people. It did us a power of good to have a gregarious Welshman who was also an eminent scholar, a man of wit and imagination. Enoch Powell, his wartime colleague in India, said of him: 'Glyn was an apolaustic man, somebody with the gift of life and of knowing that he enjoys it.' Since Glyn has gone, it seems to me, an outsider, that archaeology has split into narrower and warring sects, without Glyn's broad and humane vision.

This is not the place to write Glyn's obituary. You can read about his life, if you want, in his characteristically fizzy memoirs, *Some Small Harvest*, and in the *festschrift* for his retirement from the Disney chair, *Antiquity and Man*, with a foreword by the Prince of Wales, another of Glyn's devoted pupils. I seldom agree with anything that the Prince of Wales says about the English language, or architecture, or alternative medicine. But the high seriousness combined with *haute vulgarisation* with which he makes his points was learned at the feet of the master. Only a pupil of Glyn's would take so much pleasure in potting at Establishment cows.

Here we have a small selection of his leaders for *Antiquity*. They are learned and accessible and funny, particularly when they are laying into sacred cows such as the bogus Druids. They give a brilliant aerial survey of the years in which archaeology turned into a grown-up subject, and one of the queens of the humanities. They are of just the right length for bedside or bathroom reading. For those of us who loved Glyn they are a memorial that brings tears to our eyes, as we recognize that unique voice from the past. But for any young scholar who wants to see how to write deadly serious stuff without being pompous or obscure, and for any young journalist who wants to learn how to write compulsively readable stuff without fudging or twisting from the highest standards, they are essential, copybook reading. For the rest of us, they are such fun. And, as Glyn demonstrated by his life, that is no small merit.

PHILIP HOWARD

ANTHOLOGY OF EDITORIALS

March 1958

❦ This, the 125th number of ANTIQUITY, is the first issue which does not contain from the pen of O. G. S. Crawford some of those Editorial Notes which, for the last thirty years, have enlivened our reading at the beginning of each quarter and endeared the late Editor to us all. As he sent the December 1957 Editorial Notes to press Crawford had just heard of the death of Gordon Childe, and wrote: 'He will be mourned by archaeologists all over the world, and not least by the writer of these words, who had known him for over thirty years.' In the same week as these words were being published the writer of them was buried in Nursling Churchyard. He died in his sleep during the night of Thursday/Friday, 28/9 November. That evening he had returned home from giving evidence at a public enquiry held by the Minister of Town and Country Planning in Southampton about Southampton Corporation's proposals for the replanning of the city. He was there as President of the Friends of Old Southampton and had handed to the Ministry Inspector his own plan of medieval Southampton.

It has not been the practice of ANTIQUITY to devote any pages to obituary notices − to what the French, in a phrase that always seems peculiarly appropriate to archaeological journals, call *nécrologie*. If it had been so, this issue would be full of praise of the dead, for 1957 saw what seems to a member of a younger generation a holocaust of great men who had founded and practised modern archaeology. It suffices here to mention only Professor Seán Ó Ríordáin, Dr J. F. S. Stone, Dr Paul Jacobstahl, Dr Charles Seltman, Dr George Leisner, Professor A. J. B. Wace, and Professor Gordon Childe, as well as Crawford himself, to show what a loss good scholarship and sound learning have sustained in the last twelve months.

We are happy to be able to publish a photograph of Crawford [Plate 1], taken by Mr Irwin Scollar, on the Roman road from Southampton to the Isle of Wight as it crosses Beaulieu Heath. Mr Scollar writes of Crawford: 'He was, as you know, very shy about posing for photographs, and I obtained this one through the ruse of asking him to step into the photo of the road to give it scale.' The photograph was taken in July 1954, and shows the late Editor as many knew him and as all will like to remember him.

Crawford left no mandate as to who was to succeed him in the very considerable and worth-while task of editing the journal he had started in 1927 at the age of forty-one. In *The Times* for 31 December 1957, there appeared this letter from H. W. Edwards, the publisher of ANTIQUITY:

Sɪʀ,—In the obituary of Dr O. G. S. Crawford in your columns on 30 November it is recalled how he had founded ANTIQUITY as a quarterly review of archaeology in 1927, and had edited it for thirty years. In that time it achieved an international status as a vehicle for archaeological studies and interests and, as its publisher, I have received many inquiries as to its future.

While appreciating the essentially personal character of Crawford's editorship, a number of leading archaeologists have agreed that its continuance is highly desirable and Dr Glyn Daniel, of St John's College, Cambridge, has consented to become its new Editor. He will be assisted as advisory editors by Professor Gerhard Bersu, Dr G. H. S. Bushnell, Professor M. E. L. Mallowan, Professor Stuart Piggott, and Sir Mortimer Wheeler, and publication will continue without a break.

Although Crawford did not approve of new-fangled devices like telephones, typewriters and motor cars, he had kept neat records of his plans for articles and reviews in his own clear hand.

June 1958

❧ We once asked Dr Bernabó Brea why he dedicated his *Sicily before the Greeks* to Gordon Childe, and he replied: 'Because I did not begin to understand European prehistory until I had read *The Dawn* and *The Danube*.' How true this was for so many people, who learnt, in the twenties and thirties, when they learnt post-Palaeolithic prehistory, Childe's prehistory.

The great puzzle of Childe at all times was to what extent he was a Marxist (or a Marrist) and to what extent he paid lip-service to an Outsider philosophy. He used to complain in public at breakfast in hotels that there was no *Daily Worker* available for him to read, although he had ordered *The Times* to be delivered to his bedroom with his morning tea. To what extent was his avowed love for Russia and his intellectual contortions in *Scotland before the Scots* a pose? He has himself described his post-Oxford job in Australia as 'a sentimental excursion into Australian politics'; his Marxism/Marrism was also a sentimental excursion into the use of new archaeological and historical models. It was, most certainly, no conscious pose, for as 'Retrospect' so clearly shows, Gordon Childe was always deliberately seeking the answers to historical problems. [Eleven of ANTIQUITY's retrospective essays were published in 1989 as *The Pastmasters*.]

For a while he sought them in the works of Russian prehistorians and we remember vividly the delight with which he would quote the passage from Mongait's 'The Crisis in Bourgeois Archaeology', which has now been made available to all of us in Mikhail Miller's *Archaeology in the U.S.S.R.* (London, 1956):

Bourgeois archaeology, like history, is distinguished by extreme idealism (A. Goldenweiser). The English historian Collingwood goes even further . . . and Daniel follows after Taylor. . . . Contemporary bourgeois archaeologists serve the political aims of their governments. . . . More and more often even the scholars who are hostile to us are obliged to turn to the achievements of Soviet Scholarship. . . . Among bourgeois scholars there are not only our ideological enemies, there are also progressive scholars who are friends of our country and who understand very well the universal significance of our science. One of these persons is . . . Gordon Childe. Childe has not yet succeeded in overcoming many of the errors of bourgeois science. But he understands that scientific truth is in the socialist camp and is not ashamed to call himself a pupil of Soviet archaeologists.

Of one thing we can be sure: Childe's attitude to Soviet archaeological scholarship changed during his lifetime. He had been asked to write a volume on Russia for the series of books entitled 'Ancient Peoples and Places', and wrote in the last few days of August 1957 to the editor of that series:

I gather you're still hoping to get a book on Russian prehistory out of me. But you won't. . . . Even if one did explore the unpublished collections in remote museum magazines . . . I shouldn't find the evidence to produce a coherent story that would convince me, for I don't believe it yet exists. One cannot just enumerate a number of archaeological 'facts' in any old order; they must be set at least in a chronological frame. But the relative and absolute chronology for the neo- and palaeometallic stages is just hopelessly vague. The official Russian schemes are really guesses that do not even attract, still less convince me. Passek's division of Tripolye is terribly subjective and I see no reason why Tripolye A (whatever it is) should be put nearer 3000 than 2000 BC. An equal uncertainty affects the absolute dating of the Kuban culture. . . . I don't feel inclined to choose between such divergent guesses without convincing evidence. And I think to publish one guess, however often its guesswork character be repeated, is positively harmful and misleading. Yet the choice must be made in arranging the material for a book and the arrangement is thus the assertion of one hypothesis that no amount of reservations will banish from the reader's mind. . . . Until there be evidence to support one well-grounded hypothesis on the main issues a book on prehistoric Russia would be premature and misleading. We may expect C14 dates to resolve the major issues. But a summary of the Russians' guesses, as though they were facts, à la Hančar, is worse than useless.

We publish these words not only because they are intrinsically interesting, but because they are written by a man who wrote *Scotland before the Scots*. The great value of Childe's retrospective essay is that it shows the mental adventure of one of the most distinguished and learned of prehistorians, and shows how he ventured sentimentally and seriously into Marxism and ventured away again. The comments which he wrote in the last few years of his life (and which we have quoted) on Russian prehistory are devastating.

❦ These words are being written in the eastern marches of Finland and the view from our window over the famous Imatra rapids shows four factories – two in Finland and two in Russia. It is even more ridiculous to draw these hair-line frontiers in archaeology than it is to do so in the modern world – because the modern world demands political entities and affiliations, and in the study of the prehistoric past we have no affiliations. The prehistoric past is illiterate, anonymous and unpolitical. We are all, whether we be in Leningrad or Peking or Harvard or Oxford, studying the same problems, and the nature of our results is an index not only of our knowledge but of our objectivity. It is to the enduring fame of Gordon Childe that his work and his worth were uncurtained, and that the whole world has been the wiser for his scholarship (as for his scholarly adventures) as it is the sadder for his death. Here was a truly great man who did not know how great was his scholarship and his influence, and who was not fully aware from time to time of the ideological camps into which his scholarship was leading him. We mourn his passing and hope that his greatest monument to scholarship and to the revolution in European prehistory associated with his work, namely *The Dawn of European Prehistory*, will be, from time to time, brought up to date and kept in print. But we realize that as scholarship intensifies, there must be very few who will have both the broad vision and the detailed knowledge which Gordon Childe combined in such an excellent, endearing and authoritative way. [Plate 11 shows Childe and Stuart Piggott together in 1952.]

December 1958

❦ Rouffignac is now coming again into the news as more and more archaeologists are able to visit it, and see for themselves the disputed paintings and engravings about which there was such a furore when they were first 'discovered' by Professor Nougier and Monsieur Romain Robert in 1956. The cave has been equipped with electric light and a railway, and by Christmas (or at latest February) it will be possible to take a seat in a miniature train and travel along the winding galleries while lights pick out the paintings in the Galerie Henri Breuil and elsewhere. The speech of Professor Nougier describing the discovery of the Rouffignac paintings and engravings has now been made available in the *Compte rendu* of the Poitiers-Angoulême Congrès Préhistorique de France, the Abbé Breuil has published a full account of his analysis of the site (*Gallia*, 1957, fascicule 3), Nougier and Robert have written a book which is now available in French and English, and Pierret has published his *Précisions sur Miremont*. We print below a review of the Nougier–Robert book and of Pierret by Dr Dorothy Garrod, who brings to the question of Rouffignac a lifetime of expert study of Palaeolithic art, and whose views will command the highest respect.

Miss Garrod served on the International Commission which studied the Glozel forgeries and it is worth thinking back over Glozel at the present moment. *L'affaire Glozel* and *l'affaire Rouffignac* have much in common, most of all in the passionate over-advocacy of distinguished scholars. Many French archaeologists were convinced of the authenticity of the Glozel finds, as was most of the learned world convinced of the authenticity of Piltdown Man. The late Editor of ANTIQUITY suspected Glozel from the beginning and ended a remarkable article in the second number of this journal with the words: *We conclude by repeating our opinion that the inscriptions, the engravings, and the majority of the other finds are forgeries, and that those who believe in their authenticity have been the victims of a hoax.*

L'affaire Rouffignac, like all tales of disputed antiquities, has four aspects. There is first – though it ought to be last – the subjective judgement of expert art-historians, archaeologists and artists. Secondly there is technical evidence. Thirdly, there is the history of the site, particularly the gossip of the last twenty years. And lastly, there is the treatment of the issue by the protagonists. It is this last issue which comes first in the eyes and mind of a jury in an English court – the demeanour and character of defendants and witnesses. If any book could do harm to the defence it is *Rouffignac ou La Guerre des Mammouths*, as Miss Garrod so clearly shows.

Four members of the Cambridge University Speleological Society visited Rouffignac on 31 March 1939; they spent a considerable time in the cave and were themselves keen, and fresh from examining the known painted caves near Les Eyzies. Yet they saw nothing, as Martel had seen nothing during the eighteen hours he spent in the cave in 1893. It does need saying clearly that it is not difficult to see the Rouffignac paintings; they are clear and boldly done. It seems highly improbable that intelligent visitors from 1893 to 1939 could have missed them – if they were there. The evidence of people like Martel, the 1939 Cambridge speleologists, as well as the clear assertions of recentness made by men like William Martin and

Bernard Pierret and Séverin Blanc – men who would only have been too glad to discover an authentic Palaeolithic cave in the Dordogne – suggests that Rouffignac is, to put it mildly, a 'salted' site. It looked that way to the present Editor of ANTIQUITY in 1956, and a further visit in September of this year suggested that one might say of at least some of the Rouffignac paintings, in Dr Crawford's words, that 'those who believe in their authenticity have been the victims of a hoax'. We may be proved wrong; what is certain, as Dr Garrod argues, is that there should be an impartial non-archaeological enquiry into the history of Rouffignac. We ourselves have been convinced of this ever since it was realized that some of the paintings 'discovered' in 1956 were clearly shown in Pierret's *Le Périgord Souterrain* published in 1953. Pierret now says that they 'appeared' between September and December 1948 and this statement alone should be rigorously examined before anyone writes any more about the paintings as authentic and Palaeolithic.

And if it should be thought that there is too much in these Editorial Notes and in this number of ANTIQUITY about forgery and detection, our excuse is that it is the December number and that Christmas is the season of fun and games, *farces et attrapes*, false red noses and long white beards. Whenever I think of Glozel I think of Mistinguett's cruel sketch in the Moulin Rouge when, wearing a long white beard, she excavated busily, triumphantly unearthed a chamber pot, and deciphered on its sides the names of several distinguished archaeologists.

December 1960

❧ These words are being written in the bright September sunshine on the terrace of a café in Saint-Véran in the French Alps (Saint-Véran in the arrondissement of Briançon in the Hautes-Alpes; there is another village of the same name in the Côtes-du-Nord). Saint-Véran is the highest village in Europe and it is a surprise to those amateurs of records who find *The Guinness Book of Records* such an entertaining bedside book, that the highest European village is in France (just as the highest road in Europe is the Col d'Izère in France: it is 2770 m. and the Stelvio is only 2760). The height of Saint-Véran is given in guide books as between 1990 and 2040 m.; it is a village on a slope and perhaps the best datum to take is that the top of the church belfry is a trigonometrical point and is 2071 m. This picturesque village, well over 6000 ft. up in the Alps (and this is a fair figure for those who are not prepared to sit on the trigonometrical point on the belfry), has, according to that bible of tourism, the *Guide Michelin*, 422 inhabitants.

Its wooden chalets, haylofts, granaries and ovens are set in five separate groups to combat fire risks and in each group the houses are set *en espalier* to catch all the available sunshine. The area was occupied as early as the Middle Bronze Age (*Dictionnaire Archéologique de la Gaule*).

We walked through the village, noting the stocks of wood and hay stored underneath the houses and the way in which each house was a unit of animal quarters, fuel and forage store, and house for human beings. But there were no animals anywhere to be seen; and yet from the lingering fresh sweet-sour smell of cows and the *gaz de fumier* rising from the newly rotting dung heaps, it was obvious the animals must be somewhere. Consumed with curiosity we enquired at the post office-cum-village shop (which sold everything from skis and suncream to tinned tunny and *pâté de foie gras*). The answer was a simple one, and yet not one that appears in the classic studies of transhumance like those of Vidal de la Blache, Jean Brunhes, and Pierres Deffontaines. Here was not normal transhumance or even 'inverted transhumance' in the terminology of the human geographers, and certainly not the complicated fourfold transhumantic rhythm so brilliantly described by Jean Brunhes in the famous Chapter VII of his *Géographie Humaine*, where he seems to give the inhabitants of the Val d'Anniviers no peace in their complicated movements from pasture to pasture.

The fascination of Saint-Véran is that it is in itself a *montagnette*, a *mayen*, a *stavolo*; but one that is permanently occupied. Here is the *Hafod uchaf* which is never deserted. Like a Finnish farm, when the snows come, the animals and humans bed down – the animals to sleep, the humans to work precious stones and to carve wood. In the spring the sheep are taken up to the summer pastures on higher slopes, and return in the autumn from their long transhumance. The cattle of Saint-Véran on the other hand are taken out by day *en masse* and pastured on the high alps. Curious, we walked out from Saint-Véran up the valley towards the Chapel of Our Lady of Clausis, where, on 16 July each year, the devout from the French parishes of the Queyras, and the Italians from the Varaita meet to celebrate the Festival of *Notre Dame du Mont Carmel*. We walked for a mile and a half along a road past quarries and rock cuttings from which came the green marble used to make the base of the tomb of Napoleon I in Les Invalides in Paris. And, suddenly, rounding a corner, there were a hundred and fifty cows grazing in the high pastures, guarded by an old crone knitting and nodding to the music of the cow bells.

It seemed, in a moment, living prehistory. We ought, in our interpretation of the prehistoric archaeological material of the Neolithic and Chalcolithic, at least, and probably the Bronze Age as a whole, to think more and more in terms of the semi-pastoral, semi-nomadic transhumantic patterns which we know to exist at the present day in so many parts of Mediterranean Europe. Colonel Louis has emphasized this point in his studies of the prehistory of the Languedoc. It is possible that the 'dolmens' on the *causses* of southern France are the tombs of transhumantics who lived in the winter in places like Fontbouïsse. And is it not more than possible that the *drailles* are transhumance roads dating from at least 2500 BC? Here is a line of research for archaeologists and historians interested in the economy and ecology of the 3rd millennium BC in Western and Mediterranean Europe.

June 1961

[*An exhibition of forgery and deception had opened in the Department of Prints and Drawings in the British Museum.*]

❦ A former distinguished member of the staff of the British Museum, when given a preview of some of the exhibits as they were being assembled, said 'What fun it is when someone takes an enormous amount of trouble to be really naughty', and in a recent BBC talk, Mr Cecil Gould, of the National Gallery, discussed the role of what he called 'super-annuated schoolboy naughtiness' in the creation of fakes. There are some who have suggested that the Piltdown hoax started as such a piece of superannuated schoolboy naughtiness by a member of that fascinating group of young men led by Horace de Vere Cole who appeared here, there and everywhere – in Cambridge, in Portsmouth, in Piccadilly, variously disguised as the Shah of Persia, the Sultan of Zanzibar, or roadmenders. Mr Gould turned a pretty phrase when he said 'A fake only begins to be a fake when someone says it is genuine', and we were reminded of the American impresario who wanted to hire Rouchomowsky and the Tiara of Saitaphernes for a tour of American music halls, but only on condition that the French Government who had bought this piece of period jewellery in all good faith as antique, would give him a certificate that he was getting 'the genuine fake'. Mr Cecil Gould's talk has now been printed in *The Listener* under the title of 'The Ethics of Faking'. What were the ethics, and what the truth of the astonishing Piltdown affair? Is all yet known that can be known? Mr L. F. Salzman writes reminding us that this is the fiftieth anniversary of Charles Dawson's 'discovery' of Piltdown Man and says 'As 3 May is the "Feast of the Invention of the Holy Cross", I feel we might inaugurate a "Feast of the Invention of the unholy cross between Man and Monkey": April 1st seems a suitable date.'

Of course there are many reasons for forgery apart from schoolboy naughtiness, and while there is hope of monetary gain, and the existence of wealthy private collectors for whom the fact of ownership gives rise to passionate wilful thinking, we must be prepared for forgeries and deceptive copies in the whole field of art and archaeology from Palaeolithic Mural Art to Modern Painting, from Glozel to Van Meegeren (there is a 'genuine' Van Meegeren, the only one in England, and lent by the Courtauld Institute, in this exhibition).

We should mention here two recent books on forgery. The first is by Guy Isnard and is called *Faux et imitations dans l'art* (Paris, 1959), and a translation of Frank Arnau's *Kunst der Fälscher der Kunst* (Düsseldorf, 1959) just published in Great Britain. Arnau has a particularly illuminating and fair account of Malskat's work at Schleswig and Lübeck, and of the Fey-Malskat picture 'factory' which, after the end of the Second World War, poured out Barlachs, Chagalls, Utrillos, and Henri Rousseaus. Arnau has no dedication to his book, but merely prints before his foreword these two sentences: 'According to the enlarged edition of his *oeuvre* catalogue, Corot painted over 2,000 pictures. Of these more than 5,000 are in the United States.' (Compare Sonia Cole's *Counterfeit*: 'New York customs statistics revealed that over 103,000 Corots were imported from Europe over a period of twenty years during the present century! An eccentric old Frenchman bought up 2,000 such.')

September 1961

❧ Two very controversial archaeological issues have been much discussed in the British Press in the last few months. The first is the suggestion – not made now for the first time – that the Elgin Marbles should be returned to Greece; the second that Stonehenge should be prevented from becoming a centre of neo-Druidism and hooliganism at Midsummer. The controversy about the return of the Elgin Marbles was started on this occasion by Mr Francis Noel Baker, M.P., who asked the Prime Minister if the Government would return the marbles to Greece. Mr Macmillan's refusal was backed up by a leader in *The Times*. A heated discussion followed. On one side it was said that as we had rescued the marbles we had a right to keep them, and that they are better preserved in a museum than being left on the Acropolis at Athens. (Those left on the Parthenon have badly weathered, true, but does it have to be a museum in London?) On the other side it was argued that the marbles were an integral part of the Parthenon and that our title to them was uncertain since they were removed with Turkish, not Greek, permission.

The facts about the removal of the marbles from Athens to Bloomsbury are not in dispute. The Earl of Elgin was Ambassador to Constantinople from 1799 to 1803. He very wisely used his mission for archaeological research and from 1800 onwards had a band of artists drawing, measuring, recording, and taking casts of the antiquities of Greece. In his *Greek Studies in England, 1700–1830*, M. L. Clarke writes, 'At first Elgin's intention was only to make drawings and casts, not to take away any of the sculpture, but as he learnt more of conditions in Athens and saw the constant destruction and defacement to which the antiquities were subject, he changed his plan, and determined to remove as much of the sculpture as he could.' In 1801 the Porte gave him a firman which included permission to take away 'any pieces of stone with inscriptions or figures'. The Elgin collection included, in addition to the great majority of the sculptures from the Parthenon, four reliefs from the temple of Nike, and one of the Caryatids from the Erechtheum. It might have contained much more. His chaplain, Dr Hunt, when supervising the work of clearing the Caryatid porch of the Erechtheum, wrote to Elgin, 'If your Lordship would come here in a large Man of War, that beautiful little model of ancient art might be transported wholly to England.' Elgin's collection was shipped to England, and in 1807 was displayed in a room at the back of his house in Park Lane; it was bought for the British Museum for £35,000 in 1816.

Elgin himself was quite sure of what he was doing and why; it was to rescue ancient Greek art for posterity. 'The Turks have been continually defacing the heads', he wrote, 'and in some instances they have actually acknowledged to me that they have pounded down the statues to convert them into mortar. It was upon these suggestions and with these feelings that I proposed to remove as much of the sculpture as I conveniently could.' It was clear to him at the beginning of the 19th century, as it appeared clear to many for decades after this, that it was our duty as a nation to collect and house art treasures from other countries too backward or too negligent to look after them themselves. The famous second leader of *The Times* for 4 November 1861, which begins with the passage 'The crowded state of the British Museum has been for a long time the reproach not so much of any particular person or set of persons as of the administrative system under which these vast national treasures are placed ...' contains a splendid passage about the problems of housing in London the treasures of the world:

We have got to lodge Halicarnassus, Cyrene and Carthage and we absolutely know not where to put them. The impending disruption, if not the present feebleness of the Turkish Empire, seems to throw open to us all the many treasures of Asia Minor. Who knows what objects of art may be brought to light by the exertions of a liberal and energetic Government in the whole territory of Naples, where every step the traveller takes is over crumbling ruins of ancient Greek and Roman art? Who can tell what may be found in the bed of the Tiber, from the candlesticks of the Temple of Jerusalem to the masterpieces of PHIDIAS and PRAXITELES? We are going to Mexico: what may we not discover in the halls of the MONTEZUMAS or in the buried treasures of Palenque! Egypt is but half-ransacked, and Arabia and Mesopotamia have still much with which to reward the exertions of an intelligent traveller.

This was 1861 – fifty years after E. Daniel Clarke had exclaimed on finding what he thought was the 'Tomb of Euclid' in Athens, 'Such an antiquity must be for the University of Cambridge, where the name of Euclid is so particularly revered', and the very time when the Mudir of Keneh was stealing Mariette's finds, Belzoni and Drouetti were fighting each other for possession of an obelisk and Rassam was pirating other people's excavations to find Assyrian treasures for the British Museum. We would not do these things now; we now possess and parade an archaeological conscience, the development of which has been studied so interestingly by Seton Lloyd in the last two chapters of his *Foundations in the Dust*.

The real issue is this: does our archaeological conscience work retrospectively to change what we did in the past when viewed in the circumstances of the present? In his *Journey through Albania*, written in 1810, Hobhouse said: 'I have said nothing of the possibility of the ruins of Athens being, in the event of a revolution in the favour of the Greeks, restored and put into a condition capable of resisting the ravages of decay; for an event of that nature cannot, it strikes me, have even entered the head of anyone who has seen Athens and the modern Athenians.' By today Greece has been an independent country for 140 years and a great number of archaeologists have seen 'Athens and the modern Athenians'. It does enter the heads of all of us that the Elgin Marbles might now in justice go back to Athens where they belong and where there is a modern, vigorous nation deeply conscious of its ancient past and aware of the need for conserving and protecting its antiquities.

But if we begin with the Elgin Marbles, where do we stop? The Rosetta Stone must surely by the same token go back to Egypt. Indeed, it has less claim to be in the British Museum than have the Elgin Marbles. Found by accident in 1799 by a French soldier digging near the old Fort Rashid five miles from Rosetta in the Nile Delta, it was taken to Cairo and studied by the scholars of Napoleon's Institut d'Egypte. Later it was placed in the private house of the French General, Jacques-François de Menou. General Menou was forced to capitulate to the British Army in 1801 and the French were ordered to give up all the Egyptian antiquities acquired by them during the previous three years. Attempts were made to keep the Rosetta Stone by saying it was the private property of General Menou and outside the terms of the surrender. But the English General, Lord Hutchinson, insisted on the stone being handed over; it arrived in Portsmouth the following year and was sent to the British Museum, where, wrote Turner in his report on it, 'we hope it will remain for many years...as a glorious trophy of British arms...not captured from a defenceless population, but conquered honourably and according to the rules of warfare'. *Many* years? *How* many years? It is the rules of archaeological warfare that need formulating, and the ethics of the retention of other peoples' archaeological treasures that need thinking out. But with the full knowledge that a logical application of these rules and principles might mean that it is the Louvre and the British Museum which would be half-ransacked!

❦ Stonehenge is our own national affair, and what we do with it and to it is perhaps no direct concern of any other nation. The Greeks are not going to say that, because it may be inspired by Mycenean architecture and may have on it the representation of a Mycenean dagger, Stonehenge should be set up in the Peloponnese. Even the most rabid Welsh nationalist born on the slopes of the Presely mountains is not going to say, 'Give us back our stones.' But the British Government, through its Minister of Works, guards Stonehenge in trust for all posterity. In their Annual Report for 1960 the Ancient Monuments Board for England suggest very clearly to the Minister of Works that all is not well at Stonehenge during the annual Midsummer celebrations. They say to him, 'While we see no objection to you allowing a ceremony to be held, we deprecate the behaviour of some of the large crowd of onlookers and fear the possible harm to the monument. Last summer spectators forced their way through the boundary fence and a large crowd assembled in the centre of the monument. Many individuals climbed the stones to use them as vantage points and outside the boundary visitors parked their cars on prehistoric earthworks. As much of this activity takes place in darkness, we fear that there is a serious risk of accidents to a supremely important monument. There is no excuse for anyone at any time forcing their way through the fences and there should be an absolute prohibition on climbing the stones.'

This report was published just before Midsummer this year and we waited with considerable alarm to learn what happened at Stonehenge at the summer solstice of 1961. We quote from the report in *The Times*: 'Nearly 3000 people, it is estimated, watched the dawn ceremony on this day of longest light. As on previous occasions, unruly elements sought to lessen the dignity of the proceedings by their behaviour. On the lighter side was the man who on being asked by a custodian for his 6d. entry ticket replied that he had not bought one as he was only attending a party in the circle to which he had been invited. More serious was the litter of broken bottles – eight barrowfuls were later removed from the enclosure – and the groups of jeering louts perched on top of the stones. Strenuous efforts by the police kept the dawn ceremony moving, but lack of numbers prevented them from keeping more than a watching brief on earlier antics, which began in the late hours yesterday and continued until after the dawn broke. A strong force of military police was also on duty.'

This is a monstrous, wicked and most undesirable state of affairs and one which the Minister must bring to an end; and certainly by next Midsummer. We see *every* objection to his allowing a ceremony to be held and for two good reasons. The first is that the Ancient Order of Druids has no claim to an association with Stonehenge, and the second that the existence of these strange ceremonies attracts crowds some of whom behave deplorably. We are no spoil-sport and we love the minor faiths that flourish away from the main stream of religion as we love the lunacies that flourish away from the main stream of archaeology; but Dr R. MacGregor-Reid, Chief Druid of the Companions of the Ancient Order of Druids, should be told that, in the best interests of Stonehenge and British archaeology, the Minister of Works can no longer give permission for these grave Midsummer antics. Next June there should be, we suggest, no admission to the monument at Midsummer and a completely adequate guard of civil and military police. After all, Dr MacGregor-Reid and his Druids can do what is done by the Gorsedd of Bards of the Welsh National Eisteddfod, who build their own stone circle in a different place each year.

The Ministry of Works, we understand, is asked each year by the body concerned for permission to hold a ceremony at Stonehenge. The line that has been taken by the department ever since Stonehenge came into its care in 1919 is that any applicants may hold a religious ceremony at the monument provided they pay the appropriate entrance fee and observe the department's general rules. It is understood that in the past forty years quite a number of bodies claiming the name of Druid have sought and received permission on this basis. All these claimants, we feel, should no longer receive this permission, on grounds of archaeology and the conservation of our ancient monuments. We do not expect the Minister and his advisers and staff to evaluate what of religion and what of fantasy, what of truth and what of rubbish, exists in the claims of these bodies. They are all foolish people confusing fact with fiction. If it makes them happy – splendid. But their private happiness must not endanger one of our great prehistoric monuments – a piece of our ancient heritage which it is our duty, from the Minister of Works downwards, to conserve and preserve.

December 1961

☎ The Rouffignac controversy, now more than ever alive, was commented on in the Abbé Breuil's obituary notices in two reputable English daily newspapers. *The Times* of London wrote (24 August 1961): 'The controversy which arose in 1956 over the paintings in the cave of Rouffignac was rather a sad anticlimax to his great achievements in this field: his vehemently held opinion that the paintings were entirely genuine was seriously questioned by many of his colleagues.' And that distinguished French correspondent of what we must now learn to call *The Guardian* was even more outspoken: 'In later life', wrote Darsie Gillie (22 August 1961), 'his fellow prehistorians showed less and less confidence in his opinions. His assignment of the "White Lady" in the Brandberg, south-west Africa, to the second millennium BC on the basis of a comparison with Egyptian and Cretan antiquities (a field in which he was not competent) aroused sharp dissent. The seventeenth century AD has been proposed with perhaps greater probability. He also failed to carry conviction with many competent prehistorians when he declared authentic all the paintings in the Rouffignac caves. When the *Académie des Inscriptions* of which he was a member declined to discuss a communication he made on the subject...he swept out in a memorable whirlwind of soutane. He did not take his seat again for a long time.'

We, in this journal, and elsewhere, have tried for the last few years to suggest that all is not well with Rouffignac and perhaps some other newly discovered caves in the Midi. While the Abbé was alive many of our colleagues kept their views on Rouffignac to themselves: now, we understand, we may hear many things and many points of view. We would think that the time has come for an independent commission on Rouffignac *et al.*, and perhaps also for the French Government to take powers to own all the painted and engraved caves in France, so that there shall be no incentive for private enterprise in these matters – and we use these words 'private enterprise' advisedly. But of course, whereas it is easy to schedule dolmens and hillforts, it is much more difficult to deal with caves. Yet the painted and engraved caves of France and Spain are an international heritage.

Perhaps the most surprising comment on Breuil's death was in *The Sunday Telegraph* for 27 August, in a paragraph entitled 'Painting the Lily' in the 'London Week by Week' feature. This is what it said: 'Many cave-paintings in France owe their fame and authentication entirely to the Abbé Breuil, whose death was announced last week. Some of the most charming at Les Eyzies in the Dordogne are, however, still inaccessible. When I last visited them, I was told they were "closed for re-painting".'

Although we have been assured by the Editor of *The Sunday Telegraph* that this is a correct piece of reporting, we can find no one else who has seen such a notice. If it really existed it no doubt referred to something like the *Château Fort* at Reignac, an interesting attempt to provide a museum of life in Palaeolithic times in the Dordogne, with walls deliberately painted – and very well painted – in Palaeolithic style by a modern artist, and with life-size scenes of men and animals. It certainly is *not* true that any of the Les Eyzies caves are 'still inaccessible'. But of course with even such a trivial example of genuine misapprehension, may a *canard* begin.

It is always difficult to nail a lie, to rub out a *canard*, finally to dismiss unreasonable belief. There is no smoke without fire, we say; and it is perhaps as one of the pleasures of unreason that the desire to be convinced by the fictitious will persist, long after it has been proved that the smoke was merely Scotch mist and that there never was a fire. Such mist is far from being exclusively Scotch: it is an international agent of wish-fulfilment, the acrid tang of which can be savoured only by those prepared to shut their eyes and be led by the nose of faith. Otherwise, how are we to explain the strange story of the alleged Palaeolithic paintings at Bacon's Hole, near the Mumbles in the Gower Peninsula? The facts about this discovery are not in dispute and we are grateful to the present Lord Swansea for permission to quote from his father's notebook and press-cuttings.

In *The Times* for 14 October 1912, under the heading 'The Most Ancient Painting in Britain: A Discovery in Wales', we read: 'The first example in Great Britain of prehistoric cave painting of the kind already familiar to palaeontologists from the caves of the Dordogne, the south of France, the Pyrenees and the peninsula of Spain has recently been discovered on the walls of Bacon's Hole, near the Mumbles, by Professor Breuil and Professor Sollas.' We read how, after a survey of all the caves of Gower, Breuil and Sollas went into Bacon's Hole. 'On entering this, one of the investigators cried, "Les voilà" and the other "There they are".' The article goes on to describe them – a series of red bands – and to say 'a deposit of stalagmite has formed over them and sealed them up, so that none of the paint can be removed by rubbing. . . . Similar bands have been described from the walls of Font de Gaume in the Dordogne. Thus Upper Palaeolithic paintings have been found, and now that they are known to occur in our islands further discoveries may be expected.'

The painted bands in Bacon's Hole were made in 1894 by a man called Johnny Bale from Oystermouth, an interesting character who made a fine Gower rabbit soup. An old Norwegian barque, the *Althea*, outward bound from Swansea with a cargo of anthracite coal, was driven ashore. The salvage firm who bought the wreck of the *Althea* used Bacon's Hole to store their material. Lord Swansea, in his notebook for 17 October 1912, says 'Mr Hodgens...asserted before us that he himself had seen the marks made by a workman with a ship's paint brush about 17 years ago. His firm bought the wreck of the barque *Althea* close by the cave. They used the cave to store salvage and the men often sheltered there from the wet. There was ship's paint there and one man whose name he gave picked up a paint brush on the shore and took it with him, and when larking in the cave, splashed paint at his mates and daubed the wall.'

The Palaeolithic paintings at Bacon's Hole are therefore without any doubt 'Johnny Bale his marks'. This fact was clearly apprehended by the first Lord Swansea, Colonel Morgan and others in October 1912, was widely known, and was well published in *The Cambrian Leader* of 19 and 21 October 1912. It is therefore saddening and surprising, but salutary, to note that in his Huxley Memorial Lecture for 1913 Professor Sollas still proclaimed their authenticity. Miles Burkitt in his *Prehistory* (1925), was, wisely, more cautious: they were 'of unknown age' or 'of any age'. But in 1957, Geoffrey Grigson, in his *Painted Caves*, is deliciously savouring the acrid smoke of the non-existent fire when he describes the cave as perhaps exhibiting 'a very few markings in red ochre which are perhaps Aurignacian...what may be, after all, the only cave painting of the Old Stone Age in Great Britain'. Grigson was impressed by the fact observed by Sollas and Breuil, namely that the marks were covered by a thin glaze of stalagmite. That glaze had formed between 1894 and 1912 and anyone who uses the stalagmitic-cover arguments to authenticate Palaeolithic painting (it is used at Rouffignac) should remember this and should observe the thick stalagmitic manifestations in many of our railway tunnels in western Europe. Johnny Bale is, in a kind of way, a minor hero in the history of archaeology, like Edward Simpson and Marcelino de Sautuola's daughter and the little dog Robot.

☉ We warmly recommended the various bogus Druid and Neo-Druid organizations that lay claim to Stonehenge to build their own stone circles elsewhere (ANTIQUITY, 1961) but we were surprised to learn that at least one of these odd bodies, in connexion with some of their autumnal equinoctial celebrations in Hampstead, had asked for permission to build a stone circle on Primrose Hill. Now it is surely within the rights of anyone to build a stone circle anywhere or to construct a fine transepted gallery grave to receive the remains of himself and his friends and relatives; the intriguing thing about the request of these 'Druids' was their allegation that they wanted to build this circle because there had been one on Primrose Hill in 1792 and the *Gentleman's Magazine* said so.

28

Let us try to nail this lie once for all. There has never been a stone circle on Primrose Hill, and there was not one there in 1792. But first, the account in the *Gentleman's Magazine* for October 1792, under the heading 'Domestic Occurrences' and dated Saturday 23 September: 'This being the day on which the autumnal equinox occurred, some Welsh Bards, resident in London, assembled in congress on Primrose Hill, according to ancient usage.... The wonted ceremonies were observed. A circle of stones formed, in the middle of which was the *Maen Gorsedd*, or altar, on which a naked sword being placed, all the Bards assisted to sheathe it.' Now all this was an invention of Edward Williams (*Iolo Morgannwg*), that remarkable stone mason from the Vale of Glamorgan who mixed so much of a genuine knowledge of the past of Wales with fancies, frauds and false imaginings. And what he set out on Primrose Hill was not a megalithic monument but a circle of pebbles. It was these pebbles he took with him to the Eisteddfod in Carmarthen in 1819 and in the grounds of the Ivy Bush Hotel laid them out as a circle for the Gorsedd of Bards. Those who want to know more about Iolo should consult Elijah Waring's *Recollections and Anecdotes of Edward Williams* (London, 1850) or G. J. Williams's *Iolo Morgannwg* (Cardiff, 1956), with a warning that the latter splendid book stops at 1788 and is written in Welsh.

But the absence of authority for a proper stone circle on Primrose Hill should not deter the Druids or any other unreasonable religious body from constructing megalithic monuments. Stone circles are annually built by the Gorsedd of Bards of the Welsh Eisteddfod. A circle was built on a cliff overlooking the Columbia River at Maryhill (Washington) in the twenties of this century. It is called *Stonehenge* and was erected by Samuel Hill as a World War I memorial. It consists of two circles and two ovals with an altar stone in the centre. We quote from the official description: 'The outer circle has 30 upright stones 16 feet in height, and the inner circle consists of 40 stones 9 feet in height. The ovals consist of five pairs of trilithons ... rising gradually to a height of 28 feet. The center altar stone is 18 feet in length.' We understand from Professor Cohen of Harvard that there is another Stonehenge built in Connecticut after World War II.

Conscious antiquarianism is one thing: Stonehenges in Washington and Connecticut like stockbrokers' Tudor in Surrey are fun, just as the Margate Grotto and all follies are fun. The problem in archaeology is when to stop laughing. It is not fun to make fakes of cave paintings and perhaps, incidentally, fools of genuine and serious archaeologists. But the genuine and serious archaeologists must always be on the look-out for folly, fraud and someone else's fun. And they must always examine the facts. That was the real trouble about Rouffignac: the evidence of discovery and the facts of the affair were not properly studied because it all became involved in the personal act of authentication of the greatest-ever French archaeologist, whose death we mourn.

It would be sad if we allowed a divorce between the subjective judgement of archaeologists and the almost police judgement of facts. Breuil and Sollas never seem to have taken into account the known facts about Bacon's Hole, which would have stopped them from the error of their pronouncements in lectures in Cardiff and London. Lord Swansea wrote in his notebook: 'If one desires to see similar marks there is no need to go down to Gower. There are plenty to be seen in the Swansea dry dock walls against the side of which brushes are cleaned everyday of the week.' We do not need a Maigret for Bacon's Hole, and we no longer need one for Piltdown Man, although the unravelling of that fake made, as Ellery Queen said, the best detective story of the year. But Inspector Maigret should take a few weeks off from the Quai des Orfèvres and sit in the cafés in Dordogne. I can see his thick-set form clutching his pipe as he travels in the railway that runs through Rouffignac. But we can only guess at what he says to Sergeant Lucas when, a glass of *Calvados* in his hand, and a *truffe sous la cendre* ordered for dinner, they exchange experiences as the mist settles on the river, the limestone cliffs fade out of sight, and the whistle of the Agen-Paris train reminds them that the provincial affairs of Périgord are the concern of the whole archaeological world.

December 1962

❧ The Rome Congress of 1962 had one thing in common with all other congresses and conferences we have attended recently – the far too frequent bad standard of lecturing by *congressistes*. This is infuriating because the rules of lecturing are so simple; they are:

1. *Audibility*. Do not begin to speak or go on speaking unless you can be heard by all your audience, and check your audibility after a third and two-thirds of your lecture by thinking about it and lifting your voice.

2. *Brevity*. If you have been asked to speak for an hour prepare a script for fifty minutes. If you have been allotted a half-hour in an international conference prepare a paper of twenty minutes. Fast – too fast – talking is 120 words to a minute. Lecturers with slides rarely achieve more than 80 to 100 words. An hour's lecture should be no more than a spoken script of 5000 to 5500 words. An international congress talk of twenty minutes must be restricted to a spoken script of under 2000 words.

3. *Economy*. Start your lecture with what you want to say, say it and then stop. There is no time for preludes and postludes. Cut, and cut again.

4. *Control*. Never apologize to your audience. The lecturers who say, 'I am sorry I did not have time to get a slide made of this', or 'I'm afraid my drawing of this is very bad' should be shot; and probably will be one day.

5. *Modesty*. You are not being honoured by performing; you are lucky to be asked to give a talk, and if you don't feel this way and observe the rules you won't get asked again.

The trouble is that so few people are ever told how to speak in public to an educated audience. It is quite scandalous, for example, that our British Universities do not run every summer a course for potential or appointed new University teachers on how to teach and how to lecture. It is assumed that public speaking is something everyone can naturally do: yet it is not assumed that one can naturally talk or read or write.

The five rules we have set out are counsels of perfection, perhaps, but then we want in congresses and public places more people achieving these standards. There are of course good excuses which must be respected. The lecturer whose excuse was that his slides were impounded by customs officials because they thought they were obscene would be sympathetically received by an archaeological audience, as was the undergraduate who rushed distraught to his tutor carrying frayed sheets of paper saying, 'Sir, during the night my essay has been partly eaten by marauding mice.' The interference of customs officials and mice in our affairs is fortunately rare. The average lecturer can concentrate on achieving audibility, brevity, economy, control and modesty in the sure hope that his sixth slide is not going to be that of a bearded but naked woman portrayed upside down on a large mushroom. This happened to an acquaintance of ours recently as the result of a bold undergraduate prank. It says much for the skill of this lecturer that, unperturbed, he looked at the slide and then said coolly, 'I think this must be the wrong way up'; and, when it had been adjusted, looked at it with equal coldness and, turning to his audience, said, 'Ladies and gentlemen, I beg your pardon. This illustration should not have been shown to you. It has strayed in from the slides that properly belong to another lecture course of mine. Next please.'

March 1963

❦ The Council for British Archaeology is to be warmly congratulated on organizing a Conference of Editors. It was held in the Institute of

Archaeology of the University of London on Saturday 17 November 1962 under the Chairmanship of Professor C. F. C. Hawkes. It went off with a bang – or rather a series of three bangs when Sir Mortimer Wheeler in his opening remarks in the first lecture said *first* that only one author in ten can supply a manuscript and illustrations in a form wanted by an editor, *second*, that only one editor in twenty knows how to prepare his material for press when he has it satisfactorily from a good author, and *third*, that only one printer in thirty knows how to print the material properly when he has received satisfactory material from author or editor. With this splendid indictment of them the conference of authors, editors and printers got down to discussing the problems of writing, editing, printing and publishing.

June 1963

❧ A birthday which should not go without comment in this journal is that of His Majesty Gustav the Sixth, King of Sweden, of the Goths and the Wends (yes, this is the official title of the King of Sweden) who was eighty on 11 November 1962. King Gustav has been a subscriber to ANTIQUITY since its first issue, and is, as everyone knows, a keen archaeologist. We hope the story on which we were brought up is true, that on one occasion when he was excavating with Oscar Montelius, the future king was told by the great Montelius, 'Young man, if only you did not have another job to go to, you would make a first-rate archaeologist.' (The mythology of archaeology must not be deprived of its good stories: the Abbé Breuil did us a great disservice when he insisted that de Sautuola's daughter had not said *Toros! Toros!* in 1879. If this debunking goes on we shall not be able to believe that Augustus John said 'Still digging?' when Mortimer Wheeler met him in London, and received the reply 'Still sketching?')

September 1963

❧ The public, thwarted at Lascaux, will turn more than ever to Rouffignac. The French Government should now turn its attention to this site. That great French archaeologist, the Abbé Breuil, is now dead; it is now high time for an impartial enquiry into this site. Recently we had occasion to be corresponding with Monsieur Bernard Pierret, now a Professor in a Lycée in Morocco. It was Pierret who published, several years before the 'discovery' by Nougier and Robert, the frieze of rhinoceroses. In a recent letter which he has kindly allowed us to publish Pierret sets out clearly his testimony, and it is this: (1) there were paintings when he and his colleagues first visited Rouffignac in 1945, and he particularly recalls those on the Grand Plafond, (2) during their visits to the cave between 1945 and 1949 paintings appeared progressively and in places where they knew that the walls had hitherto been blank – one of these areas was the wall with the frieze of rhinoceroses, and (3) when, in 1949, Pierret and his colleagues discussed the paintings with Séverin Blanc he said that *all* of them were false. Pierret does *not* agree with this view and regards most of them as authentic, but some as certainly painted in the late forties. With its new lease of life French archaeology must find out for us how many of the Rouffignac paintings were done in the late forties of this century. Lascaux, Font de Gaume, Les Combarelles and the rest of them may be geographically in France as Altamira and Hornos de la Peña are geographically in Spain; but they are all part of our common, primary heritage from the prehistoric past. General de Gaulle, Monsieur André Malraux, and Monsieur Henry de Segogne are in these matters not merely Frenchmen, but the agents of the world, and the eyes of the world are on them and their staffs as, this summer, they battle with their prehistoric problems in Dordogne.

June 1964

❧ Why did ANTIQUITY succeed when many of its predecessors died? The simple answer is O. G. S. Crawford with his enthusiasm and personality which would not let it fail. He had to nurse it through the late twenties and again in the years of the 1939–45 war when it was very much touch and go. We should remember that our debt to him is not only for founding this journal but for seeing that it did not founder in the early forties. In the sixties we are in a different climate of thought; to look through the list of our subscribers is to see that they include all the major libraries and museums in the world. The circulation grows from year to year: many of our subscribers and readers in the British Isles may not know that well over half of our subscribers are *outside* the British Isles. Here's to all those who make the journal possible – subscribers, associate and assistant editors, printers and publishers, and, to quote Milton, 'That indigested heap and frie of Authors, which they call Antiquity'. And here's to the next fifty numbers. The present Editor, if he is alive in 1977, will be a strange old party then, darting from megalith to megalith in a jet-propelled bath-chair well equipped with portable library and cellar – impatiently awaiting on the first of March, June, September and December the ANTIQUITY his successor is editing.

September 1964

❧ Stonehenge was closed to the public from 7 p.m. on 20 June 1964 to 9.30 a.m. on 21 June but was open to the dotty Druids Lair! 'Stonehenge Rite for Druids Only' is the memorable headline in *The Times*. And what happened? An eye-witness reports: 'Stonehenge was encircled with two lines of Dannert barbed wire coils; there were 50 civil and military police, and four police-dogs with their handlers, the contents of 30 cars of journalists and photographers, 16 Druids and a little orderly crowd of not more than 100 spectators who obediently watched in the dim and drizzling dawn from the road outside.' More ceremonies took place at noon on the 21st, by which time the public were allowed in; it was raining, and the lady harpist had to have an umbrella held over her by the Chief Druid to prevent damage to her strings.

What a ridiculous, ludicrous, silly affair! There should be a total ban on all solstice ceremonies from now on. These strange neo-druidic organizations have no claim in history and archaeology to Stonehenge. The Minister should accept the advice of his Ancient Monuments Board. Indeed it is to us most mysterious why these latter-day Druids were ever allowed their junketings at Stonehenge, and why the permission is annually continued. There must be some very special reason. Could it be that the staff of the Ministry of Public Building and Works is riddled with secret Druids? Shall we hear, if we visit the Ministry, a curious melodious twang echoing down the corridors, and, suddenly turning a corner, find a harpist with furled umbrella at the ready?

❧ In 1955, at the height of the BBC's programme *Animal, Vegetable, Mineral?*, when anyone connected with that programme or with a museum was being inundated with parcels containing objects grave and gay, a Mrs R. G. Carter called at the Cambridge house of the present Editor of ANTIQUITY bearing in her hands a small parcel containing an object which she said she had dug up in her dahlia bed at The Old Vicarage, Markyate, Hertfordshire. With trembling hands we opened this little parcel wondering what worthless bric-à-brac was here, what odious rusty knife, what yellowing bone handle, what folding shaving-set from the Great Exhibition! The phrases were ready: 'Not I am afraid of much intrinsic interest or value, but it is always right to bring things you have found to an archaeologist. One time in a hundred, what you find *may* be of interest and value.' They were not necessary; the ready words froze as the wrapping was removed. This was one time in a thousand. Mrs Carter had found a Hiberno-Saxon gilt-bronze mounting of the 8th century, which she and her husband were happy to place on loan in the British Museum. This is a moral tale, and it has many morals. First, bravo Mrs Carter! Secondly, we must urge the men and women of England to dig more assiduously in their dahlia beds – indeed in every kind of bed and everywhere. We are said to be a nation of gardeners as well as shopkeepers and dog-lovers. Dig that ground. But, thirdly, what about all those unopened parcels that lie in the dusty corners and on the high shelves of every archaeologist's inner office? There ought, perhaps, to be every year, an opening day, an examination of the unconsidered trifles, a study of the fine things found by accident in dahlia beds, and sewer trenches. Never mind about that; dig, as Rudyard Kipling said (not in his *In the Neolithic Age*):

> ...take a large hoe and a shovel also
> And dig till you gently perspire.

Your exciting finds should be sent to your local museum curator and not to the ANTIQUITY office.

December 1964

🐚 Finally, we must correct a most curious error (for which we and our printers apologize) in the Editorial in our last issue. Writing of Stonehenge, we were made to say that at a certain time the monument was closed to the public but 'open to the dotty Druids Lair!' The exclamation mark should, of course, have followed 'Druids' and the sentence ended there; 'Lair' intruded after the final proofs had been passed.

The Editor of ANTIQUITY, patronymically equipped to be at home in *dens*, tends to be uneasy in lairs, Druidical or otherwise. Unable to account in any other way for the intrusive word, he is inclined to lay the blame squarely upon the 'very powerful properties' (*vide* Brewer) attributed to the Druids' Egg, and to hasten unobserved from the oak-grove.

March 1965

🐚 Someone, someday, and someday soon, ought to publish an anthology of archaeological cartoons. It would provide an amusing reason for thumbing through *Punch* and *The New Yorker*. Such an anthology would have to include all the classic archaeological jokes such as the Peter Arno of the be-topee-ed female archaeologist, protesting, as she was being embraced in the shadow of the Great Pyramid, 'But, Professor, forty centuries . . .', and the splendid cartoon – which we think appeared in *Dublin Opinion* – of a workman tearing down the wallpaper of a room, revealing, as he did so, Upper Palaeolithic paintings of Franco-Cantabrian style, and turning to the owner of the house with the mild query, 'And how long did you say this paper had been up?' *Punch* has, particularly in the last ten years, had an amused eye on archaeology. Indeed, as we write, the current number has a most entertaining drawing of a funeral procession going round and round a great pyramid, with one saying to another 'We can't seem to be able to find the secret entrance!'

September 1965

❦ We salute at a centenary moment some giants of the archaeological past. We know that our readers would like to join with us in also saluting at this moment our Senior Advisory Editor: he cannot yet claim his century, but we can congratulate him on his seventy-fifth birthday this month. Sir Mortimer Wheeler is certainly of the company of archaeological giants and to a younger generation has seemed co-existent with the great ones of the past, and like them, in the history of archaeology, co-eternal. Indeed, sometimes on a foggy evening in Piccadilly it has seemed to us that his tall, trim figure – 'para-military' was Jacquetta Hawkes's phrase – striding purposively from Burlington Gardens to the Athenaeum, was accompanied by others, shades in a London particular perhaps, but surely including General Pitt-Rivers himself. The General seems always a few steps behind – he is of course much older, but then no one in this day and age walks through central London as quickly as the Brigadier.

The present number of ANTIQUITY has some things which reflect in various ways Sir Mortimer's interests. As his interests have been so widespread it has not been a difficult task to do this. But here we have Wales and Roman Britain and the Indus Civilization (or at least its end in mud), and Archaeological Draughtsmanship (including the 1922 Segontium section), and even something on archaeology in France (though more complimentary than Wheeler in ANTIQUITY, 1932). This is not, and was never intended to be, in any way a formal tribute, and we are with Sir Mortimer in his oft-repeated criticism of the wastefulness of *festschriften*. This is a passing compliment from an Editor to his Senior Adviser, and we add to it a drawing of him done by another Advisory Editor in India many years ago. Professor Stuart Piggott, whose draughtsmanship is by no means confined to archaeology as many know, was, on one occasion together with the present Editor, laboriously explaining to the newly arrived Director-General of Archaeology in India the difficulties of working in the field in the Indian heat of the summer and the Indian wet of the monsoon. After several years of such weather they perhaps spoke as old *quai-hais*: Wheeler rapped on the table and said sharply, 'I propose to ignore the hot weather', and this drawing of Stuart Piggott's shows him doing so, with the results which are now part of the history of archaeology in India and the world as a whole.

'I prapose to ignare the haat weathah!'

December 1965

❦ Many of our younger readers will not remember Glozel; now is the time to recall it when Dr A. Morlet, its chief and constant protagonist for forty years, has died at the age of eighty-three. In May 1925 Morlet rented from the family Fradin at Glozel, a hamlet some twenty miles south of Vichy, the field Duranthon which he renamed *le Champ des Morts*, because he found there two graves.

One had thought that the whole business was forgotten until Morlet published his *Glozel II* (Macon, 1962) and M. le Chanoine Côte his *Glozel, trente ans après* (Saint-Etienne, 1959), and the whole business started again. André Billy wrote in *Le Figaro* (9 August 1962), Antoine Bonin in *Les*

Nouvelles littéraires (28 June 1962), and Robert Charroux produced an article entitled 'La maffia de l'archéologie' in *Le Monde et la Vie* for August 1963. What was more serious was that Charroux and Robert Arnaux produced a television programme on the RTF *France I* chain on 6 August 1963 entitled 'Chronique glozélienne', in which there were interviews with Morlet, Emile Fradin and le Chanoine Côte but none with the anti-glozelians, some of whom were vilified in the broadcast.

In *La Feuille d'avis de Lausanne* (admittedly a journal which does not often come our way, and will have little circulation in scientific circles), Dr Bénitte declared on 30 November 1964 that 'On a enfin les preuves de l'authenticité des découvertes préhistoriques faites à Glozel.' Are we then back at the beginning? Just before his death, Morlet published yet another fantastic book: this is entitled *Glozel; Corpus des Inscriptions* (Montpellier, 1965), and here he tells us, *inter alia*, two things of great interest to those who, like ourselves, find false archaeology and the growth of archaeological legends fascinating. Morlet says that had he not rented the field, there would never have been a Glozel '*car la famille Fradin avait décidé de remettre son champ en culture*', and then adds:

En effet, en dehors des fouilles dites 'de contrôle' faites par les savants aux endroits choisis par eux, j'ai pratiqué moi-même, avec un long et fort couteau, toutes les fouilles de Glozel, aidé de M. Emile Fradin et de ma femme. Nous ne prenions des ouvriers ou mon chauffeur que pour déblayer les couches superficielles de terre végétale, situées au-dessus de la couche archéologique.

So Glozel was excavated by three people with no competence or training in fieldwork and no apparent knowledge of comparative archaeology whatsoever!

In his last book Morlet gives a summary of the 1932 proceedings in the case Fradin *v*. Dussaud which, he had persuaded himself, established the authenticity of Glozel: they established only that Dussaud had libelled Fradin; and, in this delicate connexion, what about the footnote on page 61 of A. H. Brodrick's *The Abbé Breuil, Prehistorian* (London, 1963) which says, of Salomon Reinach, 'he was strongly in favour of the authenticity of the crude Glozel frauds, fragments of pottery and "inscriptions" forged by the . . . . and designed to prove the western origin of later human cultures'. The seven-letter word is deliberately omitted on the advice of our solicitors.

Morlet quotes with pleasure the words of Monsieur Mosnier of the Monuments Historiques, who at the Fradin *v*. Dussaud trial said, '*Chaque objet porte en soi sa propre authenticité.*' We went to Glozel for the second and, we hope, the last time in September; it was a wet day and everything was sad, *vieux-jeu* and forgotten. The Museum remains the same; in our view every object carries in itself clear proof of non-authenticity to anyone reasonably well acquainted with the material remains of the pre-Roman past. We had hoped for some good photographs of these bad forgeries; none was available, only a few delicious faded postcards of the twenties, green on the back in that curious fashion of the time. No. 10 shows a café erected on the main road with the caption 'Glozel-Restauration: "A l'Homme des Cavernes" — ses poulets cocotte — ses vins fins.' Alas, the café is gone; we needed restoration after half an hour in this sad museum of fakes and forgotten French hopes, but there were no fine wines and chickens en cocotte to restore us.

We had to take restoration further on at St-Pourçain, and there we were able to study the bibliography in Morlet's last book. It is called *Bibliographie Glozélienne*, with hundreds of items of rubbish, many written by himself. He says 'J'espère avoir un jour le plaisir de publier la bibliographie anti-glozélienne.' But he has gone from us, and his *long et fort couteau* will no longer unearth palpable forgeries. Had he survived to produce this additional bibliography, Crawford, Vayson de Pradenne and perhaps this present Editorial, would have featured in it. He remained to the last quite furious at the *Commission Internationale* and had a special spite against Dorothy Garrod. This is perhaps not unnatural; she it was, a very experienced fieldworker, who rumbled what was going on and how. We have asked her to write for us an account of what really went on in the twenties — her memories of the Commission and all those stirring days. She has agreed to do so and we hope to publish 'Glozel quarante ans après' in 1966 or 1967; and we have no objection if *Figaro, Les Nouvelles littéraires, Le Monde et la Vie,* and for that matter *La Feuille d'avis de Lausanne* wish to reproduce this article in whole or part.

Dr Curtis D. MacDougall, Professor of journalism at Northwestern University, in his absorbing book *Hoaxes* (1940, revised edition 1958), says that Hunter Charles Rogers, arrested in England for the sale of some spurious relics of William Penn, confessed that *he* had done the Glozel forgeries; he said that he placed a few genuine articles among the fakes. This is nonsense; there are no genuine articles, as Dr David Riesman, of the University of Pennsylvania, who made a detailed study of the Glozel affair, made quite clear.

March 1966

❦ The publication of the Vinland Map discovered in the library of Yale shows a large island S.S.W. of Greenland in which appear the St Lawrence

Gulf and the Hudson River. This has set all the crackpots going again merrily in their perpetual battle against the Phuddy Duddies. But what new comes out of all this? No one in their senses has ever doubted that the Vikings got further south than Greenland, just as no one in their senses believes they got to Minnesota, at least on the evidence of the forged Kensington Stone (ANTIQUITY, 1958). But how far south did they get? Vinland has often been identified as somewhere so far south that the Vikings met wild vines, but Professor Tanner of Helsinki in his *Newfoundland–Labrador* (1947) says that *Vinland* means grassland – pasture suitable for cattle. Helge Ingstad of Oslo has been excavating for five seasons between 1960 and 1964 at the site of L'Anse aux Meadows, Cape Norman, Pistolet Bay, on the most northerly point of Newfoundland. We have already referred to this work (ANTIQUITY, 1964) and we now hear that a major campaign of excavation is being mounted this year. Already Ingstad has found Norse ruins and artifacts which were datable on archaeological grounds to about AD 1000 and material yielding a C14 date of AD 1080 plus/minus 70 has satisfactorily confirmed the archaeological dating.

The locality of Newfoundland coincides, as Dr N. E. Odell pointed out (*The Times*, 20 October 1965), with that shown as Vinland on Sigurd Stefansson's Icelandic map of the 16th century. It begins to look as though the Vikings never got further than Newfoundland and, being unable to hold their own against Indians and Eskimos, were driven out of Vinland. But they preserved a memory of an island south of Greenland, and that island appears on many maps of the 15th and early 16th centuries. Its origin on the maps may not be a legendary history from the Viking voyages and settlements: it might be myth – the myth of Avalon, or St Brandon's Isle, the Fortunate Isles, the Isle of Seven Cities, Atlantis. What is not in dispute is that Antilia was on the map, and Roscanelli's chart which Columbus consulted in 1474 showed it in the direct line from the Canaries to Japan.

Columbus is always said to have been looking for the Indies, but was he not also, perhaps, looking for Antilia? And this he found.

The reopening of the Vinland–Columbus issue has allowed all the mad dogs to bark, and it was not surprising to read that an Italian professor lecturing recently in Florence declared there were traces of Etruscans in British Guiana. And so it goes on in those delicious and dangerous lunatic marges of archaeology and ancient history, the bogus learning which seems sometimes to discredit serious scholarship and undermine the widespread faith in scientific archaeology as a serious discipline. We have often thought what fun it would be if an experienced scholar took a few weeks off from his main work and wrote clearly and fairly a readable book about all these nonsenses. And now we find, a little belatedly, that it has been done. The book is Robert Wauchope's *Lost Tribes and Sunken Continents* (Chicago, 1962).

The archaeologist must always be on the lookout for false archaeology in one of its two forms – falsified facts, or false theories. Our comments on the resurgent interest in France and Switzerland in the possibility of Glozel being genuine (ANTIQUITY, 1965) have brought several letters saying 'How can this be?' The answer is a simple one; the whole Glozel affair is a classic example of people seeking the comforts of unreason, eschewing the orthodox line in archaeology (and incidentally this is often a very good thing!), and, being persuaded beforehand of some fact or theory, never again turning back to look or question. Elliot Smith and Co. were the most respectable and apparently scholarly version of all this, and it is interesting to learn from Professor Wauchope that 'Egypt in America' is still a widely held belief in the United States. But examples of the comforts of unreason in archaeology occur every day. Noah's Ark is one and the Druids another.

In 1964 a Mr George Vandeman, chairman of the board of directors of the Archaeological Research Foundation of New York and secretary of the general council of Seventh-day Adventists, said he was convinced that pieces of wood brought back by an Anglo-American expedition to Mount Ararat, from a site 14,000 ft. up, were part of a giant boat. There were several hundred tons of wood under an ice pack; the timber was tooled and it was a type of oak so hard that electrical blades had been broken in cutting it! Mr Vandeman went on to say that his expedition estimated that Noah's Ark had been a vessel two-thirds the size of the *Queen Mary*!

And on 13 September 1965, *The Daily Telegraph* published a remarkable photograph claimed to be the outline impression of Noah's Ark on Mount Ararat: it was 400 ft. long and thus not so far away from the Biblical description of 300 cubits (i.e. 450 ft.). The Photogeological Division of the Overseas Geological Survey at Chessington in Surrey, however, formed the opinion that the boat-like feature was caused by erosion of the volcanic rocks on Mount Ararat perhaps a million years ago. We are sure they are right, but this curious photograph is the very sort of thing which makes those on the edges of the lunatic fringe of archaeology plunge headlong down the lush grass that leads to Atlantis and Tiahuanaco, and by long straight green tracks to Glozel and the Druids at Stonehenge.

Last year, a splinter group of the neo-Druids started up rituals at Hunsbury in Northamptonshire, so this Early Iron Age hillfort must be added to Stonehenge, Primrose Hill and the Tower of London as the secret sacred places of our ancient past. In an interview on Anglia Television, the Chosen Chief of the Stonehenge neo-Druids, when asked why nothing much had been heard of the Druids from the 4th to the 17th centuries AD, said, 'The Druid is always present: he only emerges when society requires and demands him.' And his predecessor as Chosen Chief told the Heretics Society of Cambridge University that there were two ways to the truth of the past in regard to Stonehenge: one was to read books like Atkinson's *Stonehenge* and study what archaeology had revealed, but the other – and, he naturally claimed, the more reliable method – was 'to go to Stonehenge and lie down there and let the past and its true meaning seep into one's body and bones'.

As we reread Wauchope and *Ancient Ruins and Archaeology*, and contemplate those three red files in front of us as we write, marked 'Lunatics', the first containing material inherited from O. G. S. Crawford, we remember that *Alice in Wonderland* also celebrated its centenary in 1965, and we mutter 'Curiouser and Curiouser!'

September 1966

❦ All the English newspapers just before Midsummer carried the Ministry of Public Building and Works' notice that Stonehenge would be closed on Midsummer Eve and only 'the Druids' would be admitted. How long is this nonsense going to be sanctioned by a Department of State? There are no Druids to be admitted; the Druids died out centuries ago, and in any case, it has yet to be proved that they had anything to do with Stonehenge, although, admittedly, as Christopher Hawkes and Stuart Piggott have argued, if they were a native British priesthood of the last half of the first millennium BC, there is a strong suspicion that they were heirs to, if not consciously performers of, the ancient religion that swayed the megalith builders.

But this is academic speculation. To commemorate this Midsummer, Andrew Duncan wrote a fine piece for *The Daily Telegraph* (17 June 1966) called 'The witches are ready for Thursday', in which he describes interviews with Dr Thomas Maugham, Chief Druid of the British Circle of the Universal Bond, and with Mr Ross Nichols, the Chosen Chief of the Order of Bards, Ovates and Druids – a breakaway group from the Universal Bond. 'We never recruit', said the Chief Druid. 'Our beliefs are compatible with all religions, but a real Druid doesn't believe anything. ... he builds steadily on what he *knows*. ... Advanced Druids are taught the philosophy of convenience. ... The Druid believes in the continuous life.' Dr Maugham declined to give his age to Andrew Duncan but admitted that he had been a Druid in a previous existence. The Chosen Chief explained why the OBOD have left Stonehenge: they celebrated the summer solstice last year at Hunsbury in Northamptonshire and this year on Parliament Hill in

London. Mr Nichols said he thought that Stonehenge was 'a polluted place. The Ministry of Works have put down a whole lot of gravel and it's surrounded with barbed wire.' Mr Duncan reveals that the witches, like the Druids, are split into separate groups, and that the Rollright Stones have declined in popularity with them because motorists passing along the road would lean out of their cars and shout 'Lovely night for the witches, then.'

☙ We have already referred to the controversial articles of Professor Gerald Hawkins in *Nature* on the reason for Stonehenge (ANTIQUITY, 1964). He has now expanded these articles in a book boldly called *Stonehenge Decoded*.

The main unhappiness of archaeologists about Hawkins is his ignorance of prehistory. We all feel disinclined to listen to a man who has not bothered to listen carefully to archaeologists and learn what they have to say. It is almost unbelievable that a book on Stonehenge by a University Professor should not include in its bibliography (and therefore presumably not in the Professor's reading) Piggott's *The Neolithic Cultures of the British Isles*, Giot's *Brittany*, and many another standard work on megaliths, while it bothers to include Thomas Hardy's *Tess of the D'Urbervilles*, Sibylle von Cles-Reden's ill-informed *The Realm of the Great Goddess*, and – believe it or not – Marcel Baudouin's *La Préhistoire par les Etoiles*. (Surely the ghost of Vera Collum should now be haunting Hawkins for not having included in his bizarre bibliography her dotty reports on Tressé and the Déhus.)

Let us, a glass of Perrier in the hand to preserve us from extravagance, look at one page of Hawkins's *Stonehenge Decoded*: that unhappy page 88. First we are told that the rows at Menec lead to 'an irregularly-shaped circle which encloses a gallery grave covered by a mound bordered by stone slabs. One tall menhir stands above the grave.' *Completely inaccurate*. Then that it has '13 rows in a column about 900 yards long and 140 yards wide ... all three of the columns are oriented northeast-southwest'. *Doesn't make sense.* And then that 'the probable time of construction of these stone armies (*sic*) of the Morbihan region vary from considerably B.C. to a little A.D.'. But the dates of the Breton megaliths determined by C14 techniques have been published over the last few years in accessible publications like *Radiocarbon* and ANTIQUITY. And on the same solecistically rich page we are referred to megalithic sites in 'Crete and Greece'. Professor Hawkins does not tell us more about these, and here he is wise. *For there are none.*

Hawkins may be right about Stonehenge, and Palmer may be right about Knossos, but archaeologists initially dislike them because they rush at us like bulls, and we are very much pottery shops. What archaeologists have always welcomed is the informed, interested outside view – the outside specialist with something intriguing to say, like Sir Gavin de Beer or Sir

Julian Huxley; or the non-professional with a new line, like Tom Lethbridge in England and Henri Eydoux in France. What archaeologists have always disliked is the men from other disciplines who think they can weigh in, and with a half-baked appreciation of the facts of ancient history, pronounce on complex matters of prehistoric archaeology. There is no closed shop in archaeology, no trade union. All we ask of those whose non-professional views we welcome is: Please do your homework.

September 1967

❧ Here is a passage written by the present Editor of ANTIQUITY in *The Cambridge Review* for 20 May 1967:

Maitland once said at a meeting of the Eranus Club that anthropology had either to become history or become nothing. Archaeology *must* become history: years ago I warned against the danger of the new antiquarianism when the classification of flints, the typology of megaliths, and the analysis of dreary Bronze-Age pots became a substitute for the difficult task of wresting a few facts of history from the defaced antiquities and dry bones that survive (*A Hundred Years of Archaeology*). There are, broadly speaking, five archaeologies. The first concerns man from the moment he could be so called and had artifacts, to the beginnings of agriculture in the Near East, China and Mesopotamia, until what Elliot Smith called the Food-Producing Revolution and Childe the Neolithic Revolution. This is, to use the out-worn neo-grecisms, the Palaeolithic and Mesolithic: what the present Disney Professor in his inaugural lecture called 'primary prehistory'.

The second archaeology is that of the early peasant village communities of the world which in due course and in seven different regions of the world led to the first civilizations – those of Sumer, Egypt, the Indus valley, Shang China, the Olmecs, the Maya, and Peru. The archaeology of these protohistoric civilizations and the many others that followed them, like the Hittites and Phoenicians, the Minoans and Myceneans and Greeks, the Aztecs and Incas, is the third archaeology: protohistory in its widest and most exact sense. This third archaeology is also the archaeology of those societies whom Kroeber and Toynbee and others would not classify as civilized: the barbarian Celts, the Anglo-Saxons, the Vikings, the Scythians, the Sarmatians. The fourth archaeology is that comprised at present by the Society for Medieval Archaeology and reflected in its journal. And the fifth that comprised by the new Society for post-Medieval Archaeology, whose work carries on to the new and fashionable Industrial Archaeology.

All these five archaeologies need to be taught and practised in a University such as ours which, in the second half of this century when many of the new University experiments in Britain may collapse, is one of the three or four which can, with difficulty, survive with world status. What we need is a School or Institute of Prehistoric and Protohistoric Studies where the techniques and practices of archaeology can be taught and where students, whatever...they may be reading, can attend courses ... varying from Palaeolithic Cave Art to the beginnings of Agriculture, from the origins of City Life in the Near East to an analysis of Viking Ships, Anglo-Saxon linear earthworks, and Teotihuacán. . . .

When, recently, in a review in *The Spectator*, I criticized adversely some of the remarks made about prehistory and protohistory by Professor Jack Plumb in his editorial preface to *Prehistoric Societies* by Grahame Clark and Stuart Piggott, he retorted that I was not a historian. And here is the essence of the matter: we are all historians, we are all studying the past of man, whether we concentrate on Walpole, *Beowulf*, Stonehenge or Lascaux. Manuscripts, microliths, megaliths – it is all one. The past is the goal of the historian whether he is text-aided or not ... there are historians, in the strict sense of the word, who are frightened when they see archaeologists advancing toward them with dirt on their boots and a briefcase full of air photographs and Carbon-14 dates. Dugdale, Aubrey, Lhwyd and Stukeley did not think they were other than historians, and, for that matter, historians who could be members of the Royal Society. We have taken the distinction between a history that is mainly derived from material sources and one that is derived from the aid of texts, too far.

Thus ends that polemic. All universities, old and new, have this problem of organization: it should not be difficult to organize in a wide variety of ways if the end is always the right one: to pursue the whole story of man and his past from the beginning to the end examining all sources and using all auxiliary methods that the natural sciences and others can offer. It is a mistake, and of this there can be no doubt, to divide the study of the results of the five archaeologies from the study of the way in which those results are obtained, and this is why so many study-bound historians still look with wonder and dismay at men who dig and look through microscopes and use computers and still claim to be historians. It will be interesting to see, in a decade from now, how the new universities have matched up in planning and achievement to the new opportunities for archaeology, and what changes the older universities will have made. There are persistent and credible rumours of reorganization and development in Oxford: and more than rumours in London that an Honours Degree in Archaeology will appear on the Statute Book there in the next few years. Perhaps we could persuade our Advisory Editor, Sir Mortimer Wheeler, to comment on this when it happens, in the light of what he said in his Foundation Oration in Birkbeck College in 1957, namely, 'Archaeology was still on the substantive B.A. syllabus of this university; and it is a not irrelevant source of gratification to me to reflect that I was able twenty years ago to play a part in the seemingly perverse act of securing its removal from that syllabus' (R. E. M. Wheeler, *Alms for Oblivion*, London, 1966). From the seemingly perverse of the thirties to the seemingly reverse of the sixties is an intriguing way of looking at the development of academic archaeology in Britain in the last thirty years.

September 1968

There can be few serious prehistorians alive today who have any doubts about the false nature of Glozel. This was of course not so in the twenties and for a while the archaeological world was divided, as it now is about Rouffignac. Professor Dorothy Garrod was one of those involved in quarrels over Glozel in 1927 and we print in this issue her recollections of the affair. The *Encyclopédie des Farces et Attrapes et des Mystifications*, edited by F. Caradec (Président-Général of the A.F.E.E.F.A.) and N. Arnaud (Chancellor of the I.F.F.A.) is a most entertaining and valuable book (Paris, 1964) with a good section on archaeological *farces* and *attrapes*, ranging from the Cardiff Giant through Glozel and the Tiara of Saitaphernes to the Kensington Stone, Bill Stump's Stone in the Grave Creek Mound, and the portable dolmen sold in the Lorient tombola. The Glozel section is full of interest and records the touristic exploitation of the site by hoteliers who built a *Restaurant des Fouilles* and served *un Thé de l'homme des cavernes*, and by Felix Potin who made 'briques néolithiques' in marzipan. It also records the fact that on 25 September 1927, M. Vergne, director of the museum at Villeneuve-sur-Lot, surprised by a storm at Glozel, took refuge in a disused stable on the farm, and there discovered the tools used by the sculptor, and half-carved schist pebbles. The article reprints a prospectus circulated by E. Miguet and we are happy to give further circulation to this brilliant satire by reprinting it here.

❧ The Roskilde ship museum is going to be one of the finest of the many fine museums in Scandinavia. It is on the edge of the harbour and the windows look out into the sea: the five ships are being assembled there now and the museum will be opened in December. Looking at what is being done at Roskilde, and visiting the Ladby Ship near Odense, we wonder, as every visitor to these sites must wonder, whether the right decision was taken about Sutton Hoo. Might it not have been wiser, immediately after the war, to rediscover Sutton Hoo, and encase it in a glass box such as had happened at Ladby? Had this been done in 1946–8 we would have had Sutton Hoo as a permanent tourist attraction which might well have produced visitors in very great numbers and money from admission fees, guide book and postcard sales which would have produced moneys enough to subsidize the publication of the excavation report, now considerably delayed, and fresh research on the whole area.

❧ Fieldwork in Denmark has its pleasures and difficulties, its hazards and its compensations. After a day of climbing in and out of most of the remarkable collection of megalithic tombs on the Rosenfeldt estate in South Sjaelland, we were taken by our hostess, Hofdam Kontessa Waby Armfelt, to the far western end of this lovely estate to see the enclosure where live two bison and their friend and mentor, an old cow called Olga. Countess Armfelt had not been to see them for eighteen months, when she had found them charming and tame. We climbed the 6 ft.-high palisade and wandered around looking for these creatures. On the crest of a hill some 300 metres from the fence we paused and saw in the distance Olga and two bison. The bison looked large. They were: they were now fully grown. 'Are they friendly?' we asked in a tentative way. The bison provided the answer: heads down, they began to charge us. No one said, 'Stand your ground: they are only curious.' We ran for the fence, protecting ourselves for brief moments in clumps of trees, the bison waiting on the other side. The Production Editor of ANTIQUITY wanted to climb a tree but was urged on to the fence: when she was only a few yards away from it she heard heavy stertorous breathing and the tramp of pounding feet and thought that the bison had caught her up. There was nothing to do, she said, but turn round and open her umbrella in the face of the beasts who, surprised, might give her a moment to make the fence. She turned – only to find that it was the Editor who was responsible for the breathing and heavy tramping; the bison were a few yards behind. The gate was made, but looking back through the fence at the bison now only a few inches away, and Olga, laughing naughtily in the background, one was able to recollect, in that moment of post-action tranquillity, what brilliant artists Palaeolithic men were.

We have recovered from the bison chase, but we will never recover from our visit to the holy rag tree. It was a particularly good/bad day to visit it. A cold rain blew across the roads, the sky was dark, and what was needed was schnapps and an Elefant or FF Festival in a warm *kro*: but no – inexorably the car was driven into a muddy lane which led into a dark wood. When the road ceased to be *carrossable* we walked on and on: the wood became darker, the track muddier and the air colder. The trees joined overhead and we were overwhelmed by the sense that comes in an ordinary wood, a sense of being surrounded and out of the world. But this was no ordinary wood. We turned up a side-track – one not indicated in any way as special among many side-tracks – and, not having been informed of the nature of the exercise, wondered what was happening. In a sudden moment there was a clearing in the trees, and there, in the middle of the clearing, was a very tall tree with a hole in the middle, and everywhere were offerings of rags – and rags varying from dirty handkerchiefs to silk stockings. We were, it might be said, in the presence of a mystery. We were actually in the presence of heathendom, of pre-Christian religion and magic. We realized as one cannot realize when looking at a dolmen or a rune-stone that we were suddenly, only a few miles from a main road, in pagan Scandinavia, and that the present was the past. We glanced nervously around the circle of wet dripping fir-trees and out of the gloom for a brief moment the faces of Iorwerth Peate and Estyn Evans and Hadrian Allcroft and Hilda Ellis Davidson seemed to come and go, while the day-owls that hooted distantly were certainly Du Chaillu and Hector Chadwick. Here surely, alive in Denmark, is the sacred clearing in the trees which must lie behind those archaeological manifestations of this magico-religious life which in Britain we call our henge monuments. When we try to make alive sites like Arminghall, Avebury and Stonehenge, let us remember the dark Danish woods.

Dr Thorkild Ramskou mentioned the South Sjaelland 'holy tree' in an article in *Skalk* several years ago (*Skalk*, 1960) when he drew attention to the fact that heathendom was still alive in spite of the great words of Harald Blue Tooth a thousand years ago that he had 'made the Danes Christian'. In his article, Ramskou compared the Danish tree with La Pierre de Saint-Martin at Pitres, a holy stone from heathendom adopted by the Church. Here a wooden cross is erected in front of the stone as a special support for the rags and bits of cloth. Ramskou adds that at Pitres there is also a money box for the benefit of the parish church. What a brilliant symbiotic relationship of pre-Christian and Christian religions (see Jean Fournée, *Enquête sur le culte populaire de St-Martin en Normandie* (Paris, 1963).

Two years ago the Copenhagen newspaper *Berlingske Tidende* published an article on the holy rag tree, and a few days later (13 June 1966) published an interview with a woman ninety years old. She said: 'When I was a little girl I began to be crooked. I could neither walk nor stay upright, and I was given up by the doctors. But, fortunately, my mother, who was a courageous woman, did not give up hope. She went to a wizard, who read an incantation over me, and then advised her to take me to the "rag oak". We were living in a poor house not far from the tree. The wizard thought that someone had wished me bad luck when, playing with other children, I had passed through a window without going back the same way. My mother took me to the oak, and drew me through the hole in it, and we left behind some of my clothes on the branches. Once we were back home my mother plaited a string as the wizard had told her to do and, for the next few days, I spat through it every morning while my mother read incantations over me. I remained in bed for some while after our visit to the wood. Then I began to crawl and, in one sudden moment, I found I could walk. I am still a crooked person, but ever since that moment I can jump about like a cat. I have no doubt it was because of my visit to the holy rag oak.'

The living past must not be destroyed so neither *Skalk* nor *Berlingske Tidende* (and certainly not ANTIQUITY) will reveal the whereabouts of this living prehistoric shrine. Indeed we could not find it again without the expert guidance of one of the five Danish archaeologists who know where it is. Its existence poses the same problem as was revealed recently in a broadcast by the Opies on children's tag-rhymes. Some are in the standard books, others are the earthier ones sung only in the playgrounds ('Eni, Meni, Mina, Mo; Put the baby on the po...'), while a third group, among other things, count in Celtic like the shepherds count. To explain this is to kill it. Long may the country folk of Denmark go to their rag oaks in a clearing in a dark forest as their ancestors, and ours, went to circular clearings in non-existent woods like Woodhenge. Long may the country children of southern England count in ancient British.

℧ Recently we received the following:

To Publishers Producers & Journalists.

The following announcement will appear very shortly in the Personal column of the TIMES:

Is SILBURY HILL the tomb of BELGIUS

Keltic Commander in Macedonia, 280 BC?

Are STONEHENGE/WOODHENGE

Macedonian Peg-Calendars? Detailed evidence.

2s 6d. R. M. Twist, St. Anthony, Portscatho.

The BBC is to spend £20,000 and take three years to excavate SILBURY HILL. The Professor in charge thinks it to be of 'Bronze Age' date.

Millions will follow the programmes: thousands will already
have seen my announcement: some bought my synopsis.
Are you interested in my proof of 3rd cent date?
Of Great Historical Importance.

The BBC, which *is* spending £20,000 on the excavation of Silbury
Hill, itself printed an air photograph of it (*The Listener*, 27 June 1968)
captioned: 'Flying saucer view of Silbury Hill. BBC-2 is busy digging there
for archaeological treasure, but John Michell doubts whether they will find
anything in what is for him not a burial place but "an obvious sighting
mound" dedicated to the gods of the air.' This illustrates an extraordinary
article by Michell on flying saucers, discussion of which seems to embrace
every archaeological lunacy there ever was from the sacred tracks of Ireland
to Mrs Maltwood at Glastonbury and Alfred Watkins riding along his
straight tracks in Herefordshire. John Michell's book *The Flying Saucer
Vision* (London, 1967) – the subtitle is 'The Holy Grail Restored', should
be read by all who find the comforts of unreason so comforting, and when
they have finished it they should pause, drink a stiff Bloody William, and
ask themselves whether their fringe activities are really archaeology.

When we have written off as crosspatch curmudgeons and
cranks and crackpots the many who are writing rubbish about Silbury, we
are left with the sad fact that it is far more difficult than many of us thought
to educate the world to a fair and reasonable view of antiquity. Television
helps, but often its existence merely highlights the horrors of failed
communication. Recently in the middle of the North Sea an otherwise
intelligent and informed man who was engaged in selling British goods to
Denmark, and, apparently, very successfully, congratulated the Editor of
ANTIQUITY on the excellent television programme he had done the previous
night on Stonehenge. 'Yes', his wife joined in, and at this moment she was
only on her second Dry Martini, 'it was lovely. All so clear.' The Editor
drew himself up to his full five foot seven and a half inches, and said 'But
it was a programme about Silbury Hill and I did not appear in it.'

Even our official tourist organizations let us down. France this spring
and summer is full of gay coloured advertisements telling people to travel
to Britain. The legend says, 'En Angleterre vous pourrez croire que la
machine à remonter le temps existe réellement: vous verrez d'authentiques
ducs vivre dans leurs châteaux (entrée 3 F environ), vous assisterez à
Stonehenge aux cérémonies des Druides (entrée 1 F environ), vous entendrez
le bruit des calèches roulant sur des pavés du 17e siècle (château de York,
entrée 1.50 F environ)'; and the caption to the coloured photograph of
Stonehenge says 'L'âge du bronze: à Stonehenge, ces pierres fantastiques,
vieilles de 3,800 ans, représentent les vestiges des temples Druides.'

Those horrid bogus Druids are always with us. Again this year with the connivance of the Ministry of Public Building and Works they cavorted in the midsummer dawn at Stonehenge before crowds of British journalists and American tourists who ought still to have been abed. Recently the students who so wickedly daubed Stonehenge with paint were heavily fined: not, in our opinion, heavily enough. But what about fining the Druids who annually daub Stonehenge with their confusion, and the Ministry of Public Building and Works which lets them go there?

But there is worse than bogus Druids. Towards the end of June when being interviewed by the BBC on the value of honey, Barbara Cartland declared that when the Phoenicians got to Britain they found the island inhabited by natives who were both handsome and all ten feet high and that it is well known that both conditions were due to their diet of honey! What fantastic nonsense, even far surpassing the extravagant claims of John Twyne, Samuel Bochart and Aylett Sammes, and they were writing 300 years ago and more.

🐝 Three bodies, the Council for British Archaeology (Group XII: Wessex), the Wiltshire Archaeological and Natural History Society, and the Newbury and District Field Club, have recently passed resolutions condemning the construction of the new road through Durrington Walls, and deploring the failure of public authorities (local and national) to consult independent scholars before taking such drastic measures. Amenity and other societies are considering similar protests.

The whole affair is outrageous: we have a privately hired ANTIQUITY tumbril waiting for some of the shamateurs in the Ministries concerned. The centre of Durrington Walls might be a good place for the guillotine, except that it is a long drive from London. One doesn't want to do all that knitting.

December 1968

🐝 As a Christmas offering we have gathered together in our frontispiece some stamps which will be of special interest to archaeologists. We are grateful to Madame Anne Philippe, Mr Marcus Greenhorne, Mr H. A. Shelley, Mr Graham J. Clark and Monsieur Moisin for their help in collecting them. The French issues of Carnac and Lascaux and the Belgian stamp of the Spiennes flint-mines are particularly beautiful examples of stamp design. In making this selection we had hoped to use it as propaganda for a British archaeological stamp of some fine prehistoric object like Stonehenge or Avebury or Silbury Hill, when, to our horror, there appeared offensively on many of our letters the new 4d stamp of Tarr Steps in Somerset erroneously described as 'Prehistoric'. It seemed so sad that our first British 'prehistoric' stamp should not be prehistoric at all. How could the Postmaster-General have been so ill-advised as to label this pretty clapper bridge 'Prehistoric'? We felt this was another example of the way in which the outrageous inefficiencies of a centralized bureaucratic machine increase from month to month.

Lady Fox wrote to *The Times* (13 May 1968) as follows:

I have just received a letter with the new 4d stamp engraved with a picture of Tarr Steps and boldly labelled 'Prehistoric'. Tarr Steps is a Clapper Bridge across the River Barle on Exmoor, built for pack horse traffic, probably in the Middle Ages, and reconstructed after damage by floods fairly recently: like the similar structure at Postbridge on Dartmoor, it has no claim to be prehistoric. It seems a pity that whoever decided on the design did not consult either the archaeologists of the Inspectorate of Ancient Monuments or the Ministry of Public Building and Works, who include Tarr Steps in their Schedule of Ancient Monuments.

No reply came from the Postmaster-General during the next few weeks and on 30 May we wrote to him ourselves:

You will have seen the letter that appeared in *The Times* on 13th May from Lady Fox about the new 4d stamp showing the Tarr Steps. The stamp, as you know, alleges that these steps are prehistoric, which is certainly not so. I shall draw attention to this curious error in a forthcoming editorial in ANTIQUITY; but before doing so I would like to know what advice was taken by your Ministry before this stamp was issued, and whether you intend to withdraw the stamp now that the error has been pointed out.

I hope we may have a stamp with some prehistoric antiquity. The most obvious one would be Stonehenge. The French had, two years ago, a very good stamp of the stone rows at Carnac in Brittany, and have just issued an attractive stamp of the Upper Palaeolithic painted and engraved cave of Lascaux in Dordogne, while the Belgians have issued a very attractive stamp of the Spiennes flint-mines.

There was no immediate acknowledgement of this letter and as the weeks passed it looked as if the Postmaster-General would preserve the same indiscreet silence as he had in the face of Lady Fox's letter. And then on 5 July there arrived the following letter signed 'D. J. Ferry p.p. L. Pettit' from the G.P.O. in St Martin's-le-Grand:

Thank you for your letter of May 30th to the Postmaster-General about the Tarr Steps stamps. I am very sorry for the delay in replying to you.

In a specialist field of this kind we do not of course rely on our own sources of information but take care to consult experts. As you will know there are different views as to the age of the Tarr Steps. It used to be thought that they were prehistoric and our researches led us to this view.

As a result of your letter however we have challenged one of the leading sources and it seems that most experts consider the steps to be medieval in origin.

We very much regret putting out this inaccurate description of them and would like to thank you for the correction.

We have added your suggestion about a special stamp featuring Stonehenge to the list from which the choice will be made for the 1969 special stamp programme.

This is very good news; in the past few years we have had some excellent special stamps in Britain, and Stonehenge would make an admirable subject for a future issue. And now the Mexico Olympic Games have stimulated the production of a great number of archaeological stamps: Ecuador and the Kathiri State in Hadhramaut have delightful Greek scenes, mainly from vases, while Czechoslovakia, Sharjah, and the Mahra and Upper Yafa states of southern Arabia (two countries whose existence, let alone their stamps, was a surprise) have pre-Columbian antiquities. The Paraguay series is particularly good with pots, sculpture, glyphs and gold plaques.

☙ It is known to many that the Editor of ANTIQUITY (and the Production Editor) move to the hamlet of Zouafques-par-Tournehem-sur l'Hem in the Pas-de-Calais for four months each year (which may account for some of the delays in correspondence). When Professor Christopher Hawkes heard of this he said 'Why the Pas-de-Calais? I call it the Pas-de-Forêts department.' This is not true: the Pas-de-Calais has several large national forests, one of them the Forêt d'Eperlecques, on the edge of which is a magnificent piece of last-war archaeology, the *blockhaus* which was to have controlled the annihilation of Britain. We have often had a glass of wine in the Café du Blockhaus after showing visitors this fantastic château-fort of the last war. But in the neighbouring Forêt de Tournehem is something more interesting: in the middle of the wood is a circular clearing and in this clearing a small chapel. Notre-Dame-de-la-Forêt has candles burning every day. The great service of the year is at 3 p.m. on 15 August, the Feast of the Assumption, and great crowds gather to worship here, including men and women who are never normally seen in ordinary village churches. What can they be worshipping? Can Notre-Dame-de-la-Forêt be a Christianized version of those circular clearings in woods of the fourth millennium BC which consequently gave rise to our Woodhenges and Stonehenges?

Many people have written commenting on the Danish rag tree which we wrote about recently (ANTIQUITY, 1968), and we were thinking of that circular clearing in the woods of south Sjaelland when we drove away from the Forêt de Tournehem and parked the car in St Omer. We walked into the Basilique de Notre-Dame especially to see the tomb of Saint Erkembode, a fine 7th/8th-century tomb cut out of a single block of limestone and set on two grumpy lions. To our astonishment we saw alongside the tomb a collection of rags – pieces of handkerchiefs and underwear and socks. We went back especially the following Sunday to see whether these ex–votos were still there while mass was being celebrated. They had all been cleared away, but three days later, on top of the tomb, were more rags and a pair of children's bootees. The traces of the elder faiths are everywhere.

March 1969

❧ Following our remarks on rag offerings (ANTIQUITY, 1968), Ronald Jessup, fresh from excavating for the Service National des Fouilles a Roman barrow site deep in the forest of Belgian Luxembourg, tells us that he has seen two instances of such offerings at isolated forest shrines in the Gaumais. Both shrines, little wooden huts now dilapidated, were nailed to well-matured oak trees standing on small mounds, possible *tombelles*. 'In one case', Jessup writes, 'a forester preferred not to talk about such things, but in the other the gamekeeper felt that it did no harm to remember the Luck of the Forest in such a way especially before the opening of the *chasse au gros gibier* on the 1st October. He took it as a compliment that we should add a few blossoms of *Asperula odorata*, Reine des bois, the flower which adds bouquet to Maitrank, the white wine apéritif made once a year in Arlon. The offerings were of torn rags, good-quality woollen socks, a shirt and a pair of boots of decent enough quality to have appealed to OGSC!'

June 1969

❧ Has there ever been any unity of prehistory except that all things studied by the prehistorian are, in Christopher Hawkes's phrase, text-free? Is there anything, necessarily or actually, in common between Charles McBurney's *Haua Fteah* report and Nancy Sandars's *Bronze Age Cultures of France*? The answer is no: Palaeolithic prehistorians should not be berated because they find La Tène fibulae dreary. There is no unity in prehistory, and there certainly is none in archaeology. For too long too many archaeologists have been dancing around discussing whether archaeology is a science or an art, or saying, as Sir Mortimer Wheeler once did in one of his more colourful and extravagant moments, 'I do not know what archaeology is', when all the time we know that archaeology is a craft and a technique. Archaeologists are craftsmen and technicians just as are epigraphists and students of diplomatic. Theirs is an expertise practised in the field, the museum, the laboratory and the study. In their forthcoming *Penguin Dictionary of Archaeology* Warwick Bray and David Trump say crisply that archaeology is 'the study of man's past by means of the material remains he has left behind him. It is therefore a technique.' Archaeology is a craft, a series of techniques: we should use these techniques and crafts for the study of man from the beginnings to yesterday; we should encourage this study in depth, from the stone tools of Olduvai to deserted medieval villages and decaying railways and tomorrow's rubbish tips, and in breadth, from the driest taxonomy of Palaeolithic flints to the most subjective appreciation of Sumerian art and Olmec heads and American colonial tombstones, and all this without any feeling that any one aspect of the study – in time or place or topic – is necessarily more important than another. We do not subscribe to the view that many archaeologists are at the present day selling our birthright for a mess of pseudo-scientific pottage. We do not believe that the present state of our studies is a deep conflict between the kind humanism of Jacquetta Hawkes's article published in our pages last December (ANTIQUITY, 1968) and the brash methodological mystique of David Clarke's *Analytical Archaeology* (to be reviewed here shortly). It takes all kinds of archaeology to make the world of history.

Archaeology must be pursued in depth from eoliths to today and in breadth from the excavation report to art history. It is possible to be a distinguished and scholarly archaeologist by confining oneself to one's techniques and crafts. The brilliant excavator is in his own right a scholar in the same way as the man who makes elegant experiments in a microbiological laboratory or collates the manuscript versions of a text. Of course it is not enough to have dirt on your boots: there must also be the dust of museum cases and books on your hands, and brains in your head. But one can be a superb archaeological craftsman and technician, and no more or less: all archaeologists don't have to write, or pretend to write, history.

The work of all archaeologists may be conceived of as a broad band with at one end the dirt archaeologist and the taxonomist, the collector and the classifier; in the centre the synthesist and historian; and at the other end the art historian. Many archaeologists can achieve distinction in many parts of this band; others specialize in only one activity. The danger archaeology faces at present, and particularly protohistoric and prehistoric archaeology, is the growth of a new pseudo-scientific archaeology imbued with what Malcolm Muggeridge has called 'the highfalutin' notion of scientific exactitude – the great mumbo-jumbo of the age' (*The Times*, 11 January 1969). This new archaeology hides behind an uneasy façade of statistics and computers the fact that the study of artifacts is descriptive not analytical, and that the facts of history we can obtain from the preliterate phases of man's past are really very few. It is this realization that drives some, like Victorian parsons in cold remote country rectories, to question their faith; and others to give up any pretence of being historians and to spend their lives contemplating their own digs and their finds – the navel/cabbage-patch archaeology; or to take refuge in the mystique of methodology.

❦ The Editor of ANTIQUITY has long been an admirer of Astérix the Gaul, 'this Iron Age Popeye' as Margery Fisher has called him (*The Sunday Times*, 2 March 1969). He knows that at least three Professors of Archaeology in Britain share his admiration for these new Gauls, and in his book *The Druids* (London, 1969), Professor Stuart Piggott, long an Astérix fan, says: 'The whole series shows a real knowledge of the Gaulish scene which enriches the comedy for prehistorians.' By series he refers to the fact that the Astérix legend has outgrown the cartoon strip into books, and these books, hitherto in French, are not only being redistributed in England in their French form with cribs to make the allusions and puns better understood, but also in English translation.

Why has there been this phenomenal success? Many reasons have been suggested: the humour of the visual and verbal puns, the bold interplay of ancient and modern allusions, the mixture of fact and fancy. But the real reason is probably that the French have compared the achievements of Astérix and Co. in defying the might of the Roman Empire with their own contemporary struggle for international independence and recognition after the calamitous days of the Fourth Republic.

September 1969

❦ Prehistorians have been talking about megaliths for well over a hundred years. *The Oxford English Dictionary* tells us that the words megalith and megalithic were first used in 1849 in a book by Algernon Herbert entitled *Cyclops Christianus; or, An Argument to Disprove the Supposed Antiquity of the Stonehenge and other Megalithic Erections in England and Brittany*. There is something curiously vulgar about the phrase megalithic erections just as there is something vulgarly curious about the insistence of Victorian archaeologists referring to Avebury and Carnac and New Grange as rude stone monuments. But even Herbert could not train his printer to use correctly his neologism, and in his contents-list we meet the phrase, 'The rudeness of megalithic forms does not prove their antiquity.'

❦ Every prehistoric conference these days is informed, enlivened and often confused by recitals of C14 dates, and archaeologists sometimes appear like the legendary Stock Exchange purveyors of smutty stories, taking their colleagues into corners and saying 'Have you heard this one?' as some new date is trotted out, sometimes with satisfaction and sometimes with alarm. The Moesgård conference was, of course, beset with the very early dates of some of the Breton Passage Graves. It is not so easy to go on deriving the Breton, Irish and Scandinavian Passage Graves from Iberia when we have no large series of early Iberian dates, and the rethinking of megalithic problems must involve a rethinking of Breton Passage Grave origins in terms other than Iberia and the south. It is always forgotten, in our post-Childe diffusionist way, that Montelius suggested a northern origin for the funerary Passage Graves, and what are the houses at Skara Brae other than non-funerary Passage Graves?

The time will soon come, we all hope, when there are so many C14 dates, and when the problems of this still new technique of dating have been so resolved, that the 'Have your heard this one?' and 'But do you think all is well?' questions will disappear from the land.

December 1969

❦ We have recently read with great interest three inaugural lectures. The first is by Merrick Posnansky who is the third holder of the Chair of Archaeology in the University of Ghana at Legon. His predecessors were A. W. Lawrence and Peter Shinnie. Posnansky's lecture is called *Myth and Methodology – the Archaeological Contribution to African History*, but he has much to say about archaeology in general. He approves of Robert Braidwood's definition that 'archaeology is the way in which the actions of human beings may be understood through the study of what human beings did, rather than simply what they said of themselves', and declares it would be most honest 'though cumbersome, if we called ourselves archaeological historians in contrast to the documentary historians who have been imperialistic in retaining the ascription history for their own tiny slice of the study of man's past'. He has sharp and clear views about the modern vogue of declaring archaeology scientific or even a science. We quote:

Part of the problem lies perhaps in the conceit of the archaeologist: he forgets that neither infra-red ray examination of paintings nor computer analyses of grammatical items in Shakespeare make either the art historian or the scholar of English literature a scientist, and yet he supposes that the constellation of scientific methods at his fingertips provides him with an objective approach to his subject that was lacking to his humanist predecessors. This I think is perhaps one of the cardinal myths about archaeology. It is essentially an interpretative study. The controls over the interpretation may be exercised in a scientific manner but nevertheless the skill of an archaeologist lies in his personal judgements and the way he balances different types of evidence.

And Posnansky has the courage to say what so many are afraid to. We quote again:

There is a further aspect of archaeology which for myself at least is one of the most attractive. Archaeology can be an enjoyable subject; it provides access to a chronicle of human achievements, whether they be art masterpieces, cities of stone or new technologies. Moreover it allows contact with objects that in their making brought pleasure to their makers. It is difficult to convey the pleasure that discovering a new set of rock paintings or beating a long-silent rock gong brings to the discoverer.

This is fine stuff and the greatest encouragement to a man who wrote, 'The past that archaeology provides for us in the present is to be enjoyed as our common heritage, as well as tortured into typologies and transmuted into history. Through archaeology we own the pleasures of past time, as well as its historical witness' (G. E. Daniel, *The Origins and Growth of Archaeology*, Harmondsworth, 1967), and who said in his own 1969 Inaugural Lecture as Ferens Professor in Hull, echoing sentiments expressed by Martin Robertson in his 1962 inaugural as Lincoln Professor of Classical Archaeology and Art at Oxford, 'we must enjoy and delight in the art of preliterate man for its own sake, for the pleasure it gives us: we must make our own value-judgements, studying it *in vacuo*, and so leading to its appreciation and its connoisseurship.'

Professor Charles Thomas's Inaugural Lecture as the first holder of the

Chair of Archaeology in the University of Leicester was called 'Archaeology and the Mind'. He, in our view, mistakenly identified archaeology with prehistory and protohistory when he said that it was 'the attempt to recover that all-too-enormous expanse of the past with which no written document of any kind happens to deal'; but then went on to say many things of great interest, for example that 'on the criterion of usefulness, that is, of immediate and obvious social benefit, it would be hard to justify inclusion of archaeology *per se* in the content of any university', that Britain 'is already producing slightly more archaeologists than it can absorb', and that it is not a good thing to have Honours courses in archaeology in all Universities. Surely most people would agree with this last point, but let us wait until we can all read this intriguing inaugural.

The third inaugural is that of William Watson as Professor of Chinese Art and Archaeology in the University of London: these are some words from the lecture of this wise humanist:

For reasons which are more academic than essential the present century has witnessed a singular divorce between archaeology and art study.... I should not like to see the two aspects of my subject parted along the lines of the established specialisms. It is not only that 'art and archaeology' is a time-honoured combination. Today its continued use perpetuates a principle valuable in the study of cultures of remote time or remote tradition.

❦ The silly season of 1969 certainly produced again its crop of odd headlines and old favourites. A new expedition is being planned to find Noah's Ark, the signs of the zodiac are again observed in the fields around Glastonbury, the bogus Druids led by Dr Thomas Maughan again appeared at Stonehenge at dawn on the longest day of the year – this year their deliberations were disrupted by a crowd of 2,000 people one of whom climbed on the lintel of a trilithon and took his clothes off: 'Druids ignore stripper at Stonehenge' said the *Evening Standard*.

But it was the activities of Walter Yearick that got most publicity. We have already referred to Mr Yearick who advertised the sale of Roman mosaics from his garden in Cirencester in *The Sunday Times*. Yearick, aged forty-five, and a former Top Sergeant in the United States Air Force, first called at 10 Downing Street, and later, dressed as a Roman centurion, chained himself to the railings of Buckingham Palace. On 11 August the Bow Street magistrate conditionally discharged him for twelve months for causing an obstruction. Yearick is now a foundry inspector and says he is trying to make sure that 'people should know that officials had misappraised the site of a Roman forum in his garden'. He is planning to organize a march of at least 100 students dressed as Roman soldiers, if possible: this is in the hope of drawing the attention of the Ministry of Public Building and Works to the presence of Roman remains in his garden. 'If I don't raise public or private money 600 years of British history will be lost for ever', he declared, adding, 'I am becoming discouraged by the lack of interest in history by the British people.' (We are assured by the Ministry that they are well aware of the remains in Mr Yearick's garden, and that no injustice is being done, either to Mr Yearick or to the British people.)

We are grateful to James Dyer for kindly drawing our attention to a splendid entry in the catalogue of *Occult and Borderline Science Books* published by Neville Spearman of London W1. We reproduce it here:

Secret Places of the Lion

GEORGE HUNT WILLIAMSON

George Hunt Williamson was one of the four witnesses at the time of George Adamski's first meeting with the Venusian, as described in Adamski's book, *Flying Saucers Have Landed*. Since then Dr Williamson has established himself as a best-selling writer of the mystic and esoteric, as well as Flying Saucers.

These are some of the questions answered by this amazing volume:... Who built the Great Pyramid?... Did Lemuria and Atlantis really exist?... Where was the Last Supper celebrated?... Was Akhnaton of Egypt later Simon Peter?... Are there hidden pyramids in North America?... Is there a secret temple under the Sphinx?... Is there an ancient space ship buried under the Great Pyramid?... Was there a curse of Tutankhamen's tomb?... Where is the Holy Grail?... Did Joseph of Arimathea go to Glastonbury in Britain? Was he buried there?... Did the American Indians guard ancient Lemurian records in Time Capsules?... Is the Holy Shroud or Mantle of Turin really the burial shroud of Christ?... Where is the lost treasure of the Incas and the fabulous Disc of the Sun?... What and where are the *Secret Places of the Lion*?

Fifth Impression, Demy 8vo, 244pp. 25s

Surely this is the ideal Christmas present for someone who is losing his faith in the traditional methods of archaeological investigation? And is it not time we enjoyed a few hours by rereading the four Churchward Mu books? Colonel James Churchward, that eccentric soldier, was serving in Central India in 1868 when a high priest showed him how to interpret the tablets of Mu long believed indecipherable. (Where are the modern-day priests that could help us with the Indus script?) Armed with this forgotten language of Mu, the Colonel spent many years in the South Seas, Tibet, Central Asia, Egypt, Siberia, Australia, the Urals and Polynesia, searching for further proof of Mu's existence, and then wrote his four books *The Lost Continent of Mu, The Sacred Symbols of Mu, The Cosmic Forces of Mu,* and *The Children of Mu.* The story is worth remembering: Mu and her vast civilization spread over the world 25,000 years ago: it is claimed that the greatest tragedy of mankind occurred when Mu sank 'carrying down with her 63,000,000'. All this is fantasy and folly: what is interesting is that a century after the meeting with that high priest, Colonel Churchward's books are still selling and have already sold over 150,000 copies. The comforts of unreason are sought after widely by those interested in the past, and Spearman's catalogue is a sharp warning to us all of the credulity of the public we write for and lecture to. Everything is here – flying saucers and spacemen, Nostradamus, the Scoriton mystery, the Warminster mystery. These words are being written in the September warmth of the shores of Lake Maggiore: we can hardly wait to get back to London to buy Raymond Drake's *Spacemen in the Ancient East,* and Taylor Hansen's *He Walked the Americas.*

Hansen's book is, we are told, about an early Christian, 'perhaps a witness of the birth and execution of Jesus', who 2,000 years ago, walked from tribe to tribe among the American nations. He came to the west coast of Peru from the Pacific 'in the ocean-going canoes of the Polynesians, and, after winning to the laws of God one of its ancient trading empires, left the lands of the North'. Who was he? the advertisement of the book very properly asks, 'this white Prophet who spoke a thousand languages, whose slightest touch was a miracle of healing? Some believe this saintly man to be Sir Thomas Didymus.' The Editor of ANTIQUITY thinks it was Sir Thomas Diddle-us-not-quite-all, but it remains flabbergasting that these books are written and published and sold in the third quarter of the 20th century.

March 1970

❦ Professor Lyle Borst is at it again and goes from weakness to weakness. We noted (ANTIQUITY, 1969) his theory, first published in that year (*Science,* 1969), that peculiar misalignments in the layout of Canterbury Cathedral were attributable to the fact that the Christian builders worked on a floor-plan left by their megalithic predecessors: and we said that this theory was fantasy. Since then Professor Borst has subjected other cathedrals and churches to his specialist analysis and finds that 'the architectural plans of cathedrals at Canterbury, Wells, Winchester, Gloucester and Norwich, and churches at Wing, Bucks, and Knowlton, Dorset, disclose megalithic designs of an explicit kind' (*Nature,* 1969). There seem to be Borst Woodhenges underneath every Christian building he visits, and it is not surprising that on a visit to Scandinavia he demanded that there should have been henge monuments under Nidaros Cathedral at Trondheim and the cathedral at Turku in Finland.

And, to our great personal distress, chambered long barrows are not immune to reinterpretation from this highly personalized and deplorable astro-archaeology. Rodmarton, Stoney Littleton, and Littleton Drew are all pressed into service by the Professor of Physics and Astronomy at the State University of New York at Buffalo. It is sad that Borst manipulates his circular theories at Stoney Littleton on an inaccurate plan, and that his plan of Littleton Drew says that the scale of this well-known site is unknown. It is unnerving that he relies frequently on a non-existent book by Professor Piggott entitled *The Megalithic Culture of the British Isles*, allegedly published fifteen years ago, and that all his plans are given scales only in megalithic yards.

Is this a folly and nonsense that should be dismissed in a few lines in our Book Chronicle? No: because Borst's article appeared in *Nature* (admittedly, while we are dealing with astro-megalithismus, we should note that Norman Lockyer was once editor of that illustrious journal). The 25 October 1969 issue of *Nature* contained Borst's article entitled 'English Henge Cathedrals'. *Nature* was taken in; and so were those eminently sensible men Sir Eric Fletcher and Sir John Betjeman, who, when giving evidence against the siting of an aerodrome which would demolish Wing church, said that now it was realized that this splendid Anglo-Saxon church was on an old sanctuary going back to the 3rd millennium BC, it was of even greater importance that it should not be destroyed: this, they said, might be the oldest religious building in Britain. And the BBC was taken in. They put out a Third Programme talk by Ian Rodger which was printed in *The Listener* for 27 November 1969. It was entitled 'Megalithic Mathematics' and began with a photograph of Wing church and continued with an account of stories of ghostly headless horsemen: we were back at once to the old straight-trackers and Rodger has his 'lattice of communication' dating from the time of the megalithic mathematicians. Rodger approves of Thom's megalithic yard and of Borst's henge cathedrals and says: 'It's possible that the legends of the headless horseman are a distorted and disguised relic of the men with their standard measurement of 2.72 feet who first tried to survey this land.'

The Editor of ANTIQUITY has been accused of publishing material for fun: did our friend the Editor of *The Listener* publish Rodger's tarradiddle of nonsense for fun? Is this why he included in the same number not only Atkinson on Thom, but Geoffrey Grigson's brilliant review of John Michell's *The View over Atlantis*, one of the dottiest books to have appeared for some while? We wonder since we know Karl Miller and since he published at the end of the fantastic Rodger article the devastatingly funny cartoon by Barry Fantoni which we reproduce by the artist's kind permission and that of BBC Publications.

'This book shows how the roundabouts on the M4
are built on a system of ancient burial mounds,
and on clear nights you can see a headless motorist...'

However that may be, it is clear that Stonehenge and megalithic architecture are now so much a part of the general public's awareness of the prehistoric past that any joke will pass, as it has passed about cave men and cave art for a long time. There was a most amusing cartoon published in the *Evening Standard* on 17 November 1969 and we publish it again here, by kind permission of the artist and the *Evening Standard*.

'Don't worry about it kid, I don't know either and
I designed the damn' thing'

June 1970

✿ This is the fiftieth editorial we have written for ANTIQUITY and we feel old and decayed, but enlivened by a letter from a Professor in California who writes: 'I always read ANTIQUITY because it is the only archaeological journal that has a gossip column.' We are not sure that Crawford would have liked that, but we do. Looking back on the last fifty issues, what are immediate reflexions? Growing impatience with contributors who still send in single-spaced manuscripts, diagrams and photographs that cannot be reproduced. And much more than impatience with people who take more than a year to produce a review they have agreed to do, especially when – as happens very rarely – they have, quite properly, suggested themselves as suitable reviewers. Admiration for those who produce their reviews without reminder, and their material for articles and notes in perfect form – double spaced with Harvard bibliography and illustrations ready to be sent to the printer. And a deep and abiding and appreciative affection for all those who make the punctual quarterly appearance of ANTIQUITY possible: our secretaries, our proof and production advisers, Mr Collieson and Mr Trevitt, our blockmakers and our printers and publishers whose co-operation and friendship are more than one could normally expect from heavily charged and busy firms; and for our Production Editor, without whose skilled and devoted care ANTIQUITY – and for that matter the Editor himself – might not exist.

September 1970

✿ Mr Paul Screeton takes us to task for some of our jibes at what the previous editor of ANTIQUITY called 'the lunatic fringe of archaeology'. He says, in a letter, 'I found your comments about straight-trackers, John Michell and Professor Borst most odious and unwarranted . . . your comments reveal either narrow-mindedness or ignorance of the present evaluation and allied evidence of a highly technical civilization in Bronze Age Britain. I find what I can only assume to be utter contempt for our researches and evidence most disturbing in someone with so high a reputation in archaeological circles.' Mr Screeton was kind enough to send us a copy of a journal he edits called *The Ley Hunter*, which is certainly a collectors' piece for those archaeologists who, from personal interest, or from professional necessity (like the Editor of ANTIQUITY), have to keep abreast with the widening lunatic fringes of a subject now an accepted part of humanistic study everywhere. In his editorial he describes us as 'in a fit of paranoia, seeing the tidy present-day archaeological theories crumbling to the state of ruins', lashing out blindly at the ley-hunters and the rest of them.

I had not thought that any archaeologists who were seriously occupied with the study of the ancient past would dismiss any theory without giving it the most serious and careful consideration, and it is in this way that most people dismiss as extravagant nonsense the ideas of Professor Elliot Smith that all civilization came from Egypt, of Lord Raglan that all civilization came from Mesopotamia, or of others that America was first colonized by Madoc or Brendan or the Phoenicians. The straight-trackers, the ley-hunters, John Michell and Professor Borst are all part of this extravagant nonsense. A journal devoted entirely to scientific and learned papers would need no truck with such beyond-the-fringers. A journal like ours devoted to a wider readership, and a readership which will go into bookshops in San Francisco and New York and find Michell and Churchward side by side with Childe, Clark and Willey, needs an occasional reminder of what goes on. They should buy the current issue of *The Ley Hunter*. The second article is called 'Why Flying Saucers followed the Leys'; and the first article 'Bats, Ghosts, Old Mother Midnight, and the Wishing Stone'. As this goes to the printers, the Editor is just getting on his broomstick to fly to the great alignments at Carnac to meet there Professor Alexander Thom who has done so much to make us think seriously about the mathematical and astronomical knowledge of the prehistoric inhabitants of north-western Europe. Serious, informed thinking on these matters is what we want, not bats, ghosts and flying saucers. But: pause, what if we are all wrong? (not that we believe it for a moment). If the December number of ANTIQUITY bears the name of another Editor, it may well be that old Mother Midnight (whom I take to be the White Goddess and the Black Goddess of Robert Graves in one) has more efficient anti-broomstick missiles than we suspect. But how sad it is that so many obviously intelligent and interested people these days should spend their time writing and thinking dottinesses while the whole world of man's past endeavour and achievement is theirs to appreciate, understand and admire.

December 1970

☟ So many people want to be comforted by unreason. Which reminds us that we have just declined to print an advertisement of *The Ley Hunter*, and that years ago, Crawford was delighted by the abuse he received in certain strange quarters for declining to publish an advertisement for Watkins's *The Old Straight Track*.

March 1971

❧ We published in the last issue Professor Brian Fagan's review of A. J. Bruwer's *Zimbabwe: Rhodesia's Ancient Greatness* in which he said 'one cannot fail to be concerned at the effect which a book like this can have on public opinion about important archaeological sites. ... The archaeologist's responsibility is to reconstruct history without regard to vested interest or racist thinking. The resurrection of the Phoenician controversy at Zimbabwe could have serious effects on African archaeology.' This fear has proved, alas, to be justified. Roger Summers, until recently Curator of the National Museum, Bulawayo, has left Rhodesia and is now on the staff of the South African Museum at Cape Town; and Peter Garlake, until recently Senior Inspector of the Rhodesian Historical Monuments Commission, has left for West Africa. Garlake said he saw Government intervention over Zimbabwe as 'a personal attack on the integrity of archaeologists who have studied the subject in great detail'.

The Rhodesian paper *Property and Finance* published in October an evil and entirely misinformed and unjustified attack on Roger Summers under the heading 'Zimbabwe pamphlets encourage Black nationalist claims'. We quote from this scurrilous, unsigned article:

The announcement that a new official *Guide Book to Zimbabwe* is being prepared is a reminder that, as tourism is one of the country's major economic growth-points, the revision of some Government-produced tourist pamphlets on the famous ruins is also long overdue. The constant theme of the pamphlets, now, reflects totally unproven assumptions substantiating Pan-African claims that for centuries Rhodesia was the centre of a sophisticated Negroid 'civilization'. The political implications are clear: if the claims are justified, there should be no legitimate opposition to a Black take-over of the country. It is no accident that the banned nationalist groups refer to Rhodesia as 'Zimbabwe'.... Fortunately, the National Monuments Commission and the museums (and their associated archaeologists, whether professional or amateur) fall under the Ministry of Internal Affairs, and if that Ministry can ensure that the new *Guide to Zimbabwe* is a wholly factual presentation of the country's ancient history...it will at least remove yet another pretext for hostile political propaganda.

This is the most outrageous and wicked double-talk. Years of archaeological research have shown that Zimbabwe is a product of indigenous Bantu peoples, and no one in his senses believes any more in Phoenicians, and King Solomon's mines, and Arabs, and the lost tribes of Israel, as the historical explanation of this remarkable site; there is no evidence of foreign builders. It is clear that scientific archaeological research is to be denigrated, if not suppressed, by the Rhodesian authorities; and as a correspondent wrote to us: 'The field is therefore wide open for the smothering of Rhodesian later prehistory. The whole business is a salutary warning to students of history and prehistory that political distortion of science and historical truth is not something that died out with the Nazi regime.'

Professor R. R. Inskeep referred to some of these problems in his Presidential Address to Section F of the South African Association for the Advancement of Science, given in July 1970, and published in *The South African Journal of Science* of October 1970. He says how important it is for archaeologists to engage in works of *haute-vulgarisation* and write authoritative books which the general public can read, and refers to Summers's *Zimbabwe: a Rhodesian Mystery* as 'an excellent example of a scholarly statement presented in a form calculated to hold the interest of any intelligent reader in search of information about Zimbabwe'. We recommend the Rhodesian Ministry of Internal Affairs, who seem to be determined to pervert the facts about the early history of their country, to read Summers's book, and Fagan's forthcoming *Archaeological Guide to Central and Southern Africa*, which has an excellent chapter about Zimbabwe; and to reflect on Trevelyan's remark in his *History and the Reader* (1945): 'The harm that one-sided history has done in the modern world is immense. When history is used as a branch of propaganda it is a very deadly weapon.' It is this very deadly weapon which is now being used in Rhodesia to do harm to that country's prehistory.

☟ An apology to T. G. E. Powell who gently upbraids us for saying that we have both been writing about megaliths for half a century (ANTIQUITY, 1970). How right he is: it is only thirty-five years but sometimes it seems longer. Perhaps this is because the Editor was born, over half a century ago, in a small schoolhouse in Pembrokeshire, out of whose bedroom windows a ruined cromlech could be seen, in and around which he well remembers playing during the 1914–18 war.

June 1971

☟ Professor Walter Emery's death, due to a heart attack at the age of sixty-seven, has revived all the nonsensical journalistic speculations about 'the curse of the Pharaohs'. The *Daily Telegraph* for 12 March writes:

Inevitably, the circumstances of Professor Emery's death will revive speculation about the controversial 'curse of the Pharaohs'. According to popular superstition this rules: 'Death shall come on swift wings to him that toucheth the tomb of a Pharaoh.' The legend began soon after the opening of Tutankhamen's tomb in 1922. The Earl of Carnarvon, who financed the excavation, visited the site and was bitten by a mosquito. Soon after he died in a Cairo hotel of pneumonia. Subsequently about twenty people associated with the excavation died in unexpected or mysterious circumstances.

The only comment to make on this inaccurate piece of reporting is – poppycock. It is not the curse of the Pharaohs but the inevitable fact of death that brings the lives of distinguished archaeologists to an end in Egypt as elsewhere.

December 1971

☙ It is of course not only genuine antiquities which are being smuggled out of their countries of origin and sold by dealers in Switzerland, London and New York. There is a very large and lucrative trade in forgeries, and many experts and museums have, in the last few months, found that some of their cherished treasures are, at best, clever examples of the forger's art. That distinguished, learned and fascinating journal, *Archaeometry*, the Bulletin of the Research Laboratory for Archaeology and the History of Art in the University of Oxford, published in its Part 2 of Volume 13 in August of this year a number which deserves to stand on our shelves next to the revelations of the Piltdown forgery. First we are told that many of the pots, allegedly genuine finds from Hacilar (the site excavated from 1957 to 1960 by James Mellaart), which found their way on to the market when his work was finished, and were bought in good faith by the British Museum, the Metropolitan Museum of Art in New York, the Ashmolean Museum in Oxford and other museums and private collections in Europe and America, have been proved to be fakes. Thermoluminescence research at Oxford showed that forty-eight out of sixty-six pots allegedly from genuine Hacilar contexts were fakes. Secondly, twenty-five 'genuine' Etruscan tomb-paintings, sold for £10,000 each and now in European museums, mostly in Switzerland, are clever fakes.

Years ago, when 'Hacilar' pots were coming on to the market, James Mellaart told us that this must be due to illicit excavation after he had left the site in 1960. But now it appears that many of these were faked pots and the Turkish police have arrested a man by the name of Sevket Cetimkaya, deliciously described by *The Times* correspondent as 'a peasant...of no specific occupation'. The police chief of Burdur, in which area Hacilar is situated, said that, when Cetimkaya's house was raided, they found fifty-four authentic artifacts, twenty-three forged artifacts and 'five pounds of fragments which are being examined for authenticity'. Cetimkaya was the peasant who guided Mellaart to Hacilar in 1956. Ten years later, as Patricia Connor and Kenneth Pearson point out in *The Sunday Times* (8 August 1971) 'he was a business man of independent means, owning one or more blocks of flats and a travel agency'.

We shall see what happens in Turkey. Meanwhile the journalists have given us deliciously extravagant headlines such as 'How a Turkish peasant got rich on cracked pots'; 'A peasant's fakes may have fooled museums', and 'Fool's gold in velvet-lined showcases'. But it is *not* funny, and redounds to the great discredit of good archaeology. The Turks have redoubled their precautions at frontiers and posted archaeologists to many of their customs offices. The illicit trade in forged antiquities is far less important than the illicit trade in genuine objects. The convention signed in Paris in November 1970 by sixty-six Unesco member nations has so far been ratified by only one nation – Ecuador. It must be ratified by all countries, and certainly by England and America. There must no longer be these strange stories of museums such as those in Philadelphia and Boston buying unprovenanced finds through dealers whose names cannot be disclosed. The black market in smuggled antiquities must be stopped. The market in forgeries can look after itself, that is, if museums can look after themselves. With all the scientific techniques at our disposal these days, many of them so brilliantly deployed by the Oxford Research Laboratory, there is no longer any need for people to be taken in by the tiara of Saitaphernes and by Glozel and Piltdown. Perhaps the Oxford Laboratory could look at the paintings at Rouffignac and resolve the uncertainties that still surround that strange affair? That would be most helpful.

March 1972

☚ The Gulf *Tourguide* map that was given us when we hired a car to drive from New York to Boston last September had a special section: *Tourguide Facts: Places of Interest* and, under New Hampshire, was this entry: '*N. Salem. Mystery Hill. Internationally famous archaeological mystery.*' And then we remembered the correspondence between Frank Glynn and Tom Lethbridge in the thirties and photographs passed on to us of what purported to be pre-Columbian megalithic monuments in New England.

We drove to Mystery Hill so soon as we decently could leave the better-known famous archaeologists of Harvard. It lies some 65 km. north of Boston and is 40 km. from the sea. As we nervously approached it, we saw a great notice saying 'Welcome to Mystery Hill – the American Stonehenge', and on arrival were presented with a pamphlet describing it thus:

12-acre settlement of megalithic structures, huts, dolmens, carefully built walls, intricate underground drainage systems, carvings, rock-basins and bowls; several underground caverns. Centered by a grooved slab, with supporting table, called the sacrificial stone.

The tea and souvenir shop which issued tickets for admission, and which we approached with mounting trepidation, had notice boards with cuttings from various journals. One by Dorothy Patten, in the *Haverhill Gazette* for 31 July 1967, described Mystery Hill as:

...the largest unsolved complex of man-made stone structures ever found in the United States.... How far back in the centuries do these date? What are they and who built them? Are they products of the Bronze Age? The Phoenicians? Irish Culdee Monks? Vikings? Indians? Or the eccentricities of Colonial farmer Jonathan Pattee who occupied the site from 1826–1848?

We went round the site with interest and spent another whole day there with Paul Johnstone of BBC *Chronicle*, who was making a film of this strange complex of buildings. Pattee's Hill is 800 m. high and the stone complex covers three-quarters of an acre (0.30 ha.) on the top of the hill. At first sight it looks like a cross between a large neglected rockery, disused farm outbuildings, and the ruins of a folly, all with ghost memories of Cornish fogous, Grimspound, French souterrains, and Sardinian *cappane*. In our judgement it certainly bears no morphological or constructional resemblance to the great megalithic monuments of prehistoric Western Europe, apart from, of course, the coincidental resemblances that occur when drystone walling is used in a building for construction and large stone slabs for trabeate roofing. The pigsties of Pembrokeshire and the clapper bridges of Dartmoor are as much 'megaliths' in the proper archaeological sense of the word, as are some of the odd buildings at Mystery Hill.

The site has been known to natives of the area for more than a hundred years as Pattee's Caves. Jonathan Pattee was a French Huguenot farmer who lived there for a while. In 1936 the site was bought by a prosperous gentleman, a retired insurance executive, from Hartford, Connecticut, named William B. Goodwin. He brought the site to the attention of archaeologists and himself dug large portions of it, with, apparently, little care or attention. He decided, on the results of his diggings, that it was a settlement of Irish Culdee monks.

In 1939 Goodwin persuaded Dr Hugh Hencken of Harvard to visit the site. Hencken was unable to agree that the site was of Irish origin, and thought it colonial: he published his views in an article entitled 'The "Irish Monastery" at North Salem, New Hampshire' in the *New England Quarterly* for September 1939. His learning and argument however did not convince

Goodwin who believed the site an Irish monastery until his death in 1950; and, in 1946, published a book entitled *The Ruins of Great Ireland in New England*. In 1955 the Early Sites Foundation of New England authorized and financed an expedition to dig the site: the excavators were Junius Bird of the American Museum of Natural History and Gary Viscelius of Yale. After six weeks' digging the Bird–Viscelius expedition decided that there was nothing earlier than revolutionary days and Jonathan Pattee. One member of the expedition, Frank Glynn of Clinton, Connecticut, and subsequently President of the Connecticut Archaeological Society, did not agree with these findings and continued to excavate on his own for many years. Glynn alleged that he could point to forty-eight similarities between Mystery Hill and the Bronze Age of the Old World: he believed the site to be the most westerly extension of the European megalith builders, and he dated the site to between 3000 and 500 BC.

The site is now owned by Robert Stone of Derry, an engineer with Western Electric, and President of the New England Antiquities Research Association (founded in 1964). New excavations have been proceeding at Mystery Hill for the last six years under the direction of James P. Whittall Jr: Stone and Whittall are convinced that they are dealing with something much earlier than Pattee, and, while they agree that such evidence does not date the site, were very excited by the C14 dating of charcoal found between walling stones of one of the buildings. This gave a date of 3475 ± 210 BP or 1525 BC: the dating was determined in the Geochron Laboratories at Cambridge, Mass. (reference GX.2310).

This date shows that the site had an early occupation; but we share Hencken's views that the visible structures of the present day are unlikely to be earlier than the seventeenth century. A colleague summed up his views recently by saying that it was a classic example of 'how archaeology is used to take the great American public for the proverbial ride', and how right he was! The real interest of Mystery Hill is not that it is a great archaeological mystery, but that it is built up as such. The great American public want mystery and they passionately want proof of the settlement of their country in pre-Columbian times.

The bookstall at Mystery Hill sold copies of NEARA – the quarterly Newsletter of the New England Antiquities Research Association; and C. M. Boland's *They all discovered America*. We devoured Boland avidly. His book, described as 'an absorbing, imaginative account of the explorers who came to America *before* Columbus', was first published in 1961, and is now a paperback to be found everywhere. When Boland's book first came out the *San Francisco News-Call Bulletin* said 'Americans should read this book to learn just how long their native land has been there', and the

Indianapolis Star declared that 'If Christopher Columbus had known half as much about the discovery of America as the author of this book, he never would have taken the trouble.' Boland has nineteen pre-Columbus discoverers of America: these include Phoenicians, Romans, the Chinese Hoei-shin (and where indeed did he get to?), St Brendan, Irish Culdee monks, Vikings from Bjarni Herjulfsson to Bishop Eric Gnupsson, Quetzalcoatl, Prince Madoc, Paul Knutson, Prince Henry and the brothers Zeno, and Joaz Vaz Cortereal. Every conceivable dubious find or known forgery is dragged into service by Boland, from alleged Phoenician inscriptions through the Dighton Rock on Assonet Neck, Rhode Island, the Minnesota Stone, the Newport Tower (of course) and the Beardmore finds of 1931. There is a photograph of a carving of an alleged Phoenician ship revealed when the waters of Lake Assawompsett in Massachusetts were lowered, and of Mr Albert Wheeler holding aloft a fragment of a suspected (by whom and why?) Viking ship found on his property in Massachusetts. And as he finished writing this amazing collection of credibilities and nonsense, Boland was able to trumpet abroad the announcement of the authentication of a Roman head of the second century AD found in Calixtlahuaca in Mexico 'under three sealed and undisturbed floors, found in 1940, but announced by Dr Heine-Geldern in the International Congress of Americanists in Vienna in July 1960'. Boland coins a useful and amusing phrase: 'the NEBC principle', which means the model of thought that insisted there could be no Europeans in America before Columbus, and this model of thought is to be recorded and described in the same way as we are describing, from Boland and Gordon and others, the reverse model which we may encapsulate in a similarly useful and perhaps amusing phrase: 'the MEBC principle', which means many Europeans (and Mediterraneans and Orientals and others) in America before Columbus.

The NEARA newsletters are, unhappily, the same sort of MEBC stuff that one reads in Boland: they are full of oddities, quiddities and lunacies; they are credulous and querulous. Here are men trying hard – oh, so hard and often so honestly – to invent a past, but who often remain unconvinced of their own myth. All the current lunacies are ventilated in the NEARA newsletters, the Landsverk-Monge theory of ciphers and dates hidden in runic inscriptions, balancing rocks, astronomical alignments, bogus 'dolmens' at Martha's Vineyard, Madoc's stone forts in southern Illinois, the Paraiba Stone, the Newport Tower, the Dighton Rock, the Roman (?) inscriptions in Maine, and the second century AD Hebrew and Roman coins from Kentucky.

We returned to Cambridge, Mass., dejected and disappointed by this sortie into the maverick archaeology of New England. As we had left the little museum-cum-café-cum-souvenir shop, the headline of an article in the

Lawrence Eagle-Tribune for 11 June 1965 caught our eye: 'Antiquity Researchers Probe Secrets of Mystery Hill', but it gave us no comfort. A shelf in the Harvard Coop displayed five books, four of them new, discussing in various ways the problems of pre-Columbian America.

1. *Collectors' luck: giant steps into prehistory* by Betty Bugbee Cusack (Stonehaven, Mass., 1968).
2. *Before Columbus* by Cyrus H. Gordon (New York, 1971).
3. *The Quest for America* (ed Geoffrey Ashe) (New York, 1971).
4. *Man across the sea: problems of pre-Columbian contacts* (edited by Carroll L. Riley, J. Charles Kelley, Campbell W. Pennington and Robert L. Rands) (Austin, 1971).
5. *The European discovery of America: vol. 1: The northern voyages AD 500 to 1600* by Samuel Eliot Morison (London, 1971).

The last three books are of great importance and will receive special and serious consideration in a future number of this journal. The Bugbee Cusack and Cyrus Gordon books are *autre chose*, and must be summarily dismissed here.

Mrs Bugbee Cusack's book is a scissors-and-paste affair of cuttings about prehistory in America that have interested her. It begins with a photograph of a piece of metamorphic rock 300 to 400 million years old, found by the author at Cape Cod in 1966, and ends with a photocopy of her husband's deposit of $50 with Thomas Cook and Son 'for trip to Moon if and when trip is feasible: refundable on request' and dated 11 July 1961. In between these unusual items we are treated to all sorts of curious things from Irish monks, Vikings and Mystery Hill to an account of how herring gulls navigate in fog, runic (??) inscriptions from Maine and Massachusetts, and a delicious titbit, namely that in 1695 the town of Sandwich (which, incidentally, has in addition to its reputation for glass, the lovely spire on its Congregational Church designed by Christopher Wren), passed an order that 'every unmarried man in the Township yearly should kill six blackbirds, or three crows, while he remained single, and then should not marry until he obeyed and fulfilled that order to the letter'.

Mrs Bugbee Cusack is frivolous and futile: she is, encapsulated in a book, the uninformed conversation one hears in the cocktail hour either side of the Atlantic. She was not expecting to be taken seriously, and we respect her expectations: hers is a *jeu d'esprit* of enthusiasm and lunacy. Not so Cyrus H. Gordon who is a professional scholar and teacher, Head of the Department of Mediterranean Studies at Brandeis University in Boston. The publishers' blurb describes him as 'an internationally respected scholar . . . the author of some thirteen books' and his book as 'a revolutionary treatise by one of the world's most eminent scholars'. Robert Graves, the distinguished poet, who, even in the moments when he feels most inspired by his imaginary White Goddess, could hardly be called a person knowledgeable about the ancient history of western Europe and pre-Columbian contacts with America, writes: 'Romantic novelists and amateur historians have so often tried to sell us news of pre-Columbian traffic across the Atlantic, long before the days of Leif Ericsson, that when at last it comes, irrefutably substantiated and dated by one of the world's most dependable scholars, the shock makes us gasp. Professor Gordon is the newsbringer.'

Turning eagerly to *Before Columbus*, knowing Gordon's reputation, and rather warily brushing aside publishers' blurb and Graves's extravaganza, we read the book. What is it? Just a load of concentrated and dangerous rubbish. What has happened to Professor Gordon? He believes that the portraits illustrated and described by Alexander von Wuthenau (see ANTIQUITY, 1971) are of European and African and Asiatic types (but what does he, a Semitic scholar, mean by referring to a Semitic type? He must know better than most of us that Semitic is a linguistic and ethnic, not racial, term); and he alleges that the Greeks knew America. 'To sum up,' he says (p. 49), 'Greek classics independently and repeatedly attest transatlantic contacts between the Mediterranean and America.' He suggests that 'we visualize the founders of ancient astronomy as setting up bases in the Near East, Middle America and the West Pacific' (p. 172). He sees 'the megalithic monuments of the Bronze Age mariners' as 'tangible reminders of a world civilization, with highly developed science and technologies'. He believes in the Paraíba inscription, the Metcalf stone, the Bat Creek Hebrew Inscription, the Roman Head from Calixtlahuaca, the second-century AD Hebrew and Roman coins from Louisville, Clay City and Hopkinsville, and thinks that Mexico 'rich in silver and other metal ores is a possible identification for Tarshish'.

This is not the lunatic fringe of archaeology: this is not the world of the New Diffusionists, Black Horses, Atlantis, Pyramidiots, straight-trackers and the rest of them, the world which every student of antiquity recognizes, with an embarrassed smile, as a danger only to those whose weak and muddled heads prefer the comforts of unreason to the difficult facts of archaeology. This is dangerous stuff because it is set out as scholarship by a professional scholar. This is poisoned chocolate: attractive from the outside, decked out in good wrappings – but, beware: the filling is bitter-sweet, this is false-centre archaeology. The fantastic *Before Columbus* must, alas, be placed on one's shelves alongside Elliot Smith, Perry and Raglan. It contains sentences very reminiscent of the hyper-diffusionists, such as 'If high independently invented civilizations have existed, they were not on this planet' (p. 35). We are reminded of what Samuel Johnson said of Monboddo:

It is a pity to see Lord Monboddo publish such notions as he has done: a man of sense and so much elegant learning. There would be little in a fool doing it; we should only laugh; but when a wise man does it we are sorry. Other people have strange notions, but they conceal them. If they have tails, they hide them: Lord Monboddo is as jealous of his tail as a squirrel.

The Paraíba inscription is Gordon's tail and he dedicates his book to Jules Piccus, now a Professor of Hispanic Studies at the University of Massachusetts at Amherst, who told Gordon that he had acquired a scrapbook 'for a small sum at a rummage sale in Providence, R.I.': this scrapbook contained a new copy of the text of the inscription found by slaves of Joaquim Alves da Costa, on 11 September 1872, on his plantation at Pouso Alto near Paraíba in Brazil. Ernest Renan, at the time the leading authority on Canaanite epigraphy, but whom Gordon castigates as a person 'whose knowledge and reputation were exceeded only by his pedantry', declared the inscription to be a fake. Gordon believes it to be true and provides a fresh translation from the text in the scrapbook (the original stone having vanished), and finds that it records a crossing from Canaan to Brazil in 534–531 BC. It is this translation, his conviction of the authenticity of the stone, and its general implications, if authentic, that started Gordon off on writing this unhappy book.

Unhappy because it is frankly and outrageously partisan. The possibility of transatlantic voyages in pre-Viking and pre-Brendan times is denied these days only by a few. It is the archaeological or other proof that such voyages did indeed take place that interests us all. What evidence there is needs careful weighing: every alleged find from Paraíba to Bat Creek studied with care and both sides of each argument fairly presented. This is what Gordon does not do. He says, 'If I have learned anything throughout nearly half a century of study it is to keep an open mind and to avoid confusing majority opinion with truth' (p. 79). What an admirable sentiment, but what a pity that Gordon should now have closed his mind so that he confuses minority opinion with truth. We are reminded of Elliot Smith's phrase in his 1928 Huxley Memorial Lecture: 'The set attitude of mind of a scholar may become almost indistinguishable from a delusion.' Once after a lecture in California we were asked by an anxiously interested lady, a kind of Mrs Betty Bugbee Cusack, why scholars like Lowie and Dixon and Wauchope would have no truck with Egyptians and lost tribes in America, nothing to do with Atlantis and Mu. 'Can't we believe what we read in books?' she cried in despair (and with what joy she will seize on *Before Columbus*). Perhaps her best answer is contained in two sentences on page 38 of Gordon's book: 'Ignorance is a curable disease', and 'Not everything written as history is true.'

☿ These words are being hammered out on the Purser's typewriter aboard the t.s. *Bremen* (mark V, formerly the French *Pasteur*, and now making her last transatlantic crossing, at least under the North German Lloyd flag) in mid–Atlantic in mid-December in conditions described on the ship's notice board as *sehr hohe see* and *phenomenal*. Looking out to sea from the comparative comfort of the bar, a glass of Steinhager (as privately prescribed in his wisdom by the President of the Prehistoric Society) clutched firmly in our hands, observing the sixty-foot waves outside, and the passengers, glasses and ship's unanchored furniture within sliding from side to side with the confused regularity of the motions of the high seas, one is filled again with wonder, delight and admiration for those who, long before the compass and stabilizers, crossed the Atlantic in pre-Columbian days. We lift our glass to St Brendan, and keep a look out for friendly whales. How nice it would be to meet some modern Jasconius!

June 1972

☿ Dr A. C. Renfrew, Senior Lecturer in Archaeology in the University of Sheffield, has been appointed Professor of Archaeology in the University of Southampton to replace Professor Barry Cunliffe. This news will give much pleasure to many, but not, we fear, to Messrs Joel and Kraus, who produce, every quarter, that crabbed journal *The New Diffusionist*, and who recently wrote to the Trustees of ANTIQUITY to say what a scandalous man the Editor was in setting out honestly his views and refusing advertisements for their journal (which he had told them he regarded as a load of old rubbish). Now they have, temporarily we hope, abandoned their vilification of ourselves and turned to Colin Renfrew. His ideas are described as 'a relapse into flat-earth mentality in European Prehistory', and this impudent, ignorant and totally inappropriate phrase will give him as much amusement as it gives all of us who eagerly await the next issue of this deliciously irrelevant and ill-informed journal, in which the attack on the flat-earth Renfrew will be continued.

December 1972

☿ It is good news that the British Museum has decided to lend the Rosetta Stone to the Louvre. It is only the fortune of war that brought the stone to London. When Napoleon invaded Egypt in 1798 he took with him a number of savants interested in ancient Egypt, who collected Egyptian antiquities, including the block of basalt inscribed in hieroglyphics, demotic and Greek found by accident by French soldiers at Rosetta. On 19 July 1799 the members of the French Institute were most excited when a letter from Egypt was read to them announcing 'the discovery at Rosetta of some inscriptions that may offer much interest'. The British army which invaded Egypt in 1801 demanded the stone and other collections of the French savants as prizes of battle. General Hutchinson claimed everything under Article XVI of the treaty of capitulation. The French General Menou disputed every point and insisted that the Rosetta Stone was his private property and was not covered by the treaty.

The British force included several people interested in Egyptology, among them that delicious character Edward Daniel Clarke (1769–1822), Fellow and Bursar of Jesus College, Cambridge, University Librarian and first Professor of Mineralogy in the University, author of *The Gas Blowpipe*, who, when an undergraduate, sent up his kitten attached to a balloon, and when a young man travelled with Malthus in northern Europe and secured the Kistiphoros of Eleusis for his old University. Clarke entered Alexandria with the advance guard of the British army because, as J. D. Wortham says in his admirable *The genesis of British Egyptology 1549–1906* (Norman, 1971), 'he intended to make certain that the French did not send any Egyptian antiquities back to France'. Elgin had sent W. R. Hamilton to Alexandria with orders to seize the French collection of Egyptian remains. To quote Wortham again, 'Clarke and Hamilton succeeded in stealing from the French a great many antiquities – including a great green sarcophagus hidden by the French in a hospital ship – that the French had stolen from the Egyptians.'

Clarke immediately realized the importance of the Rosetta Stone, and that the trilingual inscription could enable the hieroglyphic alphabet to be deciphered. He got to know a young colonel, T. H. Turner, who shared his enthusiasm for Egyptology. When General Hutchinson insisted on the Rosetta Stone being given up, General Menou replied, 'You want it, Monsieur le général? You can have it, since you are the stronger of us two.... You may pick it up whenever you please.' Colonel Turner collected a detachment of soldiers and seized the stone from Menou's house. He accompanied it all the way to England and gave it into the safe keeping of the Society of Antiquaries of London until it finally came to rest in the British Museum. It was the arrival of the Rosetta Stone and the many other acquisitions of Egyptian remains through conquest of war that forced a reluctant parliament to approve additions to the British Museum. It is a pleasant thought that at last it will be making a journey to the home originally planned for it.

The reason for the journey to Paris is to celebrate the 150th anniversary of Champollion's *Lettre à M. Dacier relative à l'alphabet des hiéroglyphes phonétiques* which contained the key to the decipherment of hieroglyphs, and triumphantly succeeded where De Sacy, Akerblad, and Thomas Young had started. Is there any real reason why it should not go further, and return to Egypt whence it came as spoils of war? The whole learned world has copies of it; it has served its purpose. The key to ancient Egypt should really be back home, with those who so generously lent us Tutankhamun's treasures for so long.

March 1973

❧ The King of Sweden, the Goths and the Wends celebrated his ninetieth birthday last November and we congratulate an archaeologist who has been a subscriber to this journal since its foundation in 1927: and a television birthday interview showed him in his study, a set of bound volumes of ANTIQUITY behind him. Several books have been specially produced in his honour for this occasion; a most attractive one is *Kungen Gräver: en bok om arkeologer och arkeologi*. It is edited by Olov Isaksson with a text by Lars O. Lagerqvist and Maj Odelberg and produced by Askild and Kärnekull in conjunction with the Statens historiska museum, Stockholm. We quote from the book: 'Gustav VI Adolf has in seven decades made important contributions in northern and classical archaeology. In his time the King has taken the initiative and supported archaeological excavations in different parts of Sweden, as well as abroad. And at many of these he has often assisted the investigations in the field. Himself a keen collector of art and antiquities, King Gustav has presented many new acquisitions to the Swedish public collections, as well as initiating and advising upon the setting up of several new museums.'

The frontispiece is a charming photograph of the King, then Prince Gustav Adolf, digging with Oscar Montelius in 1905 at Kulla-Gunnarstorp in Skåne. It brings again to mind the story which J. M. de Navarro used to tell in his lectures (and which his pupils go on telling in theirs) of Montelius turning to the Prince on one such occasion as that photographed here and saying, 'Young man, if you didn't have another job to go to, you would make a good archaeologist.' An opportunity occurred a few years ago of asking King Gustav whether this story was true, or just another part of archaeological mythology. He was amused, thought for a while, and said, 'I do not recollect the occasion, but I would go on telling the story in your lectures if I were you.'

June 1973

❦ We deliberately published Dr David Clarke's article 'Archaeology: the loss of innocence' (ANTIQUITY, 1973) knowing that it would cause alarm and despondency among many. We thought it right and proper that the main British exponent of what is tiresomely called in America 'the New Archaeology', as if all archaeology was not moving to newness by discovery and interpretation every decade, should have his say, and set out his views. It was a personal statement and no one who has read *Analytical Archaeology* would have supposed that it would be written other than in the obscure jargon promoted by the Binfords. But we have been surprised by the violence of the reaction to the article, and print three letters of considerable interest. The first is from Dr Peter Salway who is now a Regional Director of the Open University, written on 9 March:

I have much respect for Dr David Clarke as a practising archaeologist. Hence I am all the more horrified by his article 'Archaeology: the loss of innocence' in the March issue of ANTIQUITY. Much of my own daily working information comes from systems analysts, data processors, social scientists and educational technologists. I find it requires no mental effort at all to write, for example, that in archaeology within certain parameters it is possible by deriving suitable structured questions from a model and translating them into an algorithm for non-subject-sympathetic operators to process survey research field data and allocate it to type cells in a multi-dimensional matrix, provided that by raising coded signals one can retrieve comparative information on file in a suitable data-base system. It is extraordinary that Dr Clarke should complain that specialists are 'unconsciously raising barriers to communication between archaeologists' and continue to write in the way he does. This misuse, not to say wilful disregard, of the English language is far more destructive. Indeed it is potentially fatal to archaeology. Communication between professionals becomes almost impossible. David Clarke's actual points, when one can cut one's way through to them, are valuable and already widely held (some, indeed, are not so new as they may appear wrapped up in this curious dialect). But they could easily be expressed in normal English, and there really is no reason why busy professionals should learn this new language. Indeed there is a real danger of separate (or do I mean discrete?) languages emerging, unintelligible between specialisms. The answer is not a new common jargon, since the worst danger is that the serious amateur with very limited time for his archaeology is likely to be baffled and repelled. This is a split many of us are anxious to avoid. Even worse, public understanding of archaeology is likely to decline into total incomprehension. *Rescue* and the multitude of local research committees were hardly founded for this.

Dr Clarke would have done better in his second paragraph to talk not of 'craft style' but of 'craft mystery', for this is what it is. Mystification is a time-honoured method of keeping a profession exclusive, but it will do nothing to gain public support and informed participation in all the fields vital to archaeology today, particularly legislation and planning. If I may be permitted one trendy word (now sanctified by Government use), in the end it is not only a matter of saving the raw material of our 'craft', it is also a matter of enabling the public to understand the information they need to judge the issues affecting their own environment – or is it 'quality of life-style'?

The second letter is from the President of the Society of Antiquaries of London. Dr. J. N. L. Myres writes:

If David Clarke and his New Archaeologists are no longer Innocent, it follows that they must be Guilty. Guilty of what? Well, clearly of at least one unpardonable sin, an outrageous misuse of their mother tongue.

If I understand aright the message of his article (and I have been at some distasteful pains to do so), the meaning behind twelve pages of tortuous gobbledygook can be stated in one simple sentence: Archaeologists now have access to more assistance of many kinds from other disciplines than was formerly the case, and, properly used, these aids are capable of adding greatly to our knowledge. These propositions are self-evident and it is not necessary to lose one's innocence to appreciate their truth. To make a new archaeology out of them apparently requires the use (often the misuse) of three long words wherever one short one will do. So we are expected to live in a 'metaphysical field space', peopled by 'paradigms', 'epistemologies', 'taxa' (what language are they?), 'postdictions' and 'theoretical hatracks'. It seems a great pity that the 'doomed race of disciplinary dinosaurs' (Dr Clarke's one truly memorable phrase) who tried to teach him archaeology, did not use their blue pencils to better effect on his literally unspeakable prose.

We agree with some of Dr Myres's criticisms and believe that epistemologies and postdictions are unnecessary neologisms of the so-called new archaeologists. The word 'paradigm' is a trendy alternative for the perfectly good word 'model'. But surely there is nothing mysterious or unusual about the words 'taxon' and 'taxa', which are back-formations of taxonomy, 'the science, laws, or principles of classification', and both words coming from the Greek *taxis*, meaning arrangement or order. Here is the definition of taxon in *The American Heritage Dictionary of the English Language* (1969): '*Biology*. A group of organisms constituting one of the categories or formal units in taxonomic classification, such as a phylum, order, family, genus or species, and characterized by common characteristics in varying degrees of distinction.' To take an example from megalithic monuments: passage-graves, *allées couvertes*, entrance-graves, menhirs, portal-chambers, statue-menhirs, are all taxa.

But if we defend some words we do not defend the spate of jargon of the Binford–Clarke school. We are reminded of what A. E. Housman said in his Leslie Stephen Lecture for 1933 entitled *The name and nature of poetry*:

1 *O.G.S Crawford (1886-1957). Founder of* ANTIQUITY *and Editor 1927-1957, photographed in 1954 on the Roman Road from Southampton to the Isle of Wight.*

2 *Lucas de Heere's watercolour of Stonehenge in ms. Add.28330 in the British Library, London, illustrating Dr J.A. Bakker's article in 1979.*

3 *The half-scale partial reconstruction of Stonehenge at the University of Missouri-Rolla.*

4 *Stonehenge as observed by Mike Wells in 1976.*

5 *A fish-eye-lens view by Brian Harris of the Druids at their Midsummer ceremonial at Stonehenge in 1978.*

6 *Excavations at Glozel in 1928: at left Dr Morlet and Harry Söderman.*

7 *Professor Audollent, a theologian from Clermont-Ferrand,*
clutching at roots (or straws?) at Glozel in 1928.

8,9 *The Greek*
bronze horse
in the Metropolitan
Museum of Art,
New York,
purchased in 1923,
and a Gamma ray
shadowgraph of the
horse, made in 1967.

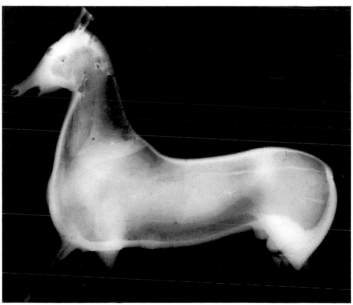

10 *'Friendship… a conspiracy for pleasure': Glyn Daniel and Mortimer Wheeler, 1971.*

11 *Gordon Childe visiting Stuart Piggott's excavations at Dorchester-on-Thames in 1946.*

12 (Above)
The Editor and
Production Editor study
the so-called
Viking mooring stone
from Jesse Lake,
Minnesota,
now in the Runestone
Park, Alexandria,
Minnesota.

13 (Right)
Viking 'Big Ole'
(20 ft high
and brightly painted),
outside the
Runestone Museum,
Alexandria,
Minnesota.

14 *HRH The Prince of Wales, ex-pupil and contributor, presents* Antiquity and Man
(Essays in honour of Glyn Daniel) *at Stationers' Hall on 25 June 1981.*

15 *Glyn Daniel with Ruth celebrating the publication of his memoirs,*
Some Small Harvest, *in Heffers Bookshop, Cambridge, on 25 September 1986.*

'When I hear anyone say, with defiant emphasis, that Pope was a poet, I suspect him of calling in ambiguity of language to promote confusion of thought.' Aspiring archaeological Popes should ponder over Housman's wise words.

The third letter was from Dr Graham Webster of the Department of Extramural Studies in the University of Birmingham. He writes:

Having made a serious effort to read David Clarke's article without understanding hardly a word of it, I began to get very worried. As an old fashioned practical excavator, was I beginning to lose my grip, or did I lack the intellectual ability to grasp the modern concept? So I gave it to a young student to read and tell me what it is about. She could not understand it either. So we are baffled. Perhaps it is not written in English at all, but some new kind of scientific language which uses some English words. . . . It is possible that the article applies only to Prehistoric Archaeology. If this is so, it is unfortunate that a gulf is being created between practitioners on the same subject in different periods. This lack of communication could lead to serious consequences, so would it not be desirable for at least a summary of such important papers to be translated into English for the benefit of those concerned with the post–prehistoric periods?

We asked Dr David Clarke if he would like to comment on the letters from Salway, Myres and Webster but he said his comments could be found in his review of the Newell-Vroomans book which we print in this issue. We wonder whether his critics will be satisfied with this answer, and we sometimes wonder whether the Binfords and Clarkes of this world realize they write in gobbledygook gibberish? The *OED* tells us that the word 'gobbledygook' was invented by Maury Maverick of Texas and means 'official verbiage or jargon'; the gobble part is, of course, talking turkey, and the gook, we learn elsewhere, may come from the Scottish *gowk*, a simpleton, or the Middle English *gowke*, a cuckoo. Certainly and fortunately the Binford–Clarke jargon is not the official verbiage of archaeology. Let us hope it may never become so. As for us, we have happily put down our blue pencil, said to hell with these gibbering turkeys and cuckoos, and are away across the road for a large stein of *Stella Artois*.

September 1973

☎ We note with sadness the death of a man who was given the Gold Medal of the Society of Antiquaries in 1950, namely Professor Dr Albert Egges van Giffen. He was the grand old man of Dutch archaeology, and in many ways, in the last few years, the doyen of European archaeology. We happened to be in Holland while van Giffen was dying and were sensible of the deep regard in which he was held by everyone. He went on working right up to the moment of his death in his ninetieth year. Only a few months before, he had excavated, with meticulous care, a megalithic tomb in Oldenburg. He seemed to have lived three lives, one in Groningen, another in Amsterdam, and a third in Amersfoort, and was also a familiar figure outside his own country. We first met him immediately after the second world war, when the British Council in their wisdom invited two dozen archaeologists from occupied countries to spend a fortnight in Great Britain. Driving across southern Britain from Cambridge to Salisbury, van Giffen described to us how he had recently had a car accident, and coined a brilliant off-English phrase which is now part of the language of many of us: 'How you say?' he said. 'Suddenly there was accident, and sault-a-somerset I was over the hedge in a field.' Never again did we hear such a fine off-English phrase until, several years later, the late Professor Laviosa Zambotti, clutching her throat, told Professor Sean ÓRíordáin and ourselves that she was certain that she had an infection of her tomkins. Ten years ago, many of us were delighted to celebrate van Giffen's eightieth birthday at Groningen: he then seemed eternal. Certainly his place in European archaeology is for ever.

❦ We asked Professor Hawkes to give us his views on the so-called 'new' archaeology, especially as preached in Britain by Dr David Clarke, and he has done so in an article which we print in this number. Meanwhile our postbag fills with letters about the David Clarke article. We print three more comments and then this is, at least for the present time, over. The first is a crisp postcard from Frances Lynch, who says:

I'm *amazed* to see from your Editorial this month that David Clarke actually *did* write that article – I'd thought it was a spoof by Hogarth! It's interesting that when he *wants* to convince, as in *Beaker Pottery*, Clarke *can* write in English.

And the second a letter from Oliver Dickinson of the Department of Ancient History and Archaeology in the University of Birmingham:

In his oblique rejoinder-by-review to his critics, David Clarke seems in great danger of persuading himself that, while protesting against his mode of expression, they are in reality opposing everything which he advocates. Nobody likes to be told that they write unintelligibly, but I feel that he should give more thought to this, and especially to Peter Salway's comments. It is not merely a matter of a few technical words, nor is it simply his august seniors who are complaining; his contemporaries and juniors are likely to have just as much trouble unless, like Peter

Salway or his own students, they have been exposed to the vocabulary over a period of time.

Part of the problem may be that he frequently uses words with a Greek base, whereas the common learned language, current for a considerable time, derives mainly from Latin. Most archaeologists will be familiar with the latter, but few nowadays will have enough Greek to work out the meaning of an unfamiliar word or the patience to consult a large dictionary, which will give a variety of definitions (when faced with bastard words like taxonomy and taxon, even the classically-trained may feel doubts; the former has the blessing of the *OED* (1933) as an irregular formation (*taxis* goes *taxeos* in the genitive), but seems to be equivalent to classification (your definition is of taxology). Why use taxonomy instead of classification, or paradigm instead of model?

But this is a relatively minor point; it seems to me that it is the form of Clarke's writings that gives most difficulty. The close packing of concepts, in complex adjective-noun groups occasionally broken by verbs or prepositions, makes for heavy going. While this sometimes appears to be gratuitous (e.g. 'rapid generational turnover' for 'short life-span'), it seems on the whole to derive from an admirable desire for succinctness (and also from the less admirable latinity to which all scholars are prey?). But it is no good straining for brevity when dealing with such unfamiliar matter; if he does not wish to remain a voice crying in the wilderness, Clarke must simplify and expand. Otherwise his prose will continue to resemble those translations of Greek and German philosophers in which the meaning is continually concealed in the terminology and syntax.

Those who run and publish excavations (of whom I am not one, I hasten to say) are forever being nagged to add to their quota of skills. The adoption of new methods of recording is one thing; but if they are expected in addition to grapple with *theory* expressed in such forbidding terms, one can hardly wonder if some refuse to try. I feel that David Clarke should leave the pulpit and mix with the congregation; he might then learn how and why what he is saying goes over people's heads.

(Mr Dickinson might also mix with a scientific congregation, who have for years regularly and usefully used the word taxonomy not just to mean classification but as the *OED* says: 'Classification, especially in relation to its general laws and principles; that department of science, or of a particular science or subject, which consists in or relates to classification.' We have always been trying hard to persuade archaeologists that taxonomy and typology are two quite different things, as they are. Taxology is new to us, and the dictionaries available in Artois, where this is being written, do not distinguish between taxonomy and taxology.)

And the third comment is from Dr Peter Salway, Director of the West Midlands Region of The Open University. We printed an earlier comment from him in the June number of ANTIQUITY and regret, as he does, that

David Clarke replied to that very sensible comment in an oblique and evasive way:

It is sad and ironical that Dr David Clarke's oblique reply to the criticisms of his article quite missed the point. My own had nothing at all to do with willingness or not to make use of techniques recently imported into archaeology from other disciplines. It was about *communication*. Dr Clarke may not like it, but the main medium of communication is still the common English language.

In choosing to reply through a review about a particular application of computing to archaeology Dr Clarke reveals an innocence perhaps even more alarming than the obscurity of his language. I am not in the least surprised that a carefully run experiment such as that he reviews should have produced a very low percentage of error. The real question is what happens when these techniques become large-scale and routine. As director of a regional organization that handles substantial quantities of computerized information daily and as chairman of a committee at the national level that takes the policy decisions for a large computer operation, it is an everyday fact of life for me that there are strict practical limits on how flexible, how complex and *how accurate* the output can be, imposed by the equipment and staff available – mostly, but not entirely, a matter of money. Some things can only be done by computer but it is often a finely balanced question whether to employ manual or computer procedures, particularly as the more computerized a system the less easy to prevent errors remaining undetected to the point where they require much time and trouble to put right. And there are some consequences – such as reputation for reliability – that cannot be quantified in terms of 'cost-benefit-analysis'.

However, Dr Clarke's innocence goes even further. We are to believe such techniques more objective. As far as computers go, this barely conceals a basic misapprehension. Current computers do not *think*. They can only answer the questions put to them. Even in an ideal world this would involve human decisions and under the pressures of the real world this means the establishment of priorities – what data to put in and what analyses to require. Since these priorities have to be established before the computer operation can be designed or run (and in the case of a system intended to produce results in the course of excavation that means long before the start of digging), it implies predicting in advance what is likely to be significant. However rigorous the 'decision-making process' the element of 'subject-ive' or 'intuitive' opinion based on experience is central to it. If Dr Clarke does not recognize the crucial role of 'intuitive' recognition of what is significant he must have overlooked the history of science and the nature of scientific method.

These controversial issues must now be discussed elsewhere. We are always happy to start a discussion and promote sensible controversy, but, with the material we hope to print in the next three numbers already bulging suspiciously large in our files, we must for a while forget the new clarke-aeology, however she is wrote.

March 1974

❡ One of the most exciting and readable books about archaeology appeared in America just before Christmas. It was *The plundered past* by Karl E. Meyer.

A central theme in *The plundered past* is a detailed consideration of the Metropolitan Museum's acquisition of the beautiful calyx krater by Euphronios: Meyer also discusses the Greek bronze horse to which we have already referred in reviewing Calvin Tomkins's fascinating book *Merchants and masterpieces: the story of the Metropolitan Museum of Art* (ANTIQUITY, 1970). In November 1972 it was announced that the Metropolitan had acquired what von Bothmer was later to claim as 'the finest Greek vase there is'. This hitherto entirely unknown calyx krater was executed by two great Athenian artists, the potter Euxitheos and the painter Euphronios. Thomas Hoving said that as a result of this find 'histories of art will have to be rewritten': he described it as 'majestic without pomp, poignant without a shred of false emotion, perfect without relying on mere precision'. He added that it was one of the two or three finest single works of art ever obtained by the museum and added, 'Appropriately enough, this unsurpassed work was acquired with funds obtained through the sale of ancient coins of its realm and time, which had not been on exhibition for years.'

We went to New York in November 1973 to see the Euphronios vase and the Greek horse, beset with the same sense of impending confusion and excitement as Crawford had when he went to Glozel in the twenties. What was going on? It had been proposed in the summer of last year that the BBC should do a programme on the Greek horse but Hoving and von Bothmer, harassed by American television and unable to believe that what they castigated as the media should contain gentleman scholars such as Paul Johnstone and his *Chronicle* team, declined to show themselves to the British viewing public. In November we were warmly received by Dr von Bothmer in the Met and by Mr Noble, now Director of the Museum of the City of New York, and listened to their well-argued accounts of the origins of vase and horse. And later, in the Blue Bar of the Algonquin, we discussed it all with Karl Meyer.

The Euphronios vase is beautifully displayed: it has a room to itself and a personal guardian − and how wise: a piece of antiquity with such public interest might easily be smashed to bits by a lunatic. It seems to a non-classical scholar magnificent, and even the most cautious British scholars are prepared to regard it as one of the great Greek vases. But where did it come from, and where has it been recently? The price paid by the Met was reported to be one million dollars. It was at first said that it had been in a private European collection since World War I, and that the name of the owner could not be divulged 'because he was the source of future acquisitions'. This was in November 1972; in February of 1973 it was being said that the pot had been sold to the Met by an expatriate American living in Rome, by name Robert E. Hecht, who had got it from an Armenian coin dealer living in Beirut, by name Dikran A. Sarrafian. Sarrafian said his father bought the vase in London in 1920, 'by an exchange with an amateur', and that he had never seen it intact: it had been lying in pieces in a hatbox. 'A *hat*box? – as Lady Bracknell might demand. Sarrafian said to Gage, of *The New York Times*: 'I wasted most of my life with whores and archaeologists', a line which Karl Meyer says is worthy of Aristophanes. The Italian police, on the other hand, believe that the Euphronios krater was found in a looted Etruscan tomb. Who is right?

As we write, the antecedents of Euphronios are in doubt: von Bothmer argued to us a cogent and, as it appeared, convincing case for the Beirut hatbox–Rome dealer story. Reading *The plundered past*, one is prepared to believe anything. But what of the horse? The Met horse was purchased in 1923, and accepted by virtually every classical scholar as one of the finest Greek bronzes in existence. Gisela Richter, von Bothmer's predecessor as Curator of the Met, and a scholar and connoisseur of great distinction, called it 'without doubt, artistically the most important single object in our classical collection', and suggested it was made by Kalamis. The horse appears in practically every book on Greek art published from that day; thousands of replicas were sold by the Met and in shops like Brentano's in Fifth Avenue [Plate 8].

In 1956 a man called Joseph V. Noble came to the Met and became its operating administrator. He had walked past the horse to his office many thousands of times when, in 1961, he noticed, what no one had before, a thin line running from the top of the horse's mane down to the tip of the nose, and also down the spine, over the rump, and under the stomach. It occurred to Noble that this mould-mark was such as is left when a sculpture is made by sand-casting, a process invented in the 14th century AD. Suspicion grew and the horse was removed from public exhibition: the incontrovertible (but was it?) proof came in 1967 when a gamma-ray shadowgraph showed the inside of the horse with its sand core and the iron wire used as its framework [Plate 9]. Noble gave a public lecture about all this in which he said of the horse: 'It's famous, but it's a fraud.' So ended Act II of the drama of the Greek Met Horse: Act I was its triumphant acceptance by Gisela Richter and almost all of her learned colleagues.

Act III begins at Christmas 1972, when *The New York Times* reveals that scientific tests have shown that Noble was wrong and that the horse is a genuine antiquity. How genuine and how antique? Battle is on, and the Met put on a first-class exhibition of the horse and all the reasons for and against it. We are especially grateful to Dr von Bothmer for keeping the exhibition on long enough for us to see it in November and for stating, with meticulous care and fairness, the arguments for and against the varying dates of the horse, which by now has gone back to a more modest place in the general classical collections.

There are four positions, at least, to adopt in relation to this most lovely bronze horse. The first is the Richter position – the horse dates from classical antiquity. The second is the von Bothmer position, that it is an eclectic work of the fifth/sixth century AD made in south Italy. The third is the Noble position, that it is a forgery made in the twenties in Paris; and here we should note that the official Met story is now that the horse was bought from Georges Feuardent in Paris who said it came from the Mahdia wreck explored by divers in 1908 (see ANTIQUITY, 1930). The fourth is the Daniel position, that we don't really know the answer for certain as yet. One thing does seem certain, namely, that the ridge which first attracted Mr Noble's suspicions was not an original feature but made by subsequent copying of the horse. Stylistic arguments are always dangerous but we warmly recommend the article by Lewis S. Brown of the Department of Anthropology of the American Museum of Natural History in that Museum's quarterly *Curator* (XIII, 1969), in which he argues on grounds of style and the representation of the horse that it is 'one of the most noteworthy cases of fraud in the field of art that has come to light in recent years'.

Our doubts relate to the acceptance of the thermoluminescence dating of the horse as final, certain, irrevocable. Three TL tests were made: the fine grain technique produced dates of between 1300 and 2800 BP, the large etched quartz technique dates of between 2000 and 5500 BP, and the single zircon grain technique 1900 to 3700 BP. We ask, in our ignorance, why do these three TL techniques produce varying dates from the same material – that of the core of the horse? And we note that the overall bracket from the TL tests suggests a date of between 1,300 and 5,500 years before the present, i.e., a date in calendar years of between 3500 BC and AD 700. This wide bracket allows the Richter and von Bothmer positions, but disposes of the Noble position. Noble however says that the horse was so bombarded by X-rays and gamma-rays that TL dating is worthless, and that the heat necessary for fusing to the horse the left back leg, admitted by all to be an addition, could have refired the clay core and rendered any TL datings worthless.

June 1974

✇ The London Sunday papers of 27 January and the daily papers of 28 January were filled by excited headlines exposing the Vinland Map as a forgery. 'Forged map that fooled the world' declared *The Observer*, 'British Agent's Part in Fake Map Deal' said *The Sunday Telegraph*, while *The Daily Telegraph* was more specific: 'Vinland Map exposed by 54 specks'. It was revealed that 'chemical analysis of 54 specks of ink, so tiny that put together they would still be smaller than a pinhead, lead to the claim that the Vinland Map, purporting to show that Vikings discovered America long before Columbus, is a fake'. The Royal Geographical Society held a special symposium on the Vinland Map on 4 February, and a huge crowd filling its large lecture hall in Kensington heard half-a-dozen speakers discuss the problem. The discussion was introduced by Dr Helen Wallis, Keeper of the Map Room in the British Museum, and concluded with Mr Walter McCrone of the Chicago firm of Walter C. McCrone Associates who had done the small-particle analysis. The text of all the speeches is being printed in the June number of *The Geographical Journal* and will make good reading.

Most of the speakers accepted that the map was false, but George Painter, Assistant Keeper in charge of fifteenth-century printed books in the British Museum, stoutly defended the authenticity of the map and the view that it was drawn by a Swiss monk about 1440, fifty-two years before Columbus left Spain. What is not in dispute is that the Vikings did get to America before Columbus: the Sagas tell us this and so surely does excavation at L'Anse aux Meadows in Newfoundland. The only dispute is whether the map adds further proof of this historical fact, and shows that the Vikings had a far greater and more accurate knowledge of the topography of Greenland than would have seemed likely. What is also apparently not in dispute is that the 11 in. by 16 in. (*c.* 28 cm. by 40 cm.) map, which we were able to study two years ago in Yale University Library, was drawn on paper made in the Upper Rhineland about 1440. Walter McCrone Associates claim that the brownish-yellow ink used contains a titanium dioxide pigment not developed until 1920. Walter McCrone said: 'The likelihood of a pigment of the crystalline size and shape of that found in the Vinland Map ink being used in a map of AD 1400 can be compared with the likelihood that Admiral Nelson's flagship at Trafalgar was a hovercraft.'

The apparent physical evidence incriminating the map did not move Mr Painter. 'I am not shaken', he said, 'I would regard this as just another episode in the dialogue between scholars and investigators. . . . Little is known about the medieval use of inks. There were many different types even on the same manuscript. A monk might well lean across and borrow some different ink from his chum's inkwell' (*The Sunday Times*, 27 January). We are indebted to Dr Wallis for drawing our attention to a most amusing pamphlet produced by Scandinavian Airlines entitled *What every Scandinavian school-child knows....* (Alas, SAS tell us there are no more copies of this brochure available.) It is a collection of Vinland Map cartoons produced, they say, 'as a contribution to the lighter side of Scandinavian scholarship'. The two Stevenson cartoons from *The New Yorker* are particularly amusing, the first in which two Vikings in their ship are saying 'Let's take another look at that damn map', and the second in which an American Indian is sitting down for a drink with some Puritan Fathers and saying 'Skoal'. Another amusing cartoon is that of two monks seated at their desks in a scriptorium: one, his pen poised over an inkwell, says to the other, 'I think I'll throw in a couple of extra islands on this map, just for laughs.'

It was only a few weeks before the RGS Vinland meeting that the BBC broadcast a programme which finally debunked the Minnesota runestone. The programme was called 'The Riddle of the Runestone'; it went out on 23 December 1973 in the series *The World About Us* and it was produced by Brian Branston, who has himself already done much original work on early Scandinavia. It was a notable contribution to the controversy about the presence of Norsemen in America, and we are grateful to Mr Branston and the BBC for allowing us to quote from the programme. Professor Erik Wahlgren (whose book *The Kensington Stone, a mystery solved* was reviewed in these pages in 1958) appeared in the programme saying firmly: 'The Kensington Stone is a fake. The stone is a genuine stone from Kensington, Minnesota – it is not a man-made block of cement. It is the inscription that is phoney. The Kensington inscription is a preposterous fraud. The language is definitely modern, mixed Scandinavian, Norwegian, Swedish, possibly even a bit of English.'

The central figures in the perpetuation of the Kensington forgery were Olof Ohman, Fogelblad and Anderson, but as Branston said dramatically at the end of the programme: 'A country churchyard near Kensington holds the last word – a report of a death-bed confession. Besides Ohman, Fogelblad and Anderson as hoaxers there was at least one other. A few months ago died a man whose voice in a secret recording comes literally from the grave – Frank Walter Cran.' This is the text of the recording of Walter Cran's statement:

I was up in Canada and my Dad got really sick so then of course they sent a telegram to say that if I wanted to see him I should hurry up and come down, which I did. I never mentioned anything about the runestone to him. He says (something in Swedish) that it was false, he says. Yeh, I am saying. That's all I am answering. Then again he would turn around and say, 'You are going to get after Ohman', he says. 'What if he should die all of a sudden?' he said. 'You know it's going to be pretty hard to prove how we made this thing.' How we made it. Why should he say *we* then? They worked together and then Dad says: 'Well sometimes on Sundays when we ain't doing nothing... he gets his knife out and we carved them letters now and then. Then a big kick and a laugh you know.' Dad says, 'Yeh it would be fun to make some scripts', he said, 'that would bluff the people around the country, especially the educated ones', he says, 'that think you are dumb.' Do you know what, they had a sculptor examine this stone and they found out there had been two men that worked on the stone – one was a left-handed man and one was a right-handed man. Well that fitted in and I thought, 'By God my Dad has been saying that the stone was false and you have been one of them that has been chiselling left handed and helping him.' John Ohman was sick on his dying bed too when I talked about this. I said, 'Dad told me that I should talk to your Dad and he would tell you how we made the stone, and I says that must be my father and your father who chiselled out the stone.' He laughed and then he says, 'Well I guess you are right.' 'I don't care', I says, 'who made it, I figure it is a hell of a good joke, and I will bet if your father or my father could come alive', I says, 'and listen to all the talk, they would get together and they would have the biggest haha they had ever had in their life.'

Well, there it is, and Cran's phrase is a good one to describe the forgery, 'the biggest haha'. As Russell Fridley said in concluding the programme, 'The Kensington runestone should be viewed for what it is – as a great monument to American/Scandinavian humour.' But obviously this is not the view shared by the Smithsonian Institute who put it on show to the nation in 1948 for a whole year, nor of those who had it displayed at the 1965 New York World's Fair. And without doubt the people of Alexandria where a giant 22-ton granite replica was solemnly dedicated do not regard it as a big haha.

In a letter to us, Mr Brian Branston writes:

Like you, I have also been interested in the story for many years, and like you for most of the time I have believed it to be a hoax. When I got the opportunity of actually digging round on the spot, I found that all the evidence to prove the stone a hoax had been there, mostly in the morgues of local newspapers and in the archives of the Minnesota Historical Society from within a few months of perpetration. It just demonstrates that you can't accept statements from no matter how august a pulpit without going back to check sources.

The one thing that worried me in my search was the number of likeable, worthy people in Alexandria who had been sold on the stone by Holand. They have taken him almost entirely on his face value, and no evidence from the archives of the Minnesota Historical Society will ever change their beliefs.

December 1974

When, in our March number, we were referring to the TL dating of the Greek horse in the Met, we wrote: 'Recently we have been told that TL dating of four tablets from Glozel, in two separate laboratories, has given a date of about 600 BC, and we will return to this problem in a later number. Hardly anyone has any doubt that most of the Glozel material was fabricated between 1924–7' (ANTIQUITY, 1974). We now return to this fascinating problem, and publish in this issue an article by McKerrell, Mejdahl, François and Portal entitled 'Thermoluminescence and Glozel', which may make the statement 'Hardly anyone' a grave understatement. They describe thermoluminescence dates for at least two dozen objects from Glozel as falling in the bracket 700 BC to AD 100; they argue that Glozel is neither a modern forgery nor an unusual neolithic site as Morlet and Reinach claimed, but an early iron age or Gallo-Roman site. Many of our readers may be immediately convinced by their data and arguments, as we know some French archaeologists are.

Perhaps there is need to remind some of our readers of the facts about Glozel. A clear and fair summary of the controversy is given by McKerrell *et al.* in their article. On 1 March 1924 Emile Fradin, then a young man of seventeen, working on his family farm 17 km. south-east of Vichy, stumbled – or rather his oxen stumbled – on a site which has become one of the most controversial issues in all archaeology – far more so than the Greek horse and the Euphronios vase. Crawford wrote in the second number of ANTIQUITY (1927) an account of his visit to Glozel and concluded with these words, 'the inscriptions, the engravings, and the majority of the other finds are forgeries, and those who believe in their authenticity have been the victims of a hoax'. He persuaded Vayson de Pradenne to write an article dealing with the whole affair and this appeared in ANTIQUITY (1930). De Pradenne concluded with these words, 'We are not so sanguine as to expect, of course, that Dr Morlet, M. Salomon Reinach and the little group of persons round them, will ever perceive their mistake. It matters little. In actual fact, whatever may be the verdict of the Law with regard to the forger, the Glozel affair has been shown up so thoroughly that *it will never more be a danger to science* (italics ours – Ed.). One must hope, also, that all the trouble it has created will not have been in vain, and that it will have taught a useful lesson.'

An International Commission set up in 1927 reported that all the finds from Glozel were not ancient. In January 1928 *The Times* published a letter from Sir Arthur Evans expressing his surprise that anyone could have been taken in by these forgeries, and later that month, Champion, technical assistant at Saint-Germain, reported that all the objects from Glozel that he had examined were fakes. 'These triple blows have demolished Glozel', wrote Crawford; 'after a short but gay life it is dead. On the field of battle lie the corpses of several learned reputations.... We shall not refer again to Glozel – unless greatly provoked' (ANTIQUITY, 1928).

The great provocation is here in the form of TL dates, and it is because we feel these dates should be widely known and discussed that we publish the McKerrell *et al.* article and invite the views of anyone who can resolve this curious problem. At least Vayson de Pradenne has been proved wrong in one thing when he said that Glozel would 'never more be a danger to science'. But to what science is it now a danger? To physics and thermoluminescent dating? or to the humanistic science of archaeology? One thing is certain: somebody is wrong. Either there is something unexplained about these TL dates, and all our scientific colleagues assure us that there cannot be anything wrong with the TL technique, or the many distinguished archaeologists from 1925 onwards who have pronounced the Glozel finds as palpable forgeries are wrong. And another thing is certain: the site of Glozel was never properly excavated. The grubbings around by Morlet and Fradin from 1924 onwards were unscientific hogging; neither had then, or at any other time in their lives, the faintest idea of stratigraphy and archaeological evidence from the ground. The 1927 International Commission spent only a very short time in actual excavation: it was a control process. The 1928 Comité d'Études had hardly anyone on it who had any experience of fieldwork. Salomon Reinach was taken to the site in an ox-cart and idly fumbled in the ground with his hand. Plates 6 and 7 show two views of the excavations being conducted by the 1928 Comité d'Études in April 1928. The top photograph is a general view of the uncontrolled, unrecorded work in hand: the two figures on the left looking at the camera are Dr A. Morlet (black hat) and the policeman Harry Söderman (grey fedora). The lower photograph shows Professor Audollent, a theologian from Clermont-Ferrand, clutching some roots which have either passed through or over some tablets. He gives an air of disagreeable surprise at having been caught in some dirt archaeology. His book *L'énigme de Glozel* (Paris, 1927) shows that this learned biblical scholar hadn't the faintest notion what Glozel was all about, or what he thought he was doing there, trowel in hand. The truth is that the Glozelians, from Morlet and Fradin to Reinach and Audollent, thought archaeological excavation was akin to digging a flower bed.

We published several years ago Dorothy Garrod's reflexions on Glozel (ANTIQUITY, 1968), and an interview between ourselves and her, from which the paragraphs in ANTIQUITY were taken, will be published in full on television in a BBC *Chronicle* programme in December. She is now, alas, dead — how fascinating it would have been to revisit Glozel with her, the Mejdahl-McKerrell TL dates in our hands — but there still lives one member of that 1927 Commission: Professor Bosch-Gimpera. We invited him to write an account of his life in archaeology and hope to publish this in full in 1975, but we quote now his memories of Glozel:

At the time of the meeting of the Congress in Amsterdam the strange finds at Glozel near Vichy in France were very much in the news. I was appointed, at the behest of Count Bégouën, to be a member of a Commission of 'neutral' archaeologists to investigate the finds.... At Vichy we of the commission stayed at the Hotel Majestic as the guests of the Syndicat d'Initiative. We were conducted to Glozel by Dr Morlet, a physician who believed that the site would be a great attraction for tourists. The find had been made by a certain Fradin, at whose family home we examined his collection of objects found in the neighbourhood. It was a most astonishing complex of things: 'palaeolithic' pebbles with engraved animals, fossilized bones, neolithic polished celts, and clay tablets with what appeared to be Phoenician signs in the style of Eshumazar of Sidon and other uninterpretable characters. Then we examined the excavations themselves in the terrain where the objects were supposed to have been found. The general public and journalists who had gathered were prevented from entering.

That evening at the hotel we discussed our impressions. The apparently genuine pebbles with engraved animals especially puzzled us.... We had already noted at the excavation one pebble in a suspect vertical position which suggested that it had been introduced from above. Further evidence of such recent introductions was obtained by our own excavation. By cutting the terrain vertically, there appeared a pocket with a clay tablet on its bottom. The pocket was filled with soft disturbed earth, which did not show the strata of the soil into which the pocket had been dug. It was easy to see how the tablets had been introduced. Smaller objects apparently had been placed beneath the strata by driving a pole into the earth to the desired level and then dropping in a pebble, for example. In some cases the pebbles had remained in a vertical and unnatural position at the bottom of the pole hole.... Later, one of the tablets was analysed. The clay included fresh grains of corn and even a fly whose organic substance was still fresh....

It is also said that Fradin was very disappointed with our report because it had spoiled his negotiations to sell the collection of finds to an American museum. Subsequently, the police made a search of his house where they found half-finished objects of the type he planned to sell. The young man was a talented sketcher and painter. When his friend Dr Morlet had loaned him books with pictures of prehistoric objects for identification, and spoken vividly of the importance of finding a prehistoric site, he conceived the idea of imitating them.... Glozel was supposed to be palaeolithic after the find of the pebbles and some genuine fossil bones which Fradin must have bought in an antiquarian shop.

There is the voice of a man, a man of the greatest distinction as an archaeologist, a man who happily is still with us, who was present in Glozel in 1927. (Alas, as we read these proofs, a letter from Mexico reports his death a few weeks ago.) His testimony and that of Dorothy Garrod, and the report of the 1927 Commission, must be weighed in the balance against the McKerrell-Mejdahl-François-Portal paper. This paper is a major document in the resolution of *l'affaire Glozel* and as we publish it we wonder if Crawford is turning restlessly in his grave. Was the 1927 anti-Glozelian Commission which said everything was a forgery entirely mistaken? Was the 1928 Glozelian Comité d'Études which said everything was genuine and neolithic equally mistaken? Now we seem to have three parties, not only the Glozelians and anti-Glozelians, but the La Tène/Gallo-Roman modified Glozelians of this paper. It is all fascinating. Is there a major conflict between TL dating and the views of archaeologists? Are there two sets of facts: those provided by physical science and those provided by students of the material remains of man? We are, editorially, at the moment, neutral, or, as the Production Editor reminds us, as neutral as ever a Welshman can be who has already written and lectured about Glozel as a classic case of forgery. Nonplussed is the word, not neutral. But what goes on? How can this strange dispute be resolved? In one way, by scientific excavation of Glozel. Here we warmly support the suggestion of the authors of the article, and are delighted to know that this may happen.

Glozel is no longer funny: it is no longer the lunatic fringe of archaeology. But at the end of the summer, as we write, the lunacy and fun still remain on the fringe of our subject.

March 1975

❡ The article which we published in our last number, 'Thermoluminescence and Glozel' by Hugh McKerrell, Vagn Mejdahl, Henri François and Guy Portal, has, not surprisingly, attracted a great deal of attention. The Archaeological Correspondent of *The Times*, in an article entitled 'Glozel: the ghost walks again' (2 December 1974), concluded thus:

What is certain is that archaeologists will now have to revise their opinions about Glozel, or about the accuracy of thermoluminescence dating, or about both. The present range of possibilities seems to be that the objects are genuine, in their original context, and mixed with earlier material there; that they are genuine but were brought to Glozel and buried in the 1920s for purposes of hoax or fraud; or that they are modern in both manufacture and context, in which case the assumptions on which the present acceptance of thermoluminescent dating rests will have to be radically re-examined. The recent reassessment of radiocarbon dating has been similarly controversial, even without allegations of archaeological fraud, but the method itself seems to have emerged modified and strengthened. Thermoluminescence may be about to undergo the same transmutation.

Many of the letters we have received ask whether there is not some factor that affects the TL data – not of course the processing in laboratories: and no one suggests that the dates produced in laboratories in Edinburgh, Denmark and Paris of the same material can be open to criticism. But what are these laboratories dating? And why have we not been given the C14 dates of the associated material and the dates of the forgeries impounded by the French police at Glozel in 1928?

The present Editor of ANTIQUITY has always approached problems like Rouffignac, and Piltdown and Glozel, as matters of history and detection: not as conflicts between science and history, between physics and archaeology, but as stories, often scandalous, that must be studied in detail. He regrets that it is only very recently that he has read Harry Söderman's *Policeman's lot: a criminologist's gallery of friends and felons* (New York, 1957). Söderman was a Swedish policeman, who was seconded to the French police at Lyons, and while there was made a member of the famous or infamous (it depends on your thinking: 'Jeune homme, êtes-vous Glozélien ou non?', as Reinach once asked Christopher Hawkes) Comité d'Études of 1928. He was reluctant to join the Comité but the Lyons police were certain no Frenchman was going to be involved, particularly when Edmond Bayle, head of the Paris Police Laboratory since the end of World War I, and almost the direct successor of Alphonse Bertillon (who died in 1914), was doing research on the Glozel finds. It was, incidentally, Bayle's report that revealed a cotton thread dyed with an aniline dye in one tablet, and a potato sprout in another, and caused the *New International Year Book* for 1928 to say, 'M. Bayle turned out to be an excellent detective.... Thus Glozel becomes a hoax and ranks among the most famous in history.'

Söderman set out from Lyons on the noon express to Vichy – a five-hour journey. His companions were Déperet, Roman, Mayet, and Arcelin, and, as he says, 'an elderly lady who soon became as silently fascinated as I by the conversation of the four savants. It was really awe-inspiring. World-famous names flashed by our listening ears. Stretches of hundreds of thousands and even millions of years obviously were bagatelles to these men dedicated to studying the origin and development of the human race. The talk had a scale and a sweep to it which I found exhilarating. Nothing like it had come within my ken before.'

He had been puzzled what to put in his kit before he set out on this curious mission. He included a fingerprint outfit, a pistol, a very small camera, some small surgical instruments, a strong magnifying glass, a flashlight, and a pair of handcuffs of a special kind which had just been given to him by their inventor M. Melon: they were called *melonettes* – a pleasant play on *menottes*, the French word for handcuffs. Old Déperet asked Söderman what police equipment he had brought with him on his Glozel enquiry and Söderman opened his despatch case. Déperet asked him 'to put them on his hands, explaining that he wanted to feel for once what it was like to be handcuffed'. 'I put them on him', wrote Söderman,

and the instant those infernal things closed around his fragile wrists a fearful doubt swept over my mind. Had I brought the keys with me? I had not. A minute search of my portfolio and all my pockets revealed the awful fact. When the truth began to dawn upon poor Déperet, his kind smile gradually became melancholy and his face grew haggard. In about twenty minutes' time we were due to arrive at Vichy, where scores of journalists, press photographers, and newsreel men would be waiting for us on the station platform.

What to do? What to do? A cold sweat broke out all over my body while I racked my brains as to how to get out of this situation. In French railway carriages there are always a few tools – at least a pickaxe, a small shovel, and the like – stored in a glass-covered case for use in emergencies. But a glance at delicate old Déperet convinced me that he could never endure harsh treatment. Next I thought of the locomotive. The engineer certainly must have tools, but he would be difficult to get to. Still, something had to be done. I was planning to perform the circus stunt of climbing over the tender to reach the locomotive.

The elderly lady, our fellow passenger, who had been observing the goings on while busily knitting, suddenly said, 'Why don't you try one of my hairpins? I have read in several detective novels that hairpins are very good for picking locks.'

She drew a hairpin from her hair and handed it to me. . . . Contrary to the bragging of their inventor, those wretched *melonettes* were easy to pick. In a short while, I had opened one of them. And high time too, because the train was already slowing down for the Vichy stop. One of the cuffs was still around poor Déperet's wrist. I tucked the rest of the gadget up into his sleeve, and to make assurance double sure, fastened it with a piece of string, also supplied by the amiable lady, who fished a length out of her big handbag. . . . Smiling genially, we alighted from the train and were interrogated by the world press.

Now in the confusion and contradictions about Glozel from 1924 until now, and, we fear, for some time to come, this is a most amusing and fascinating story. Clearly here is fact surpassing fiction: the old lady with the knitting, the hairpins, the big handbag, the ball of string, and the knowledge of detective stories, *must* be no other than Miss Marple. We consulted Dame Agatha Christie and Sir Max Mallowan and they say, alas, it cannot be. But, whoever she may have been, what was she doing in that compartment, and what happened to her when the train stopped at Vichy, and the Comité d'Études got to work?

There was one Englishman on the 1928 Comité: Söderman describes him as 'Dr Foat, an English specialist in Hellenic cultures'. There are two photographs of his backside in the Musée at Glozel. But who was he? He agreed to the report of the Comité d'Études which declared that all the Glozel material was authentic, but did he publish his own testimony anywhere? We would like to read it: it would be a primary document, as were those testimonies of Dorothy Garrod and Pedro Bosch-Gimpera that we have already published in these pages. Or has he vanished for ever like the pseudo Mademoiselle Marple with the hairpins and string – perhaps murdered on the Orient Express or the Blue Train? Information, please, about Dr Foat.

June 1975

☙ On 31 March 1853, after dining with the Bishop of Salisbury, W. E. Gladstone 'drove to see Stonehenge'. He wrote in his diary, 'It is a noble and an awful relic, telling much and telling too that it conceals more.' We thought of these words a few weeks ago, looking by candlelight at the carvings of Gavrinis, sitting on the capstone of the Table des Marchands at Locmariaquer and contemplating the Grand Menhir Brisé, and walking, as we have often done before, the long lengths of the Kerlescant, Kermario and Menec alignments. These monuments tell much but conceal more: there is no reason to suppose that we shall ever know what the scribings on the walls of Gavrinis and other Breton megalithic monuments mean, or for what purpose the Grand Menhir was cut and dressed, and why the Carnac alignments were laid out.

Professor Alexander Thom, whom we introduced to the Breton megaliths many years ago over a glass of cider in a *crêperie*, is convinced that the megalithic monuments of the Morbihan and indeed everywhere else are primarily astronomical in purpose.... Thom has shown us that there was a unit of measurement, the megalithic yard, used in prehistoric Europe, and that the circular, near circular and near elliptical stone enclosures in north-western Europe were laid out with great care to careful plans involving some knowledge of geometrical principles which were later, and perhaps independently, established as a part of Pythagorean geometry. No one in their senses ever supposed that complex megalithic sites were laid out and constructed other than from careful plans drawn on parchment or on sand tables. Because the ancient Britons had no writing that has survived, it is a mistake to suppose that they did not have good methods of communication, measurement and survey, and we must always remember Baron Nordenskjöld's remark that 'Writing need not be the only way of expressing thought.'

The great work of Alexander Thom is his demonstration of the mathematics and mensuration of the megalithic builders of Europe. His other contribution to our understanding of them, namely his insistence on their astronomy, is not one which has convinced all archaeologists. His use of the Crucuny *quadrilatère*, very possibly the work of an eighteenth-century landowner, and his insistence on the role of the Grand Menhir Brisé in astronomical sightings, is alarming. We do not know for certain that these four large bits of stone were ever part of one great menhir 23 m. long, and ever stood upright.

But our doubts are not shared by archaeologists who are much better equipped than we are to deal with these problems. The editor of the *Journal for the History of Astronomy* asked Professor Richard Atkinson to assess, from the point of view of a prehistorian, 'the octet of papers on megalithic astronomy and mensuration by Professor Alexander Thom and Dr A. S. Thom which have so far appeared in this *Journal*'; and we regard Atkinson's article, 'Megalithic astronomy: a prehistorian's comments' which appeared in *JHA* (1975), as essential reading for all. This article has been very well summarized in *The Times* for 13 March 1975 in a short article amusingly entitled 'Stonehenge: foresight saga', by Norman Hammond, who reminds us that Atkinson regarded, a few years ago, the original suggestion of Stonehenge as having an astronomical significance as 'Moonshine'.

The moon still shines bright on our wisdom and follies, our sanities and lunacies, but Professor Atkinson has written for the *Journal for the History of Astronomy* an article which can only be described, in Cartailhac's famous words, *Mea culpa d'un sceptique*. He says, disarmingly, that he has no formal grounding in astronomy, nor in mathematics beyond the age of fourteen. He is with Thom in dealing with the Grand Menhir Brisé. 'For me,' he says,

the present positions of its four fragments leave no doubt that it originally stood upright on its broader, north-western end and that it fell as the result of some vibratory event, which can only have been an earth-tremor, a number of which have been recorded for the area in historical times. I can see no other explanation for the relative attitudes and spacing of the broken pieces, which are quite inconsistent with the idea sometimes advanced that the stone fell during its erection. The local belief mentioned by Thom, that it formerly stood on its narrower end, is contrary both to universal Megalithic practice elsewhere, and indeed to common sense.

Atkinson then summarizes his views of the application of Thom's work to prehistorians and what he says must be quoted *in extenso*:

It is hardly surprising that many prehistorians either ignore the implications of Thom's work, because they do not understand them, or resist them because it is more comfortable to do so. I have myself gone through the latter process; but I have come to the conclusion that to reject Thom's thesis because it does not conform to the model of prehistory on which I was brought up involves also the acceptance of improbabilities of an even higher order. I am prepared, in other words, to believe that my model of European prehistory is wrong, rather than that the results presented by Thom are due to nothing but chance. Fortunately, recent developments in radiocarbon dating now show that some parts of the traditional picture of European prehistory will have to be abandoned, and that some innovations in the west are now to be dated so early that they must be indigenous and cannot be derived from the east.

Atkinson then refers to his paper 'Neolithic science and technology' published in the *Philosophical transactions of the Royal Society of London* (1974), and goes on to say that in this paper he tried 'to outline the implications of this new chronology for the history of the early contributions which Britain and its continental neighbours may have made to the foundation of European culture'. He concludes, 'It is within the framework of this nascent model of prehistory that Thom's astonishing contribution will find its rightful place.'

Every archaeologist concerned with these matters, which really means everyone interested in the major historical contexts of barbarian Europe, must read this article and the Thom octet on which it comments. These are issues which vitally affect our appreciative understanding of the past. People talk too much about models and about changing models as though they were changing nappies. To borrow a phrase from Peter White, whose admirable book *The Past is Human* will be discussed in our next Editorial: *the past is human*; we are dealing with the achievement of men, not astronauts or astronomers. Lyell, who died a hundred years ago, promoted the principle of uniformitarianism. Inspired by White we suggest we should promote the principle of humaniformitarianism, that is to say we should not admit as reasonable explanations of any context in the past, especially the pre-literate archaeological past, explanations which are not reasonable and understandable in terms of the societies known to us today or in the recent past. The people who lived in western Europe in the fourth and third millennia BC, and built Stonehenge and the Carnac alignments and the great tombs of Gavrinis and Newgrange, were not people outside the range of technologically neolithic societies: they were not fantastically exceptional mathematicians and astronomers, and they did not receive wisdom from space-men. They were hard-working peasant farmers, who, after all, are the backbone of much of European agriculture today: and they understood times and seasons, the wind and the weather, the good years and the bad years, life and death. We know now through Alexander Thom's fine work, that their detailed knowledge of geometry and trigonometry was of a much higher standard than we ever supposed before. We still need another Thom to tell us how they achieved their constructional skills. We recently showed a party of Cambridge undergraduates on a study field-trip of Breton sites the great *allée couverte* called La Roche aux Fées at Essé, south-east of Rennes. How were these megalithic monuments built? Many, including Atkinson, have made useful and helpful speculations. To our mind, the engineering ability of the megalith builders, and it is a proven and obvious achievement, far surpasses as a historical fact about barbarian Europe, speculations about their devotion to the moon and the stars in the setting of their tombs and temples.

☙ When we published in our December 1974 number the paper on 'Thermoluminescence and Glozel', declaring that the objects found at Glozel between 1924 and 1927, and widely thought to be forgeries, were TL-dated to between 700 BC and AD 100, we said: 'These startling conclusions are bound to provoke much discussion.' On 15 January the British Broadcasting Corporation presented a television programme in the *Chronicle* series dealing with the TL-dating of Glozel, and this, too, has provoked much discussion.

The BBC programme began with an interview between the Editor and the late Professor Dorothy Garrod which had been filmed in 1967, and the text of which we printed here the following year. Dorothy Garrod was a member of the 1927 Commission, and so was the late Professor Bosch-Gimpera whose views we have also published (ANTIQUITY, 1974); neither of these distinguished archaeologists, who have, on many occasions, discussed *l'affaire Glozel* with the Editor, had the slightest doubt that all the Glozel material was faked – and we must remember that they were there at the time and much closer to the events than any of us writing today. The programme continued with an explanation by Vagn Mejdahl and Hugh McKerrell of their methods, and their conclusions that all the material they had studied was genuine. Then there was a discussion of the material from the archaeological point of view by Professor Atkinson and Lady Brogan who went to Glozel with the Editor in September 1974. They had never been to Glozel before. Their fresh reactions to the site and the material were of great interest. We quote from the recorded notes of the programme.

Professor Atkinson said:

The first thing one has to bear in mind about Glozel is that it has never been properly excavated. Indeed by modern standards it has never been excavated at all. It's a dog's breakfast. And one can't even say of it, justly, in Sir Mortimer Wheeler's famous phrase, that it was 'dug up like potatoes'. It was worse than that. What we are dealing with, therefore, is really simply a collection of material in the museum, and here we are faced with a balance of improbabilities. There is first of all this series of TL dates running from about 700 BC to AD 100; even allowing for uncertainties of thermoluminescent dating this means, on the face of it, that this site ought to have been occupied for something like four centuries. It seems to me very improbable on a site where the soil is sandy and easily moved, that, if it was occupied for that length of time – it is on a steep slope – all this material should be in one layer a foot (30 cm.) thick, as we are told by the excavators: there ought to be a complex stratification. Now of course, it is inherently improbable that these thermoluminescence dates are wrong, and by wrong I do not mean that things have gone wrong in laboratories, but that there may be some undisclosed factor in the material itself which is causing these very curious results. Thermoluminescence has been an established method for some time, but it isn't as old as radiocarbon dating, and there have been in the past some similar abnormalities in C14 dates. I can think of two Neolithic sites in Britain where there is more than one determination from the same site and the C14 dates are consistently in error, in one case by more than 2,000 years and in the other by over 1,000 years.

Then when you come to look at the material itself there are a number of archaeological improbabilities. First of all there is the improbability of much of the material, particularly the fired clay material which has no parallel elsewhere during the period in question, or, for that matter, in any other period or place. Then the bone material: much of the decorated bone work is light in colour and actually has a polished surface, yet these objects are supposed to have been buried in the soil for some two thousand years. It was perfectly clear to me from examining both the soil and the vegetation growing on it that this is an acid soil; it is highly improbable that these things have been buried for this length of time. Many of the tablets have a smooth surface and have not been fired to a very high temperature. They are not very hard and do not break evenly and smoothly as would a dinner plate or a modern tile: the fractures are irregular and rather like the surface you get when you break a digestive biscuit or a piece of very stale cake. The pottery is soft; it is quite clear they were soft-fired, and it is extremely improbable that they could have retained their exceedingly smooth surface if they had been buried in acid soil for that length of time. So we are faced with a balance of improbabilities: the improbability on the one hand of the TL dates being wrong, and improbabilities of equal weight on the archaeological side. Which side of the scales will eventually prove to be heavier is something we must wait for.

Lady Brogan said that she had wandered around France for many years studying the immediately pre-Roman and the Gallo-Roman periods and had excavated in the centre of France. She described the Glozel material as 'this extraordinary assemblage of objects out of any context'. Why, she asked, if the site is to be dated from 700 BC to AD 100 does it not include anything archaeologically characteristic of that period? Why no pottery from Lezoux, not far away: why no Celtic or Roman coins, and why none of the metal work so characteristic of late La Tène and Gallo-Roman sites?

She emphasized that the tablets were completely alien to Celtic and Gallo-Roman contexts. She also asked why anything Glozelian had not been found in any neighbouring site in Central France.

The Editor emphasized the impossibility of all the material coming from one genuine ancient context. He said that what had impressed him most on seeing the material again was that we were being asked to believe that palaeolithic decorated bones, neolithic polished axeheads, and sexual idols and inscribed tablets of La Tène or Gallo-Roman times were all found undisturbed in one genuine *gisement*. No experienced archaeologists in their senses could believe this. The 1927 Commission had insisted these varying objects had been placed there in the twenties of this century. The only new factor was the TL dates and in thinking about them he was reminded of Sherlock Holmes's remark in *A Study in Scarlet*, 'When a fact appears opposed to a long chain of deductions it invariably proves to be capable of bearing some other interpretation. . . .'

Most of the correspondence following the ANTIQUITY article and the BBC *Chronicle* programme suggests that the answer may lie in the Glozel material having been re-radiated, and we are told that this is possible. Meanwhile we must record the fact that no one archaeologist to whom we have talked about this curious affair, and their numbers run to between seventy and a hundred, has the slightest doubt that the material is modern, or that most of it is modern, and that sooner or later some explanation will be provided for the TL dates. But the TL dates *may* be right and *all* the archaeologists wrong, just as nearly all the scientists were wrong when they were taken in by Piltdown. What we need is independent dating. We have recently all been startled by the very early dates produced for the finds of man in Kenya and Ethiopia. Dr E. T. Hall, Director of the Research Laboratory for Archaeology and the History of Art at Oxford, in an excellent article entitled 'Old bones – but how old?' (*The Sunday Telegraph*, 3 November 1974) urges on archaeologists the necessity of not relying on one scientific dating technique. He writes:

My plea is that archaeologists should exercise the right degree of caution before drawing conclusions based on these measurements. They should never find themselves in a position where a key argument or interpretation is based on a single measuring technique which cannot be cross checked by an independent method. Archaeologists must also learn which techniques are more likely to give reliable results. It must be a great temptation to an archaeologist when a unique process comes up with a date which changes his work from the merely interesting to the sensational . . . the greatest temptation is the one which leads an archaeologist selectively to believe evidence which seems to confirm the theories on which he thinks his professional reputation rests.

Fair enough. We do not want to rely on one dating technique for Glozel. Are we not right, are we not exercising the right degree of caution if we do not accept the Glozel TL dates until they are cross-checked by an independent method? We offer Dr Hall the hospitality of these columns to answer this point and to reflect on this. No one denies that the palaeolithic engravings and the neolithic hafted axe with strange scribings are fakes: if they were found associated, as the incompetent excavators of Glozel allege, with the TL-dated material of 700 BC to AD 100 and these dates are confirmed by independent methods, then they are forgeries *made in that period*, and of course there were forgeries in antiquity. Camille Julian thought the only explanation of Glozel was the equipment of a Gallo-Roman sorceress, and it is indeed a witch's hellbroth of nonsense. It might perhaps be the stock in trade of a Gallo-Roman dealer in *farces et attrapes*. These are amusing possibilities but let the scientists who are urging caution on archaeologists remember that no one between 700 BC and AD 100 *could* have forged palaeolithic art. Mobiliary palaeolithic art was not known to the general public until the last quarter of the nineteenth century. *Ergo*, Glozel was salted: it may have genuine Gallo-Roman material but everything about it stinks. We wait with interest the resolution of the dating problem and remember that the only known C14 date so far gave a zero reading and was deliberately not published by Morlet.

And has the mysterious Dr Foat been traced? Readers will remember that he was on the 1928 Comité d'Études. Söderman described him as 'an English specialist in Hellenic cultures', and Emile Fradin proudly points to him in pictures hanging up in Glozel museum, lauding him as the great English scholar who rectified, as he thinks, the grave errors encouraged by the English scholar on the 1927 Commission, Dorothy Garrod, who was his, and also was Dr Morlet's, *bête noire*. We asked for information about Foat, and Sonia Cole writes,

You may be amused to hear that a friend of mine knew Dr Foat – at least he knew *a* Dr Foat, and as the name is so uncommon and the data would fit it seems quite likely that it was *the* Dr Foat. But as he was young in the late twenties unfortunately he does not know if Dr Foat ever mentioned excavation in France. He also thinks it unlikely that Foat had a family so I'm afraid you are no nearer to discovering his testimony on Glozel.

My friend's father was Dr George Farquharson, who was a doctor and town councillor in Southampton, and both he and his wife were well-known for their 'progressive' views. Dr Foat became a friend of theirs in the late 1920s, but my friend, Maurice Farquharson (former Secretary of the BBC), thinks that Foat was a bird of passage and did not actually live in Southampton. Foat apparently expounded on many subjects and was generally regarded as a savant, but Maurice said his father was sceptical about him. Foat regarded himself as an expert on the obscurer poems of Browning, and particularly *Sordello*, and he and the Farquharson parents used to act Shakespeare parts in the drawing room. He was then grey-haired and probably in his early sixties. Maurice says he never discovered what kind of doctor Foat was, nor does he connect him with Hellenic studies, though he thinks this sounds quite likely. He remembered him mainly as a very talkative extrovert. In fact, from the description, he sounds just the sort of chap who might be mixed up in Glozel and – if he was the same chap – his testimony would presumably not be very reliable.

Thank you, Sonia Cole and Maurice Farquharson. Perhaps someone else has recollections of this character. Everything that can contribute to the history of the events of 1924 to 1928 is important for here is the key to the Glozel mystery. Of course in the passage of fifty years facts get forgotten and memories fail, but the documents from the time are with us: surely our colleagues who make these TL determinations and boldly speculate on the archaeological and historical implications of their new dating of Glozel do not deny that the French police raided a barn at Glozel and found inscribed tablets waiting to be fired, and various tools suitable for inscribing bones on what was the forger's desk. Incidentally, where is this material which was then impounded by the French police?

Do the authors of the December (1974) article really know what they are subjecting to their machines? The authenticity of their material is much open to question. Some of us think they are dealing with a rag-bag of oddities, some of which were never in the ground at Glozel, and some of which may have been re-radiated by highly skilful forgers in the last few years.

September 1975

☙ *Leakey's Luck* by Sonia Cole is an excellent workmanlike piece of writing; it is long and detailed as befits what will be the main sourcebook for the work of the Leakeys in East Africa up to 1972. It is a sympathetic, understanding and fair portrait of a man described by the publishers of his *By the Evidence* as 'one of the great men of this or any century'. Sonia Cole writes of him,

he packed more into his sixty-nine years than ten ordinary men would in their combined lifetimes. He was one of the most versatile scientists of his generation, even in an age when specialization had not yet become the god that it is today and it was still possible to be archaeologist, anthropologist, anatomist, palaeontologist and zoologist all at the same time. He was renowned in each of these roles, but they by no means exhausted his repertoire; he threw himself into anything that aroused his curiosity, which was just about everything that lived or had once lived...Louis's life had not been easy, and very often he was disillusioned by the behaviour of his fellow men, but he never lost his basic faith in humanity.

She writes at all times with clarity, fairness and understanding, and portrays Louis Leakey as he was, warts and all. She is particularly good on the most difficult problem, the so-called Kanam-Kanjera 'scandal'. The Editor remembers well the conference convened in St John's College, Cambridge, by the human biology section of the Royal Anthropological Institute in March 1933 and the subsequent *affaire Boswell*. Boswell was at the Cambridge meeting and put his name to the conclusions of the geological committee. But, having brooded over it all since, he stressed the advisability of obtaining further geological evidence from Kanam. Leakey persuaded the Royal Society to send Boswell to Kenya and study the evidence for himself. Here is Sonia Cole's comment:

How often in the months to come Louis must have wished he had kept his mouth shut; for the Battle of Boswell, fought on the field of Kanam in January 1935, was to prove disastrous. Percy Boswell, Professor of Geology at Imperial College, is said to have had a somewhat contradictory character, emotional, inclined to be humorous, almost obsessively concerned with professional conduct. He came from a poor background and may have suffered from the proverbial chip on his shoulder even after he had risen to the dizzy heights of FRS...His vendetta against the Kanam mandible – and against Louis – was no doubt prompted mainly because of his insistence on scientific exactitude, but perhaps jealousy was another motive. In addition, Boswell championed the Piltdown mandible and so was unable to accept a jaw with a chin in the Lower Pleistocene.

The Boswell visit to East Africa could not be arranged until January 1935. By that time the writer of these words had become a pupil of Louis Leakey and had been invited by him to join his next expedition to East Africa. His tutor, who was later to be Sir James Wordie, counselled successfully against this course, and advised a talk with O. T. Jones, then Woodwardian Professor of Geology at Cambridge. He was the man who set H. H. Thomas on the course of research which led him to identify the foreign stones of Stonehenge as coming from south-west Wales. We went to see him with diffidence, having only two cards to play, namely first that we were fellow countrymen, and secondly that John Daniel, the Editor's father, and David Walters, who taught him science at school, had been contemporaries of O.T. Jones at the small and insignificant grammar school at Pencader in north Carmarthenshire. Jones went straight to the point: Leakey was a brilliant man who would do brilliant things, but was brash and rushed to conclusions, and was operating in an interdisciplinary field where every specialist would be against him. 'He will work out his own destiny', he said, 'and it will be a great one. Don't join his bandwagon now. There is something very fishy about Piltdown [this was the Michaelmas Term of 1934]. I don't think there is anything fishy about Kanam and Kanjera, but some will pretend there is.'

Boswell reported most unfavourably on Leakey's work and that great and kind man Alfred Haddon, who more than anyone else had created the Cambridge School of Archaeology and Anthropology, and had taught Leakey, wrote to his former pupil:

I have been shown Boswell's report to the Royal Society and also your field report and I must confess that I am disappointed at the casual way in which you deal with the matter. So far as I can gather it is not merely a question of a mistaken photograph, but a criticism of all your geological evidence at Kanam, Kanjera and Oldoway...It seems to me that your future career depends largely upon the manner in which you face the criticisms. I am not in a position to know to what extent they can be rebutted by you with scientific evidence, but if you want to secure the confidence of scientific men you must act bravely and not shuffle. You may remember that more than once I have warned you not to be in too much of a hurry in your scientific work as I feared that your zeal might overrun your discretion and I can only hope that it has not done so in this case.

Boswell's infamous letter appeared in *Nature* on 9 March 1935. In it he said:

Unfortunately it has not proved possible to find the exact site of either discovery [i.e. Kanam or Kanjera] since the earlier expedition neither marked the localities on the ground nor recorded the sites on a map...Moreover, the photograph of the site where the mandible was found...was, through some error, that of a different locality; and the deposits (said to be clays) are in fact of entirely different rock (volcanic agglomerate)...Thus, in view of the uncertain location of the Kanam and Kanjera sites, and in view also of the doubt as to the stratigraphic horizons from which the remains were obtained and the possibility of the distortion of the beds, I hold the opinion that the geological age of the mandible and skull fragments is uncertain.

It is amazing that Leakey survived as a responsible scholar after Boswell's attack: incidentally Sonia Cole is wrong in supposing that St John's College lost faith in him; their Fellowships are normally for three years and he was exceptionally renewed for a further three. Leakey lived to prove that his perhaps hastily published Kanam-Kanjera finds were all right and Boswell was wrong. It was Boswell who was cut down. At a meeting of the Geological Society of London, O.T. Jones made mincemeat of a paper that

Boswell had given on tectonic structures in Wales, making it clear that Boswell did not know the elementary principles of structural geology. As a result of this Boswell resigned his professorship, and had a nervous breakdown from which he never recovered.

Sonia Cole writes with a fine sense of humour and tells us many curious episodes in the Leakey saga. It is almost unbelievable that Olduvai was discovered by an absent-minded professor with a butterfly net, yet in 1911 an entomologist from Munich called Kattwinkel was so intent on pursuing an alluring specimen that he fell 300 feet down a spectacular gorge: Olduvai is invisible from the plains above until one is standing almost on its very edge. And how fascinating to learn the origin of the name of the site called Apis Rock. The Masai called it Nasera. Allen Turner accompanied Louis Leakey and Donald MacInnes on a reconnaissance to Nasera, and Louis was in a great state of excitement at finding a stagnant pool at the rock shelter. 'There's water!' he cried. Turner looked at it with distaste and said 'That's not water, that's ape's piss.' And Apis Rock it has been called every since.

Leakey was always especially interested in the Piltdown affair. He firmly believed that the refusal of many scholars (including, as we have mentioned, Boswell) to accept the authenticity and antiquity of Kanam and Kanjera was in part due to their conviction that modern man could not have existed at such an early date and must have an ape-like ancestry. Piltdown fitted the pattern of a character half-ape, half-man. While we have no recollection of Leakey suggesting Piltdown to be a forgery, and there is no suggestion of this in Sonia Cole's book, he was immensely suspicious of the remains. In the second edition (1934) of *Adam's Ancestors* he wrote: 'If the lower jaw really belongs to the same individual as the skull, then the Piltdown man is unique in all humanity ... It is tempting to argue that the skull, on the one hand, and the jaw and canine tooth, on the other, do not belong to the same creature. Indeed a number of anatomists maintain that the skull and jaw cannot belong to the same individual and they see in the jaw and canine tooth evidence of a contemporary anthropoid ape.' He referred to the whole affair as an enigma. In *By the Evidence* he says, 'I admit ... that I was foolish enough never to dream, even for a moment, that the true explanation lay in a deliberate forgery.'

Once the forgery had been demonstrated, Leakey was as intrigued as most people as to who was responsible. He did not accept the solution proposed by many that Charles Dawson was the hoaxer. He was convinced that it was first of all a practical joke played on Dawson by Teilhard de Chardin. When, argued Leakey, Teilhard found that Dawson had taken the material to the British Museum, he told Dawson that he had himself tricked him. Dawson then said they must continue the hoax together to see to what extent the pundits could be taken in. 'From then on,' wrote Leakey (*in lit.*), 'Teilhard and Dawson continued jointly with the hoax, with Teilhard playing the more important role of providing more of the fossils and helping with the chemistry.' In 1972 Leakey was engaged in completing a book in which he set out these theories and he discussed the whole affair with us fully in conversations and letters.

We differed in our views of Teilhard's role and we based our views on Teilhard's letters. If we may treat these as a primary source, Teilhard met Dawson between 1 July and 25 July 1909. On the latter date he describes how he took 'my new friend, Mr Dawson, the geologist, to the cliffs to show him the iguanodon tracks'. The first mention of Piltdown is in a letter of 26 April 1912. 'Last Saturday, my geologist friend, Mr Dawson, came for a visit. He brought me some prehistoric remains, flints, elephant and hippopotamus, and, especially, a very thick, well-preserved human skull which he had found in the alluvium deposits not far from here.' [The Jesuit seminary at Ore Place, Hastings.] A letter written from Bramber dated 3 June 1912 gives an account of Teilhard's first visit to Piltdown [first according to our reading of the evidence from his letters]. He wrote:

We planned an excursion to the famous alluvial deposits at Uckfield (north of Lewes): the prehistoric remains I mentioned in one of my letters over a month ago came from there. I began with a hearty English breakfast in Mr Dawson's very tidy home: it's a very comfortable dwelling nestling right in the middle of the ruins of the old castle which overlooks Lewes. Mrs Dawson is an Irish woman born in Bordeaux. One son is in the colonial army in the Sudan and is cluttering up the house with antelope heads.

I was received cordially. Around 10 o'clock we were in Uckfield, where Professor Woodward joined us. He is director of the British Museum's palaeontology division, and is a little man with salt-and-pepper hair, plus a rather cold appearance. At three o'clock, armed with all the makings for a picnic, we started off in the car. After going across Uckfield Castle's grounds, we were left off on the hunting ground; a grassy strip 4–5 metres wide, which skirts a wooded path leading to a farm. Under this grass, there's a centimetre layer of gravel which is gradually being removed to be used for roads. A man was there to help us dig; armed with picks and sifters, we worked for several hours and finally had success. Dawson discovered a new fragment of the famous human skull; he had already three pieces of it, and I myself put a hand on a fragment of an elephant's molar; this find made me really worth something in Woodward's eyes. He jumped on the piece with the enthusiasm of a youth and all the fire that his apparent coldness covered came out. To catch my train, I had to leave before the other two had to abandon their search.

In September Teilhard returned to Uckfield with Dawson and Woodward and it was then that he found the canine tooth of what was thought to be Piltdown Man. It is just possible that the finding of the canine tooth was a piece of legerdemain by Teilhard who was known to be a practical joker and a conjurer of ability. This is certainly what L.S.B.L. thought. We think he cannot have started the whole affair and accept the letters to his parents as truthful accounts of what was happening. Teilhard was not involved in Piltdown until on 26 April 1912 his geologist friend brought him the thick well-preserved human skull. Teilhard was certainly *not* the person who *started* the Piltdown hoax; here we are entirely against L.S.B.L. But did he improve on it? The whole incident of the canine tooth stinks and we all wait to hear Professor Weiner's considered views on that strange day, 30 August 1913.

We are certain that Teilhard was not involved in the beginning of Piltdown: he just could have been curiously involved in the affair of the canine. Leakey insisted to the last on Teilhard's complete involvement. Writing to the Editor on 11 September 1972 he said:

Dear Glyn,

Thank you for your letter of 25th August from France. Many of the points you make on pages 1 and 2 are easily answerable. I will answer them as soon as I can. I still do not think your facts are all correct and certainly not that 'the 3rd June 1912 was the first time that Teilhard was at the site'. There is a record somewhere in a letter of his of *seeing* Dawson collect two pieces of skull.

Anyway, I will write further. Also you make no comment of the time when Teilhard found one of the best artefacts.

Yours sincerely and in haste,

Louis

He died three weeks after writing this letter and there was no further communication. Of his book about Piltdown and Teilhard, Sonia Cole writes in *Leakey's Luck*: 'After his death Mary [Leakey] was very anxious to prevent its publication: Louis had no new evidence to put forward and she felt that the imputations he made would damage his reputation – she was far more concerned about Leakey's reputation than about Teilhard's.' Sonia Cole's own comment is this: 'Louis had no real evidence, only a hunch: Teilhard had once told him that Dawson, the main suspect, was not responsible, but had refused to elaborate.'

September/December 1976

☙ Sir Mortimer Wheeler, CH, CIE, FRS, FBA, died on the morning of 22 July. We were driving to London at the time and heard of it on the one o'clock news. That afternoon we had to walk to Thames and Hudson, his publishers, and back through Whitcomb Street to Piccadilly and on past the Athenaeum to Pall Mall. Memories of the great old man crowded in on us – and then we saw in the streets, everywhere, posters for the evening papers declaring 'Sir Mortimer Wheeler dies', and we thought for a moment that we heard behind us a ghostly voice saying 'Well, well, dear boy.' His vanity and his sense of humour would have been pleased: his essential good sense would have realized that to have made the posters of the newsboys of Central London was a tribute to a great archaeologist who had succeeded more than anyone else in getting archaeology to the public.

Jacquetta Hawkes described him as 'one of the truly heroic figures of the later Heroic Age of British archaeology' (*The Sunday Times*, 25 July). He was born in the year that Schliemann died: he was ten years old when Pitt-Rivers died. He knew Arthur Evans and Woolley and Alfred Clapham. He is now a part of the history of archaeology and one of the most distinguished and important parts that Britain has ever contributed.

By a series of strange accidents the present Editor of ANTIQUITY was involved in the 1950s in the projection of Wheeler to the public through *Animal, Vegetable, Mineral?*. Friendship has been described as a conspiracy for pleasure: Wheeler has often been said to cultivate enemies rather than friends. All we can say here is that from 1950 onwards we built up a friendship – certainly not a mutual admiration society – which survived a quarter of a century. There were ups and downs, but mainly ups and levels. And when, largely due to him, we became Editor of ANTIQUITY in 1957, there were two decades of most fruitful, helpful, and always kindly co-operation. We lunched together each month alternately in his club and ours ('I cannot understand, dear boy, why the food and wine in your club is so much better than in mine'), and built up the closest possible relationship with a man who knew he was brilliant, and slightly resented any criticisms of his advice and judgements until what he had decided to say, as he strode quickly from Piccadilly to Pall Mall, had been changed by two dry martinis, a bottle of claret, and his ready awareness that there was another point of view. It is nonsense that he cultivated enemies rather than friends. A few weeks before his death he insisted on coming to the annual lunch of the Antiquity Trust and making the most generous speech about the Editor and the Production Editor. He was a man of many parts and those who forget his humanity and kindness and sincerity will get a wrong picture of him. Certainly ANTIQUITY in the twenty post-Crawford years would have been much the poorer but for his constant encouragement and advice. There were battles, and we sacked him from being advisory editor for a short while (bibliographers note), but the axe was buried. He found, not unnaturally, the Production Editor more interesting than ourself, but looking back at it, we did conspire together for pleasure and, we think, good over the last quarter of a century; and if the trumpets blow for him on the other side (he never thought there was such a place) they must blow not only for his well-known career set out so often and so well, but for his honest kindly affection for his friends and his devotion to ANTIQUITY.

March 1977

☕ We have been reading Jean-Pierre Adam's *L'Archéologie devant l'imposture* (Paris: Robert Laffont, 1976). Adam is a pupil of Professor Roland Martin and Pierre Coupel, and, since 1970, head of the *Bureau d'architecture antique de Paris*. He writes with a rapier-pen dipped in vitriol 'pour le secteur de l'archéologie, disons qu'à chaque information authentique présentée par un savant, correspond, hélas! la publication d'une sottise ou d'une mystification'. What a pity the English language has not such a fine word as *sottise* with its delicious under- and over-tones of rubbish. Alas, *hélas*, this is sadly what the Gordons, Michells, McKerrells and the too many rest of them are at; they *débitent des sottises*.

Adam is brilliantly scathing about Glozel which he describes as a *delirium atlante*, and the whole affair *rocambolesque*, a word to set beside Professor Renfrew's description of it all as 'a load of rubbish' in the BBC's *Science Now* programme on 24 July. Adam republishes the fascinating photographs from Bayle's report showing the allegedly ancient Glozel tablets dissolving in water and then addresses himself to the basic problem of the Glozel forgery. 'L'auteur de la mystification glozélienne avait indiscutablement une culture archéologique d'un certain niveau; c'est pourquoi Fradin, modeste cultivateur, s'il a participé à la réalisation des objets, a du reçevoir l'aide ou les directives d'une personne, demeurée dans l'ombre, le "cerveau" de l'entreprise.'

Colin Renfrew in his BBC broadcast said that the forger of Glozel was still alive and living in the south of France. We think that the 'cerveau de l'entreprise' died many years ago and lies with his evil secrets in a cemetery in Vichy. McKerrell, Mejdahl, François, and Portal should pay a sentimental visit to Morlet's tomb: we shall be happy to accompany them and to read over the grave the words from page 269 of Adam's book: 'Que deviennent alors les objets "magdaléniens" présumés vieux de 15,000 ans et destinés à dater les tablettes? Les analyses faites à Gif-sur-Yvette commencent à faire la lumière sur cet étonnant bric-à-brac, où les dents de vache modernes côtoient les os authentiques?'

Those who have followed with keen interest the second *affaire Glozel* will have read with growing excitement the Barbetti and Peacock papers in the June and September issues of the *Journal of Archaeological Science* (Barbetti's paper was summarized in *The Times*, 30 June 1976). As Peacock says this is no longer a dispute between archaeologists and scientists but a dispute between scientists, and a test of the reliability of TL dating. We have already said that we found the TL Glozel dates 'inconclusive and unconvincing'.

July 1977

☙ We feel it is time that the second *affaire Glozel* should disappear from the pages of ANTIQUITY as the first *affaire* did after a few years in the twenties. And this for three reasons. The first is that the TL dates give us less and less assurance that they are a primary and reliable chronological document. We think there is some unexplained factor at Glozel. We were not at the Archaeometry conference this spring in Philadelphia. There was a Glozel session, and a correspondent writes:

Glozel at Philadelphia was in a fairly low key and confined to reporting ten dates which grouped fairly convincingly around 100 BC (falling within the range 350 BC to AD 250), one at AD 900, one at AD 1100 and one at AD 1750. The last is the tablet in which there was vitrification over the lettering.

The second reason is the work of Dr T. D. Crawford who is a Lecturer in Linguistics at University College, Cardiff. Dr Crawford wrote to us in November last year:

I became interested in the Glozel material some four years ago, before there was any question of its being genuine. I was planning to do some research on the way that the structure of natural languages of different families shows through a syllabic form of script and I acquired the *Corpus des Inscriptions* as a 'control' set of data because I assumed that there would be no natural language represented in it.

We wrote to Dr Crawford in January as follows:

I wonder how you are getting on with your linguistic examination of the Glozel material? Isserlin sent me a copy of his paper published in France but it was the same paper that he had submitted to ANTIQUITY and I had turned down because it merely said what languages and scripts might have been available if Glozel was authentic, and this of course we knew before. I think that if you read through all the material – and it is very extensive – you will see that the high probability is that the Glozel inscriptions were forged in the twenties of this century. We may, of course, all be quite wrong about this, and if your statistical analysis of the material tells us that the whole thing could really be a possible genuine language then we would all have to think again. If, on the other hand, your researches show that the material is not a language at all, then those of us who believe that the whole thing was an impudent forgery between 1925 and 1927 would be helped in our ideas. Do let us please keep in touch. I have failed to get any replies to the last few letters I have written to McKerrell.

Dr Crawford kept in touch and sent us a copy of his paper 'The inscribed tablets from Glozel' which we hope will be published in the near future in some specialist journal: it is too detailed and specialized for ANTIQUITY. But Dr Crawford has kindly allowed us to quote the summary of his paper. He says that the Glozel inscriptions contain at least 133 signs of which 34 occur only once, which is of the greatest interest and significance. He says, 'One can safely rule out the possibility that the script is alphabetic, since the signs are far too numerous.' These are his conclusions:

The corpus examined does not exhibit the characteristics to be expected of texts in a natural language and linguistic methods are therefore not appropriate to the determination of the genuineness of the material. It is for representatives of other disciplines to assess the possibility of a non-linguistic function for the tablets as opposed to that of their recent fabrication. Certainly in this respect it is unlikely to be attained except by further study of the technique of thermoluminescence dating and by the reopening, under properly qualified direction, of the excavations at Glozel.

Dr Crawford's linguistic findings are fascinating and convincing. The writings at Glozel are not then in any natural language. They are in the very unnatural language invented by Morlet and Fradin to deceive us.

The third reason is a letter from Dr Baumgartel which she wrote to us two years ago, before her death, and which we now feel it is appropriate to publish:

Who would have thought that after so many years the ghost of Glozel would wander again?

I happened to be in Paris in the summer of 1927, just after Dorothy Garrod had given her verdict on the fakes of Glozel. I had been accepted by the late Professor Breuil at the Institut de Paléontologie Humaine to study flints under him for which I have always had a special interest. The etiquette of the Institut demanded that I had to visit the director of the Institut, the late Professor Boule first, before contacting Professor Breuil. Boule had his study in a house in the Jardin des Plantes. There I went, and after paying my respects Boule turned and showed me the Glozel finds. He then took a pin and lifted from one of the lines of an engraved bone a thin film. All at once the scratch stood out white from the yellow colour of the old bone.

That the thermoluminescence dating gave such an odd result only goes to show how careful one has to be when dealing with the latest help provided by our science colleagues. Few archaeologists will be able to understand the process by which they have been evolved, and we have to accept them on trust, though I too hope that one day they will give us the longed-for tool to date the far distant periods. Thermoluminescence is the latest of these methods, and, I think, just as with C14 we shall have to wait a little until all possible sources of error have been detected before we accept its result as unquestionable.

We do not propose to darken the pages of ANTIQUITY any more with Glozeliana: but we leave with our readers this tale. At a conference at Saint-Germain – and we have this from three sources – Henri Hubert asked Salomon Reinach why, if he thought Glozel was so important, he had not insisted on some examples of the finds being in a special exhibition in the Musée des Antiquités Nationales? Reinach flew into a rage and said 'Not while I am Director of this Museum!' How right he was: he must have realized, in his old age, how he had been fooled by Morlet and Co., and it may be this realization, admitted only to himself, that is responsible for the Bouzonville flagons being in the British Museum and not, where of course they should be, in Paris. And perhaps the memory of the Tiara of Saitaphernes haunted him all down the years.

No, there is one simple answer to those who go on asking our views about Piltdown and Glozel, and the answer is Bunga-bunga. This phrase may need some explanation to some of our readers. In 1910 a party of six people led by the arch-hoaxer Horace de Vere Cole (who had already hoaxed the Town and University of Cambridge by a bogus visit of the Sultan of Zanzibar's uncle) inspected *HMS Dreadnought*, flagship of the Home Fleet, then anchored at Weymouth. The party consisted of Cole and Adrian Stephen, his sister Virginia (later to be Virginia Woolf), Guy Ridley, the artist Duncan Grant, and Anthony Buxton, naturalist and author. They were supposed to represent the Ethiopian Emperor and his entourage. They were received by the Commander-in-Chief, the Home Fleet, Admiral Sir William May. It was perhaps one of the greatest hoaxes of all time. Cole had armed himself with a Swahili grammar under the mistaken impression that it was Swahili and not Amharic that was spoken in Abyssinia. Buxton was the Emperor, Cole was the Foreign Office official escorting the party; the others were supporting princes except Adrian Stephen who was, oddly enough, a German interpreter called Hauffmann travelling round Europe with the Ethiopian party.

Let us tell the rest of the story in the words of Norman Moss in his fascinating book *The Pleasures of Deception* (London, 1977):

Stephen was very unsure of his ability to speak either Swahili or plausible gibberish. He got out three words of what seemed like Swahili to him and then he had an inspiration. Drawing on his rigorous classical education, he spoke chunks of Virgil's *Aeneid* to them, mispronouncing it just enough so that it was not immediately recognizable as Latin. Later, when he ran out of Virgil, he spoke some Homer, bringing the same mispronunciation to the Greek. He added plausibility by using the same phrase for a repeated situation: as they had to duck through several doorways, one line from the *Aeneid* came to mean 'Mind your head, your Majesty.' The princes repeated back to him a few of his words. Virginia Woolf, who was Prince Mendex, was worried that her voice would mark her as a female, and, pleading a cold, said only in a gruff tone, 'Chuck-a-choi, Chuck-a-choi.' But the others found a phrase to express their admiration and delight at the things they were shown: again and again they threw up their hands and exclaimed 'Bunga-bunga.' They Bunga-bungaed their way around the ship appreciatively. The officers smiled at their simple excitement at seeing an electric light.

The only full account of all this remarkable nonsense was published in a small book written by Adrian Stephen called *The Dreadnought Hoax* (1936, from The Hogarth Press run by Leonard and Virginia Woolf). It is all very well summarized in Moss's book which was, appropriately enough, published on April Fool's Day of this year. It is brilliantly good and for the most part accurate, though it does not venture much into archaeology and art history: there is no mention of Glozel, although Piltdown is treated but not very accurately. If Glozel had been dealt with we feel that Moss would have agreed with us that the epitaph of that strange story, revived to confuse us and blind us with science in the seventies, would be 'Chuck-a-choi, Bunga-bunga.'

November 1977

☏ One of the pleasures of being an editor is the rude letters and abuse that one receives. We thrive on it: more please – it not only shows that ANTIQUITY is widely read but tells saddeningly what a lot of loonies there are about. We eat our eggs Brillat-Savarin, our kedgeree, our grilled kidneys, our marrow toast, whatever it may be at breakfast that day, with renewed zest when the post brings copies of *The new diffusionist*, or *The Stonehenge viewpoint*, or *The ley hunter: magazine of earth mysteries*. The day is made, but never so happily as when we read No. 75 of that misguided publication *The ley hunter*. In its review of Peter Lancaster Brown's interesting book *Megaliths, myths and men* it says that the book 'details some of the reactions exhibited by the editor of *Antiquity*, whose steadfast refusal to consider that Stonehenge could be anything more than what his fellow archaeologists stated it to be, will surely be noted by posterity as a prime example of scientific obscurantism'. Bravo! What splendid stuff!

Crawford declined to advertise Watkins and so do we: we may poke fun at the lunatic fringers who dwell on the wilder shores of archaeology, preferring the black comforts of unreason to sense, but we should not make money out of them. He was not keen to take notice of dotty books although he did print reviews by R. C. C. Clay of Massingham's *Downland man* and *Pre-Roman Britain*. The latter review, one of the briefest ever published, contains those classic sentences: 'This book possesses all the faults of *Downland man* of which it is a *rechauffé*, but nevertheless the publishers demand the exorbitant price of 6d a copy. The style is bad, and the meaning (if any) of the extraordinarily long sentences very obscure...Scotchmen, who value their sixpences, should beware!' (ANTIQUITY, 1928).

We have just received from G. P. Putnam's Sons in New York the advertisement of a book which we eagerly await. It is called *Psychic archaeology: time machine to the past* and is by Jeffrey Goodman, former President of Stratigraphic Oil Company. Apparently Goodman had a dream which showed an American location where human artifacts were to be found dating back 100,000 years. He consulted Aron Abrahamson, a well-known clairvoyant, who identified the site as Flagstaff, Arizona. 'Archaeology today', writes Goodman, 'is in the throes of a revolution where ESP is replacing the spade as archaeology's primary tool.' Dr Paul Henshaw of the University of Arizona calls it 'a fearless – even fearsome – document'. It sounds like it. In the preface to Massingham's *Downland man*, Elliot Smith wrote: 'What is most needed at the present time is the elimination of learned nonsense.' Those words, written fifty years ago, apply equally well today.

March 1978

🐚 It was a great excitement to visit Lascaux again a few months ago and to marvel anew at its beauty, the freshness of the colouring and the vigour of its art. It is one of the seven wonders of the prehistoric world of Western Europe. We first visited it with Dorothy Garrod and Suzanne de Saint-Mathurin in 1947 before it was opened to the general public, and then many times in the years following until it was closed to the public in 1963 because the paintings were fading and being covered by a fungus. These troubles have been solved but not so satisfactorily that the general public can be admitted, or, so far as we understand, will ever be admitted as they were in the fifties, in their thousands each day. We found ourselves (Production Editor and Editor) waiting anxiously with four other people. On time there arrived the guide and it was Jacques Marsal, one of the original discoverers of the cave, whom we had known since he had first shown us round in the late forties. He is now a sound and very well-informed guide. In conversation after our visit I asked him about the dog Robot who is a standard part of the story of the discovery of Lascaux. We quote from our own *Man Discovers His Past* where we wrote:

...The most exciting discovery was made on the 12th of September 1940, at Lascaux. It was made by four boys who were out rabbiting with their dog Robot. The dog fell through a hole in the roof of the cave – a hole made by the uprooting of a tree in the previous winter's gale. The boys climbed down to rescue their dog, and found themselves in a large cave, the walls and roof of which were decorated with painted and engraved animals.

Marsal was scornful: 'Yes', he said, 'we did have a dog, but it was not involved in the discovery of Lascaux. The story, as you and others have often set it out, was a piece of sentimental propaganda to amuse and encourage foreigners, particularly English and Americans.'

The true story is set out in Pierre Fanlac's book entitled *La Merveilleuse découverte de Lascaux*, written, printed and published by himself (Périgueux, 1968). The traditional story must now be varied in several ways. First: the cave of Lascaux had been known – as a cave, not as a painted cave – for a long time: it was called *le trou du diable* and the entrance to it was revealed *twenty* years before the events of 12 September 1940 by the collapse of a tree. Secondly, there were five not four boys. There were three locals, Jacques Marsal, Marcel Ravidat, and Pierre Fanlac, and two *réfugiés* from Paris, Simon Coencas and Georges Agnel. Thirdly, they were not rescuing a dog: they were a local adolescent gang engaged in warfare with another local gang of *réfugiés* whom they called *les étrangers*. *Le trou du diable* was to be their secret headquarters and in occupying it they found Lascaux and made one of the greatest archaeological discoveries of all time.

So perishes another archaeological legend, and we recollect how the Abbé Breuil once told us that when, in her old age, he taxed the daughter of Marcelino de Sautuola about the *Toros! Toros!* story, she said she had no recollection of it – which is sad, unless it merely means that the memories of old ladies, like old men, often fade. But we shed a tear for poor Robot: he seemed such a nice part of the history of archaeology as did the little girl of five at Altamira. We can only hope that the young Kurdish boy 'who had come from a distance' and who is supposed to have enabled Rawlinson to copy the Behistun inscriptions in 1847, will never be debunked.

November 1978

✪ Our plate 5, taken by Brian Harris, was published in *The Times* on 22 June and is reproduced here by the kind permission of the photographer and *The Times*. It shows, in an unusual and dramatic way, the modern bogus Druids at their midsummer frolics. This year there has been more than usual comment on Stonehenge at midsummer. There are two problems. The first is the invasion of Stonehenge by members of a bogus nineteenth-century organization purporting to be Druids. They have no right to be there. Imagine what would happen if a similar bogus organization asked to celebrate midsummer or Beltane in Westminster Abbey. The Dean and Chapter would very properly regret. Presumably these bogus Druids apply each year to the Ancient Monuments Board or the Department of the Environment. Next year those notably spunkless organizations should very properly regret that permission is not forthcoming. Let us in 1979 clear Stonehenge of modern Druidic follies.

The second Stonehenge problem is the thousands who camp illegally on the land of a farm near by – land belonging to the National Trust. 'Once again', says the Director-General of the National Trust, 'the National Trust, the police and the local authority have been powerless to prevent the heavy loss suffered each June by the Trust's public-spirited farm tenant' (*The Times*, 22 June 1978). A Mr Sid Rawle, giving his address as Stonehenge, in his reply to the Director-General's letter tells us some surprising things:

What has happened at Stonehenge over the last five years is that for the week of midsummer thousands of pilgrims from many religious persuasions have come here. There are over 50 recognized groups on site at the moment: many different groupings of Christians, Buddhists and Hindus, a Church of England minister solemnizing a marriage, a Catholic priest consecrating Mass, all celebrating the unity of one God. We come to Stonehenge because in an unstable world it is proper that the people should look for stability to the past in order to learn for the future. The evidence is indisputable that Stonehenge and the surrounding area is one of the most powerful centres in Europe. It is right that we should meekly stand in the presence of God, but it is proper that we should sing and dance and shout for joy for the love and mercy that He shows us. (*The Times*, 28 June 1978.)

The only possible comment is Christ Almighty! But what is a more rational comment? Jacquetta Hawkes has said that every generation has the Stonehenge it deserves. But what does our generation deserve? Have we quickly passed through the generation of astro-archaeologists and are now in a generation of mystical archaeologists?

We all have a problem here. It seems simple to urge the Department of the Environment and everyone else to ban Stonehenge and its environs to everyone for the octave of midsummer. But what if these characters are really using Stonehenge as a cult-symbol, and in all sincerity? It would be fascinating if, after 4,000 years, the magic of this astonishing monument still ensnared the public of today. There is a strange American magazine called *Stonehenge Viewpoint* and its spring catalogue for 1978 shows how strong Stonehenge is in the American market. There are pendants and stars and brooches for sale: we are tempted by the megalithic pendant at $8.50. But, we ask, why is all this happening?

☎ As we go to press we have heard the sad news of the death of Max Mallowan, a most valued member of the Antiquity Trust and one of our most helpful and wise Advisory Editors.

His relations with Sir Mortimer Wheeler were always interesting to observe and we well remember Max greeting Rik on one occasion with these words, 'And what evil ploys are you pursuing today, you old monster?' After the 1978 meeting of the Antiquity Trustees we walked with him down the steps of the United Oxford and Cambridge University Club. With an imperious wave of his stick he summoned a taxi, said 'Wallingford' to the driver and was gone to his house in Oxfordshire fifty miles away. The Editor now realizes that he would not have been surprised if, getting into his London taxi, Max had said 'Nineveh' or 'Ur'. And now he has gone to those Elysian fields where there are no taxis, where time and chance are meaningless, and he can talk freely with Wheeler, Woolley, Layard, Rawlinson, Gilgamesh, and of course Agatha, beneath the gaze of the eye-goddess herself.

March 1979

☎ Dr Aubrey Burl writes (*in lit.*, 9 November 1978):
I have just been reading your comments about the state of Stonehenge. Ironically, I went there last month, too late for the barbed wire but just in time to see 'Save

the Ponys' red-daubed on the Outer Circle. A cohort of paint-removing workmen added to the general obscurity of the monument which now has to be viewed from an outer periphery where one has the choice of the 'short' or the 'long' walk, the difference in distance being something of the order of a hundred yards (Imperial, not megalithic).

Damage to Stonehenge will persist so long as people are allowed to visit it. Even on a cold, late afternoon in October, with the sun setting, I counted three coaches and 27 cars in the car-park, and that must have represented at least 120 looking at the stones. As nearly all of them will have had two feet a lot of walking was being done and I'm rather doubtful as to whether a shuffling, claustrophobic queue along a series of duckboards is any answer.

Just for amusement, in the way that most archaeologists are somewhat unbalanced, I did some calculations about the effect visitors must have upon Stonehenge. An average of 2,055 people go there each day and if each one of them walked around the central area of the sarsen circle just twice – and most visitors meander much further than that – they would have taken 460,320 paces. This is the equivalent of a man jumping up and down on the spot 62 times daily on each square foot inside the ring, day in, day out, throughout the year – whether the ground was wet or dry. If we look at the spots where a bowler's feet have landed at the end of 10 overs we have a good idea of how the ground is being affected. And cricket pitches are given rest and treatment between matches and a long fallow period during the winter.

This is not to mention the inevitable damage to stones where children climb and where ladies in dagger-like heels teeter on the Altar Stone, and where the more knowledgeable do even more harm by prodding at the axe-carvings, and running fingers around the Mycenaean/British dagger/axe.

Perhaps the most sensible solution would indeed be to increase the entrance fee and create a good long walk to the site, perhaps from the Winterbourne Stoke cross-roads where the visitor could start in a prehistoric context with the prospect of a mile and a half ramble across the Plain.

After these interesting comments on Stonehenge, Aubrey Burl goes on to more general issues:

The problem is not at all confined to Stonehenge. How much worse it must be in a confined area like the passageway at New Grange or along the crests of banks like Arbor Low. And sometimes the damage is deliberate. Last year I myself had to prevent some French visitors from removing some stones of the chamber tomb at Callanish! They were quite indignant at my protests but I suspect my French was dreadful enough to restore their good humour and they put back the sideslab they had dragged out of the turf.

Did you know that the south-west quadrant of Avebury has been closed to the public this summer? It is no longer possible to saunter around the top of the bank, tumble into the ditch, or embrace the Barber's Stone. Instead, there is a roped aisle through the field well away from the popular areas where, once again, half a million feet a year were wearing a hollow way round the bank's summit.

We showed Burl's letter to Professor Atkinson and here are some of his comments:

Aubrey Burl is quite right about the erosion of Stonehenge by its visitors; but I don't think myself that the solution is to put the car-park so far away that visitors have to walk several kilometres to visit it, in the rain in the winter. And what about the disabled and the aged and infirm?

We know from experience that the grass in the centre will stand no more than 250,000 visitors per annum in normal conditions, and fewer if the summer is particularly dry or the winter particularly wet. The current number of visitors is in excess of 800,000, and in a year or two it will be a million. Given this demand it seems to me quite impracticable to reduce the numbers to one quarter by increasing the price or the distance. The present policy of excluding all but educational parties from the stones themselves is a compromise, certainly, but one which seems to me the only solution in the circumstances. The same goes for the fencing off of Silbury Hill and the south-west quadrant of Avebury, much though I regret both. Somewhere the line has to be drawn between the requirements of preservation of unique monuments and the demand, always increasing, for full public access. In a sense these necessary restrictions are a comment on the part played by ANTIQUITY and by television in the popularization of archaeology.

Before we make our comments may we bring to your attention another piece of correspondence which started when a friend of ours, who took a party of students to Stonehenge, had the same reactions as James Dyer and refused to pay the admission fee to view the monument under such conditions. A letter of sensible protest was sent to the Department of the Environment and the reply is such an unbelievably classic example of bullshit bureaucracy that it must be allowed to sully the clean page of ANTIQUITY. We quote from the second paragraph dated 30 June 1978:

The Druids have been allowed to perform their Solstice rites at least since just after the First World War. *If they were forbidden entry they would allege religious persecution and force their way in unless physically stopped by the police* [Italics ours – Ed.]. The latter would not welcome the job especially under the eye of the TV cameras. Do you really expect Ministers to agree in these circumstances to stop what has been a traditional event, no matter how dubious the historical connexion? Incidentally we opened the monument to all comers on Solstice Day.

This letter was written by an Assistant Secretary in the Ancient and Historic Monuments Division of the Department of the Environment. If this rubbish really reflects the policy of the Department, where are we? In cloud-cuckoo-land. How could anyone with even the slightest knowledge of prehistory and antiquity write in such a way? When we reread those bland phrases 'religious persecution', 'traditional event', 'the eye of the TV cameras', we boil with such rage that the platen of our typewriter is endangered.

If this policy is seriously pursued by the Department of the Environment then surely any religious sect can claim entrance to Stonehenge? Traditions can easily be fabricated, and so we shall find Salisbury Plain at the Summer Solstice full of rival bands – Druids, Moonies, Loonies, Boobies, Straight Trackers, Bent Trackers, Geomantics, Pyramidiots, Atlanteans – the lot. Elizabeth Fowler (*in lit.*, 7 November 1978) says: 'Perhaps the archaeological body as a whole should apply to hold some sort of "rite" at Midwinter, as Robert Newall used to suggest, and force the D of E to the absurdity of their position.' Another idea is to institutionalize the subscriber readership of ANTIQUITY and register ourselves as a religious body: the Backward Looking Curious Brethren? Not to embarrass our friends in the Department of the Environment or get mixed up with bogus Druids and Lunatic Fringers, we might march to Stonehenge at Beltane or Samhain. What a jolly procession it could be, led by Richard Atkinson and Stuart Piggott! During the ceremonies, carefully devised by Professor Piggott from forged manuscripts, the Editor would be happy to play ancient Celtic hymns (including 'Sospan fach') on a portable baroque organ, supported by an orchestra of old musical instruments devised by John Coles, Vincent Megaw and Graeme Lawson, with Rupert Bruce-Mitford plucking plaintively at a lyre on the Altar Stone.

The Stonehenge problem is as real as the Lascaux problem and that was solved by banning the public, organizing restricted entry for small accredited groups, building a replica of the cave near by, and having a special cinema show. It doesn't seem to us that the building of a replica Stonehenge would serve a good purpose. The present Daniel plan has three proposals: 1. Ban all special entry for religious, social and secret societies. 2. Close the monument in perpetuity to the public – that is to say the central important part, but allow accredited parties of scholars in from time to time. 3. Build (perhaps underground?) a cinema and museum. The cinema would show all day a short, detailed documentary film of the site, explaining its origin and construction. Entrance to the cinema show and the small museum would be part of the admission ticket.

July 1979

❦ We publish in this issue a very interesting article on Prehistory and Marxism which is in itself a bibliographical curiosity: it was written by Gordon Childe eight years before he died and has lain in our files for thirty years. We were reminded of it because of the receipt of two letters from Australia relating to the last few weeks of Childe's life and commenting on the strange circumstances of his death. The first is from Dr Laila Haglund of the Department of Anthropology, University of Sydney:

It is time this myth about Gordon Childe's suicide was knocked. It seems to be prevalent in Europe; I sometimes wonder whether some of his colleagues and contemporaries there think that he *ought* to have felt suicidal.

I had the pleasure of knowing him at the time of his death and remember him as ebullient and full of enthusiasm. As a fellow guest of the Stewarts and a budding archaeologist I saw several different aspects of him. At first he seemed shy, but he soon mellowed and obviously enjoyed conversation, food, drink and his pipe. Maybe it was my pipe-smoking that broke the ice. He seemed highly amused and always remembered to bring me some good pipe tobacco from Sydney. Such luxuries could not be had locally in those days.

We often sat by the fire, puffing away, while Childe talked about prehistory, sometimes almost through the night. He was full of plans. There was so much he wished to see done in Australian prehistory, some of this he wanted to do himself. But it was all part of a large co-ordinated scheme. Listening to him was at times rather like hovering over the continent and looking down in a godlike manner. I have often regretted not making notes. At the time what he said seemed unforgettable. He was definitely much interested in the geography of Australia in relation to problems in prehistory. At the time of his death he was particularly interested in the geology of the Blue Mountains, and I am convinced that it was this interest that brought him to his death. Though mentally alert he was physically somewhat tottery. I can easily see him fold his coat, put it down on the rocks, place the compass, take off his spectacles to do some sighting, peer around, perhaps step back a bit to line up certain features – quite forgetting that he had a cliff edge behind him. I cannot imagine him stepping – bleakly or desperately – over that edge to end his life!

Our last long talk was only a couple of days before his death. It was largely Childe's enthusiasm that influenced me to turn to the study of Australian prehistory. He could hardly have faked enthusiasm so convincingly. When he left he was clearly intending to come back soon and looking forward to it.

The second letter is from Mrs Eve Stewart, widow of J. R. B. Stewart, who was Professor of Near Eastern Archaeology in the University of Sydney until his death in 1962:

A copy of *Mallowan's memoirs* has just reached me and I have been reading it with much pleasure and interest. However, one thing distressed me, namely his suggestion that the late Professor V. G. Childe 'felt that life, for all his interests, held but a bleak prospect. . . . There is little doubt in my mind that he committed suicide' (p. 235). I cannot agree with either of these statements.

My husband and I came to know Prof. Childe well, because he stayed with us several times in 1957, at our home near Bathurst. The two had long discussions about archaeological problems and also Prof. Childe's plans for his latest line of research, which concerned the geology of the Blue Mountains. I got the impression of a man full of enthusiasm for a new project. There was certainly no hint of a bleak future; I would have said that he was rejoicing in his retirement because he was free to devote *all* his time and energy to the things which interested him. The enthusiastic tone of the letters he wrote us, between April and October 1957, endorses this impression.

As to suicide – definitely NO!

He spent a few days with us in mid-October. When he left, only two days before his death, he was as cheerful as usual and was looking forward to returning a few weeks later.

Mrs Stewart goes on to say that naturally the Australian papers carried an account of his death. We do not quote these verbatim but it is clear that the *Sydney Daily Telegraph* and the *Sydney Morning Herald* accepted the police view that 'mislaid spectacles caused Professor V. G. Childe to fall 900 ft. to his death at Govett's Leap'. One paper reported: 'People who knew Professor Childe said that without his spectacles he was almost blind, except for looking at close objects.'

Mrs Stewart states that as soon as her husband learnt the tragic news he phoned Mrs V. Clift, the secretary of the Carrington Hotel in Katoomba, the hotel where Professor Childe always stayed. Professor Stewart received a lengthy letter in reply, of which Mrs Stewart sends us these relevant portions:

As promised, I am writing to tell you a little of the dear old chappie's last days. We were all so fond of him at the Carrington. . . .

Apparently he asked the taxi to take him to Govett's Leap, and either to wait for him, or to come back for him so that he would be back at the Carrington for lunch. He was to get the afternoon train down and was to be at Bundanoon today. When the Professor did not arrive at the meeting place as arranged, the taxi-driver [Mr Newstead] became worried and went looking for him.

He found the Professor's coat on the edge of the cliff, with pipe and spectacles on top of it, and the compass on the rock beside it. . . .

As he had gone out before breakfast, and the day was fairly hot, we think that he must have taken his coat off, and feeling the heat, combined with an empty stomach, had had a giddy turn and over-balanced.

As soon as the taxi-driver notified the police they phoned us and I happened to answer. Constable Morey wanted to know if I thought he would have suicided. I assured him that the Professor was definitely not that type, and that he was far too interested in life, and his archaeology, to do anything like that....

Mrs Stewart finishes by saying that not long ago she happened to meet the taxi-driver, who remembered Professor Childe well, having been his regular driver when he was staying at the Carrington. He, also, is convinced it was an accident.

Also in our files we discovered a note from Crawford to Childe, and Childe's reply (he often signed his name in Russian in letters to friends).

Sorry Just off to Australia on May 17 Don't know when if ever I return & the books sound too heavy to read on boat

Togorr

❦ The lunatic fringes close in on us and the ley-hunters have us marked down. The Institute of Geomancy is only a few miles away from us as we write and its editor, Nigel Pennick, kindly sends us copies of his *Journal of Geomancy* as it comes out. Volume 3, no. 2, published a few months ago, contains an article by Pennick and Michael Behrend on 'The Cambridge 7-Church Ley', a straight line from the Holy Sepulchre (the Cambridge church of that name better known as the Round Church), through St Michael's, Great St Mary's, St Edward, King and Martyr, St Benet's, St Botolph's, and St Mary the Less. After this we are told the ley 'crosses nothing else of any significance between Much Hadham and the south coast'. The geomantic ley-hunters are a little displeased that their 7-church ley goes through the Victorian Emmanuel United Reformed Church (formerly Congregational) and say 'the significance of nineteenth-century churches on ley-lines remains enigmatic'. They declare triumphantly that the ley-line goes through 'The Flying Stag, at present the home of Glyn Daniel, Disney Professor of Archaeology at Cambridge University, and staunch opponent of geomancy'. This is fame indeed, actually to live on a ley-line – although we are bound to say that the significance of the

ANTIQUITY office being so sited also 'remains enigmatic'. We have projected the line through Much Hadham and it seems to hit the south coast at Newhaven, where we are about to drive on our way to Normandy to celebrate our sixty-fifth birthday. Is there some strange, occult significance here? Anyhow, the merry misguided harmless ley-hunters, who give us all a lot of amusement in this hard, serious archaeological world, and who keep complaining that we refuse to accept advertisements for Watkins's *Old Straight Track* and similar lunacies, have been given a little, grudging, publicity by this journal: which they firmly believe (and they will believe anything) shows at its worst the unacceptable hard face of the dyed-in-the-wool and out-of-date archaeological establishment.

November 1979

❧ Some of the issues that have been written about in these editorial pages so frequently keep coming up again and again in correspondence: Stonehenge (and who was it that first noticed the Post Office trench being dug through our most publicized ancient monument?), Rouffignac (and is it true as we are told that more mammoths have appeared this year and that there is now incontrovertible proof of an alleged prehistoric painting superimposed on a written signature?), Piltdown (and we understand that soon a letter is going to be published proving the complicity of Teilhard de Chardin in the affair), Mystery Hill (when can we and how can we explain to intelligent Americans that colonial root-cellars are not dolmens or cromlechs, however widely and unwisely we extend those well-worn words?), and Glozel. How jejune all these issues can become, as are the well-meaning lucubrations of bullshit pseudo-archaeologists from Barry Fell to von Däniken.

But from time to time Glozel breaks through boredom to renewed interest. We recently asked Dr Vagn Mejdahl of the Risø National Laboratory at Roskilde in Denmark what were now his considered views about this strange affair. He writes (6 June 1979):

It might interest you to know that a society called 'Association pour la Sauvegarde et la Protection des Collections de Glozel' has been formed. The main task of the Society will be to ensure the conservation of the objects in Fradin's museum, but another declared objective is to work for a reopening of the excavation at Glozel which would be of great interest if done properly.

Together with French archaeologists I have selected a number of ceramic objects for TL dating. So far I have only had time to look at a glass-covered object which should date to the period of the glass-smelting activities. The object did not seem to be an artifact but a clay ball that had been heated accidentally. The date obtained was AD 200. There are a few other TL dates from around that period, including the date obtained by Martin Aitken, but most TL dates fall in the range 350 BC–AD 240 as indicated in the paper I presented at the Archaeometry Conference in Philadelphia in 1977. The recent measurement confirms our earlier finding that the Glozel material is well suited for TL dating. It still seems to me, therefore, that the dates obtained must represent the time of firing (*or a later heating*).

Our good friend Mejdahl readily agreed to the publication of his letter; the italics are ours. They underline and underlie the doubts of many of us: how it is that palpable forgeries of the 1920s AD give TL dates of 350 BC to AD 250? *Qu'est-ce qui se passe?* By all means let us have a proper excavation of the Champ des Morts controlled by an international Committee (Becker, Atkinson, De Laet, Krämer, Seton Lloyd, Giot and Willey?) but there is at least one person who should be *en congé* during these fouilles. Our files are always at the disposal of the French Sûreté. None of us is any longer worried by the ghosts of the wicked Dr Morlet or the misguided Salomon Reinach.

March 1980

☛ We published in the July 1979 issue letters from Dr Laila Haglund and Mrs Eve Stewart, prompted by reading *Mallowan's memoirs* in which Sir Max wrote of Gordon Childe in 1957 that he 'felt that life, for all his interests, held but a bleak prospect.... There is little doubt in my mind that he committed suicide.' Dr Haglund and Mrs Stewart strenuously deny the view that Childe did take his own life. Professor W. F. Grimes, who succeeded Childe as Director of the Institute of Archaeology in the University of London, wrote to us on 14 August 1979 about this and has readily given us permission to publish his letter:

My dear Glyn,

I have only now got round to reading your editorial in the July issue, with the further correspondence on Gordon Childe.

I forbear to comment on the views expressed, beyond saying that of the making of myths there is no end; but there may be need to look at the mental attitudes of those who create or contribute to them. May I offer the following contribution to the subject? A number of people know about it, but it won't have appeared in print, as far as I know.

Shortly after my appointment to succeed him at the Institute Childe and I dined together in Soho. We drove back to NW3 in his car. In the hundred or so yards between Primrose Hill station and Chalk Farm (where I was to leave him) the following conversation took place:

G: What are you going to do when you retire?

C: I know a 2000-ft cliff in Australia. I intend to jump off it.

G: Good god! Why are you going to do that?

C: I have a horror of a prostate operation.

G: But surely thousands of men have had that and come out of it without difficulty?

He made no further comment and seconds later I got out of the car.

The conversation is *verbatim*. I saw no point in arguing or remonstrating. Childe knew his own mind, though he rarely – very rarely – revealed it in personal matters.

In the light of his statement Childe's subsequent conduct seems to me to be consistent and in some respects shrewd. Though there are disturbing features about it I believe that he did what he wanted – and I happen to think that every man/woman has the right to do what he/she likes with his/her own life.

Yours ever,

Peter

We recently showed this letter to Professor Estyn Evans in Belfast and he told us that Childe had had virtually the same conversation with Professor Woolridge; and Miss Sally Green, who has written a book on Childe, says that she has heard this story from many people. When we were discussing it with Professor John Evans, who succeeded Professor Grimes as Director of the Institute, he confirmed that Childe had left a letter to his successor which was not to be read or published for ten years after his departure to Australia in 1957. Professor Evans and Professor Grimes now agree that this letter should be published. Here it is. There are really two items: a letter to Grimes, and a memoir. Here is the letter:

THE CARRINGTON

KATOOMBA

BLUE MOUNTAINS, N.S.W.

20/10/57

Dear Grimes,

The enclosed contains matter that may in time be of historical interest to the Institute. But now it may cause pain and even provoke libel actions. After ten years it will be less inflammable. So I earnestly request that it be deposited in the archives and be not opened till January 1968 supposing that year ever arrives.

Yours sincerely,

V. Gordon Childe

And here is the enclosed essay which deserves careful reading by all our readers, young, middle-aged, and old, and certainly by everyone who either knew Gordon Childe personally or as the great prehistorian he was. The essay is undated but must, we suppose, have approximately the same date as the letter to Grimes.

THE CARRINGTON

KATOOMBA

BLUE MOUNTAINS, N.S.W.

The progress of medical science has burdened society with a horde of parasites —
rentiers, pensioners and other retired persons whom society has to support and even
to nurse. They exploit the youth which is expected to produce for them and even
to tend them. While many are physically fit to work and some do, others are
incapable of looking after themselves and have literally to be kept alive by the
exertions of younger attendants who might be more profitably employed otherwise.
And in so far as they do work, they block the way to promotion against younger
and more efficient successors. For all in all persons over 65 — there are of
course numerous exceptions — are physically less capable than their juniors and
psychologically far less alert and adaptable. Their reactions are slowed down; they
can only gradually and reluctantly, if at all, adopt new habits and still more rarely
assimilate fresh ideas. I am doubtful whether they can ever produce new ideas.
Compulsory retirement from academic and judicial posts and from the civil services
has of course done something to open the rewards of seniority to younger men,
and has rescued students and subordinates from inefficient teachers and incompetent
administrative chiefs. In British universities the survival of the old system during
my lifetime has provided cautionary examples of distinguished professors mumbling
lectures ten years out of date and wasting departmental funds on obsolete equipment.
These instances probably outweigh better publicized cases of scientists and scholars
who in their colleagues' opinion are 'forced to retire at the height of their powers'.
But even when retired, their prestige may be such that they can hinder the spread
of progressive ideas and blast the careers of innovators who tactlessly challenge
theories and procedures that ten or fifteen years previously had been original and
fruitful (I am thinking for instance of Arthur Evans).

In fact if the over-age put 'their knowledge, experience and skill at the service
of society' as honorary officers or counsellors of learned societies, public bodies,
charitable institutions or political parties, they are liable to become a gerontocracy —
the worst possible form of leadership. In a changing world their wisdom and
maturity of judgement do not compensate for their engrained prejudices and
stereotyped routines of behaviour. No doubt the over 65s are competent to carry
out routine investigations and undertake compilations of information, and may be
helped therein by their accumulated knowledge. Yet after 65 memory begins to
fail, and even well-systematized information begins to leak away. My personal
experience is confirmed by observations on senior colleagues. And new ideas,
original combinations of old knowledge, come rarely if at all. Generally old authors
go on repeating the same old theses, not always in better chosen language.

I have always considered that a sane society would disembarrass itself of such
parasites by offering euthanasia as a crowning honour or even imposing it in bad
cases, but certainly not condemning them to misery and starvation by inflation.

For myself I don't believe I can make further useful contributions to prehistory. I am beginning to forget what I laboriously learned – forget not only details (for these I never relied on memory), but even that there is something relevant to look up in my note-book. New ideas very rarely come my way. I see no prospect of settling the problems that interest me most – such as that of the 'Aryan cradle' – on the available data. In a few instances I actually fear that the balance of evidence is against theories that I have espoused or even in favour of those against which I am strongly biased. Yet at the same time I suspect this fear may be due to an equally irrational desire to overcome my own prejudices. (In history one has to make decisions on inadequate evidence, and, whenever I am faced with this necessity, I am conscious of such opposing tendencies.) I have no wish to hang on the fringe of learned societies or university institutions as a venerable counsellor whose authority may slow down progress. I have become too dependent on a lot of creature comforts – even luxuries – to carry through some kinds of work for which I may still be fitted; I just lack the will-power to face the discomforts and anxieties of travel in the USSR or China. And, in fact, though I have never felt in better health, I do get seriously ill absurdly easily; every little cold in the head turns to bronchitis unless I take elaborate precautions and then I am just a burden on the community. I have never saved any money, and, if I had, inflation would have consumed my savings. On my pension I certainly could not maintain the standard without which life would seem to me intolerable and which may be really necessary to prevent me becoming a worse burden on society as an invalid. I have always intended to cease living before that happens.

The British prejudice against suicide is utterly irrational. To end his life deliberately is in fact something that distinguishes *Homo sapiens* from other animals even better than ceremonial burial of the dead. But I don't intend to hurt my friends by flouting that prejudice. An accident may easily and naturally befall me on a mountain cliff. I have revisited my native land and found I like Australian society much less than European without believing I can do anything to better it; for I have lost faith in all my old ideals. But I have enormously enjoyed revisiting the haunts of my boyhood, above all the Blue Mountains. I have answered to my own satisfaction questions that intrigued me then. Now I have seen the Australian spring; I have smelt the boronia, watched snakes and lizards, listened to the 'locusts'. There is nothing more I want to do here; nothing I feel I ought and could do. I hate the prospect of the summer, but I hate still more the fogs and snows of a British winter. Life ends best when one is happy and strong.

We print this essay and Professor Grimes's letter with sadness and sympathy because we knew and loved Gordon Childe and were sorry that no opportunity came to us or to many other friends and contemporaries to persuade him that 65 was not necessarily the end of things. Nor is it. It is an important moment in the ageing life of academic archaeologists and our universities are wise to have retiring ages at 65 or 67. They should perhaps be 60, and what could be nicer than a system (unlikely to happen in our present university financial crisis in England) whereby dons were retired from teaching duties at 60 and paid for the next five or seven years to do research or to publish their many unpublished archaeological reports and papers? But Childe's essay is not only of interest to readers of ANTIQUITY and to students of the history of archaeology and of the development of thought in the western world in the twentieth century – because Gordon Childe was a very formative figure in creating the climate of thought about the past in which most readers of ANTIQUITY under 65 live. His essay is of the widest interest to scholars concerned with the aged and with aged scholars in particular. We suspect that this essay will often appear in anthologies. It is a moving document: we have read it with care, and our ageing fingers that strike at the keys of our ageing typewriter remind us that the Editor of ANTIQUITY is himself (surely it cannot be ourselves?) over 65 and therefore, according to Gordon Childe, pretty gaga. (Discerning readers may have noticed this already.) Incidentally, it is worth recording that the average age of professors of archaeology in Britain at the moment is under 50, whereas the average age of the members of the Politburo in the Kremlin is 70. (There is one curiosity in Childe's letter to Grimes: it is dated 20 October 1957; Childe's death has been consistently reported as 19 October 1957 and this is the date in *Who Was Who* and the *Dictionary of National Biography*.)

There may well be in the next few years a number of books about Childe. The first to be published will be Professor Bruce Trigger's *Gordon Childe: Revolutions in Archaeology* (London, 1980).

We have had the pleasure and privilege of reading Bruce Trigger's book before publication. He naturally makes many cogent points and gives an admirable analysis of the development and content of Childe's thought. He makes two special points that we had hitherto missed. First, that Childe felt that his *The Aryans* was too close to the Kossinna master-race theory, and did not much like people referring to the book. Secondly, he was at first much influenced by the Elliot Smith–Perry Manchester school of Egyptocentric hyper-diffusionism. This point was also made to us by Daryll Forde shortly before his death. Forde and Childe were close friends and travelled extensively together in eastern Europe in the twenties. It is to be remembered by historians of archaeology that Forde's first book *Ancient Mariners* (1928) was in the Elliot Smith–Manchester school and diffused Egypt over the world. Two years later his article on 'Early Cultures of Atlantic Europe' in the *American Anthropologist* (1930) killed the Egypt–Smith view. It is fascinating to look back on those five years from 1925 to 1930 and see how Childe, Forde, Fleure and Peake rewrote prehistory and produced the model of the past which was to be our paradigm until C14 dating showed it to be an invented past.

☙ Mr Timothy Ambrose, Assistant Keeper of Archaeology in the City and County Museum, Lincoln, writes (12 March 1979):

I have been meaning to write to you for some time over a matter which I felt might appeal to the readers of your Editorial column in ANTIQUITY. Last year a little medieval bronze pilgrim's badge was brought into the City and County Museum for identification. The saint referred to on the badge is Saint Barbara, the patron saint of, among others, architects, stone masons, miners and gravediggers, firework makers and artillerymen. My colleague here, Andrew White, wrote a short note on the badge for *Lincolnshire History and Archaeology* (1978).

It struck us both at the time that British archaeologists lack a patron saint, and we felt, rightly or wrongly, that Saint Barbara was a suitable candidate for such a role. It may well be that some archaeologists would feel that other saints are equally eligible.

What, we ask, do readers think? Our own thoughts are these: did the saintly Barbara ever exist? She is alleged to have lived round about AD 200 and was beheaded by her father, Dioscorus, when she professed Christianity. On returning home from executing her, Dioscorus was, very rightly, struck by lightning and reduced to ashes. Saint Barbara is invoked during thunderstorms, her emblem is a tower (she lived as a hermit in a bath-house for a long time), and her day 4 December. The Penguin *Dictionary of Saints* says 'there is no evidence that a martyred Saint Barbara ever existed'. The new *Encyclopaedia Britannica* describes her authenticity as 'highly questionable', and the new *Oxford Dictionary of Saints* (edited by David Hugh Farmer, Oxford, 1978) says 'the very existence of this supposed virgin–martyr is doubtful'. She was suppressed in the Roman calendar of 1969.

Who is for Saint Barbara, and who for some other saint? We have always thought that Saint Samson would make a very good archaeological saint, especially for those concerned with megaliths. Of his existence there is no doubt. He was born *c.* AD 490 and was a pupil of St Illtud's at Llantwit Major; he migrated to Brittany and was Bishop of Dol where he died *c.* 565. His *Vita* is one of the earliest of any Celtic saint. What we have always found fascinating about him was that on his journey from Wales to Brittany, he discovered in Cornwall people worshipping around a standing stone, told them to mend their evil ways, and Christianized the menhir.

Saint Barbara? Saint Samson? Or another?

July 1980

℧ Our light-hearted banter about the appropriate patron saint for archaeology, which stemmed from Timothy Ambrose's letter recommending Saint Barbara, has produced more correspondence than we have had for a long time about more serious matters, which shows that in the end, and thank God for it, archaeologists and antiquaries are dilettanti; and long may they delight in the past.

Tom Greaves, who is archaeological assistant to the Dartmoor National Park, writes, 'May I suggest St Mina of south-east Europe as a candidate for the patron saint of archaeologists? St Mina was drawn to my attention and offered as patron saint of archaeologists in June 1974 by Bogdan Nikolov, Director of the Museum at Vratsna, Bulgaria.' In Bulgaria, Romania, and Yugoslavia, St Mina is the saint to whom one prays 'when one finds something and when one wants to find something'. But Percival Turnbull of the County Planning Department of the North Yorkshire County Council, thinks otherwise. He writes, 'I would like to point out that, among those concerned with stimulating due interest in the prehistory of northern England, it has long been traditional to light candles to St Jude.'

But the main support has come for St Helen. Dr Lloyd-Morgan of the Grosvenor Museum, Chester, writes, 'I suggest St Helen who may (or most probably may not) have been Welsh and the Elen of Sarn Helen, and who certainly spent much time exhuming or "inventing" fascinating archaeological material – the Holy Cross for example.' He goes on to say, 'If not you could try invoking Suphlatus, the angel or genius of dust in the Nunetemeran of Apollonius of Tyana!'

Mrs C. van Driel-Murray, of the sub-faculty of pre- and protohistory of the University of Amsterdam, has no doubts about the role of St Helena. She writes (*in lit.*, 7 March):

I am surprised that you are unaware of the fact that we have long been under the protection of St Helena, mother of Constantine the Great. Though born in Trier, her Yorkish connexions are well known. Her search for the True Cross is, technically, surprisingly up-to-date. Her hypothesis was that the Cross could indeed be found. She mounted an expedition to the Holy Land, surveyed suitable sites, as indicated by previous study of the textual material (Christian traditions: the ideal cooperation between history and archaeology), and exploited local knowledge. Though the recalcitrant Levite Judas was subjected to more pressure than would be advisable today, he was eventually converted and, changing his name, later became a saint in his own right (a suitable patron for other guardians of antiquities?). Then followed the excavation, observing stratigraphic principles in first demolishing a Hadrianic temple to Venus in order to reach the earlier wooden crosses below.

The independent test of the hypothesis (a corpse was restored to life by the True Cross) proved its correctness. The discovery was displayed in a specially built sanctuary on the site. And finally, if we are to believe later traditions, samples were spread all over Europe.

It was all financed by the State. Surely an exemplary saint? On the other hand, an archaeologist of my acquaintance habitually invokes the aid of St Clement, 'patron of hopeless cases'.

Mr J. K. Knight, Inspector of Ancient Monuments, writes from the Ancient Monuments Branch of the Welsh Office in Cardiff as follows (*in lit.* dated the Feast of St Winwaloe, 1980):

You ask for possible patron saints of archaeology. Whilst you will no doubt receive many suggestions, may I put in a word for St David, who was conceived in a Pembrokeshire megalith, and also mention one or two other possible candidates.

According to his biographer Rhigyfarch (*obit* 1099), the son of Bishop Sulien of St David's, the event took place 'in a small meadow, pleasing to the eye...in (which were)...two large stones, which had not been seen there before...one at her head and one at her feet, for the earth opened...both to preserve the maid's modesty and to declare beforehand the significance of her offspring' (*Vita Davidis, c.* 75, ed. and trans J. W. James, Cardiff, 1967). As you know, many Welsh prehistoric sites bear names like Ty Illtyd or Bedd Branwen and presumably in the late eleventh century a (chambered tomb?) near St David's was known as Bedd Nonnita, or some similar name, Nonnita being the alleged mother of St David, though there is I understand a distinct possibility that Nonnita was originally a male saint. There is a much more detailed account of an Irish chambered tomb in one of the early lives of St Patrick, who summoned up a giant who had been buried there and questioned him about the tomb (a prerogative of sainthood of some archaeological potential). This perhaps displays greater interest in field monuments, but I cannot allow St Patrick precedence over St David.

The Patrick story is one of a number where a saint's attention is drawn to an archaeological site, often by a ghost, and where he often ends up excavating the site for relics or to give the ghost Christian burial and so lay it. The basic story goes back, of course, as far as Pliny's famous ghost story of the buried treasure. One possible candidate for an archaeological patron saint on these grounds is Germanus of Auxerre, whose fifth-century life (best known, of course, for the account of his visits to Britain) tells us he once excavated a ruined Roman villa in the French countryside to recover the bodies of some executed criminals buried there and lay their ghosts. The story is of considerable archaeological interest as perhaps the only contemporary account of the state of a ruined Gallo-Roman villa in the mid-fifth century.

Much as I revere the memory and example of that Bretonophile South Walian St Samson (and wish that someone would produce a new edition of his Life to answer some of the problems raised about its date by Fawtier), perhaps it would be unwise to put him forward for archaeological patronhood for defacing an ancient monument – by carving a cross on it – an act for which he would today be prosecuted by the Department of the Environment, and no doubt castigated in the editorial columns of *Antiquity* should the matter come to your attention.

Mr Knight then offers us an article about the way people thought in the early middle ages about archaeological sites and we have readily accepted his suggestion. Incidentally for those whose dictionaries of saints are not easily available, St Winwaloe's day is 3 March and many readers will remember the old weather jingle about the saints for the first few days of March:

> First comes David, then comes Chad,
> Then come Winnol, roaring like mad.

There has been support for St Barbara, and General Sir James Marshall Cornwall canvassed the views of General Sir Henry Tuzo, the Master Gunner, who wrote (*in lit.*, 12 March), 'Poor St Barbara. In my view she has enough on her plate – The Royal Regiment, all gunners in other western countries, the RAOC and no doubt other organizations. What is more she suffered down-grading at the hands of John XXIII, along with St George. She should not be asked to take on the archaeologists even though she might stop the real grave diggers.'

Dr David Trump is also against St Barbara who, he says (*in lit.*, 5 March) 'must be too over-worked, even if she actually existed, to give the attention they deserve to the frantic prayers of a small group like the archaeologists'. He then goes on to say, 'St Samson, though historical and having some association with an archaeological site (for entirely non-archaeological purposes however) seems to be hardly more appropriate.' And he, too, comes down in favour of St Helena, excavator of the True Cross, 'eminently suitable as a patroness of archaeologists in general – and if there is any truth in the reputed connexion, of the York Trust in particular'.

❺ It is years since Emile Fradin, then a young man aged sixteen, was ploughing the field called *Duranthin* on the family farm of Glozel near Vichy when, on 1 March 1924, one of the oxen fell into a hole. The hole seemed to have been part of a medieval glass factory and/or, possibly, an earlier tomb. Since then the field has been known as the *Champ des Morts*.

Here was the beginning of *l'affaire Glozel* which has divided, confused and tantalized archaeologists and the general public ever since. Now, at seventy-one, Fradin has written his version of it all in a book entitled *Glozel et ma vie* (Paris, 1979). It is, appropriately enough, in the series *Les Enigmes de l'Univers* (which contains many bizarre books), and is said to be a 'récit recueilli par Pierre Peuchmaurd'.

It is, understandably, a one-sided account of the controversy, and contains grave omissions and some very strange statements and errors. We are told that Vayson de Pradenne, signing his name in the visitors' book as Pradennes-Lozé, visited the site in 1927, declaring himself to be an American and saying he wished to buy the site and the museum! Then there is a completely misleading account of the famous hole in the control section during the visit of the 1927 International Commission, and the row between Dr Morlet and Dorothy Garrod, in which the latter is made to say 'Eh bien, oui...c'est moi qui ai fait ça.' The true story has been clearly set out in her article 'Recollections of Glozel' (ANTIQUITY, 1968), which should be reread by anyone who dips into *Glozel et ma vie*. It is clear that Fradin and Peuchmaurd have not read Miss Garrod's article or the testimony of Professor Bosch-Gimpera which we printed in 1974.

They refer to Vayson de Pradenne's papers in the *Bulletin de la Société Préhistorique Française*, but not to his devastating and convincing article on 'The Glozel forgeries' in ANTIQUITY (1930), in which he says: 'The history of Glozel is useful as well as diverting, because it lays bare so cleverly the workings of imposture and the development of a controversy.' Crawford, in an editorial footnote, referred to official reports which 'give categorical proofs of forgery'. These are not seriously discussed in this book.

Fradin alleges that Peyrony was ill-disposed to accept the authenticity of Glozel because he thought, if properly established, it would take tourists away from Les Eyzies! But he does record that Peyrony once said to him, 'Mon petit Emile...Vous avez fabriqué une grande partie de ces choses-là, n'est-ce-pas? Allons, dites la vérité.' This book, in our view, does not do that. It ends with cries of triumph that thermoluminescence dating has at last vindicated the truth and antiquity of Glozel and that Emile in his old age can rest happy that he has been proved not to be a *faussaire*. He may think this, and as the coffin lid gapes open for him, as it does for us all, this may be comfort for his soul. But what is the truth about Glozel?

We print an interesting letter dated 12 November 1979 from Dr Mejdahl, who is now back working in the Risø National Laboratory at Roskilde in Denmark:

I read with interest your comments about Glozel in the latest issue of ANTIQUITY and noted that although your conviction is unshattered, at least your remarks seemed slightly less acrid than they used to be.

I feel that the only hope of ever unravelling the mystery lies in fresh excavations, and note with satisfaction the continuing revival of the case in ANTIQUITY and elsewhere, which no doubt helps to maintain the pressure on the French authorities.

In the publication of my letter a disturbing misprint has crept in: the date obtained for the glass-covered clay ball was AD 1200 and not AD 200. The result thus confirms the dating of the glass-smelting activity to the medieval period.

As you know, the authenticity of the glass furnace and the finds associated with it (bricks from the wall, fragments of stoneware ceramics, etc.) has never been disputed. The correct assessment of the date of the glass furnace by TL is thus a strong indication of the validity of the TL dates of the controversial finds as well.

However acrid the Editor of ANTIQUITY may appear to those scientists who work north of Copenhagen and south of Paris (there are, alas, no squeaks from Scotland these days!), he should say he is feeling rather picric as he writes these words: the problem remains. To most archaeologists and to most sensible people who have carefully studied the history of Glozel from 1924 onwards, the whole thing is a nonsense. The objects (apart from some genuine things picked up from neighbouring fields or from other collections, what was Dr Morlet doing in the Pyrenean excavations of the twenties?) are hocus-pocus, palpable forgeries. How come they have TL dates of reasonable antiquity? This is a question for the scientists to resolve. In the early days of C14 dating there were archaeologists who found some C14 dates 'unacceptable'. We think that the Glozel controversy should resolve itself around the simple issue that most archaeologists find the TL dates unacceptable.

Where do we go from here? Science or archaeology? The Editor of ANTIQUITY is, not surprisingly, on the side of archaeology.

March 1981

❧ We have been taken to task by Nowell Myres and Rupert Cook for some of the things we have said in recent numbers of ANTIQUITY. Dr Myres says (*in lit.*, 6 November 1980):

I wish people would not call my Father 'Johnny', a name never used either in the family or by those who really knew him well. He detested it and thought, rightly I believe, that it had been cooked up by those who used it to suggest a bogus familiarity to which they had no real claim. My mother always called him Jonathan, and, strangely enough, his schoolboy nickname was Thomas, which continued in use by a dwindling band of school friends, such as Bruce Richmond, to the end. But it never jumped the gap, I think, from Winchester to New College. ('Johnny' never existed at all as a genuine nickname – e.g. he never signed himself that way – and the sooner it is forgotten the better.)

We may all wish to forget things we do not like but the facts as known to us are that the great man was known familiarly to pupils and friends as

Johnny Myres and still is so remembered. We cannot decide how our friends, pupils and colleagues call us; the Editor of ANTIQUITY was for years called by his contemporaries and teachers 'Prophet' – we think it was a term invented by J. M. de Navarro, a man half-way between the time when one referred to one's pupils by their surnames, and the present when we call them by their Christian names. It never worried me, and we are sure that Professor Stuart Piggott is never worried when he is affectionately referred to as 'dear Piggins', nor was that brilliant ethnographer R. U. Sayce, who was always known as 'Uncle Lenin'. All this is affection and respect. Our predecessor as Editor loved to be known as OGS, and Sir Mortimer Wheeler was pleased when people he was only beginning to know were prepared to call him Rik, as the whole world did.

We replied to Nowell Myres as follows:

I am only concerned with the historical aspect of this matter and let me assure you that your Father was always referred to by everybody who ever spoke to me at any time when he was alive, or indeed when they think back to his life and works, as Johnny. When I began writing my *Hundred years of archaeology*, just after the war, and discussed with Rik and OGS the sort of people I should talk to who could give me a direct link with the past development of archaeology, they both said, 'Go and see Johnny Myres . . .'. This is certainly how Joan Evans referred to him and this is how his Oxford pupils, who included the Production Editor of ANTIQUITY, referred to him. Indeed, thinking back over the last ten years, I have never heard anyone talk about him except in this way.

❧ It is now a hundred years ago since Marie-Joseph-Pierre Teilhard de Chardin was born near Clermont in Auvergne. He found himself in 1908 in the Jesuit House near Hastings in England, which he described as the 'Cannes de l'Angleterre'. His palaeontological researches produced a meeting with Charles Dawson, and he became introduced to the work Dawson was doing at Piltdown where he had found what we know now to be a fake. His accounts of his palaeontological adventures in Sussex are set out in his letters to his parents. In 1912 Dawson found three more pieces of the infamous human skull and Teilhard, as he says, 'laid hands on the fragments of an elephant's molar . . .. This first tooth of an elephant impressed me in the way another man is impressed by bringing down his first snipe.' On Saturday 30 August 1913 Teilhard found a canine close to the spot where the lower jaw had itself been disinterred. There was great excitement. Dawson said, 'the tooth is almost identical in form with that shown in the restored cast', and Dr Underwood said 'the tooth is absolutely as modelled at the British Museum'. [Perhaps it was. – *Ed.*]

The war came, Teilhard was a stretcher-bearer and was awarded the Médaille Militaire. By now Dawson had died in 1916. After the war Teilhard paid a sentimental visit to Lewes and Piltdown with Smith-Woodward but nothing further was found. Indeed nothing was found after Dawson's death. In the speculation about Piltdown, and especially after the revelation that it was a fake, there has been much speculation about who were the fakers and what, if any, was Teilhard's part in all this. Louis Leakey wrote a book, which has fortunately not been published, saying that Teilhard was the forger; we argued passionately with him about all this for years. He insisted that Arthur Keith had told him that Teilhard was frequently at Piltdown. This is not true – his visits were very few. Professor Stephen Jay Gould of Harvard University published in an article in *Natural History* (1980) the theory that Teilhard and Dawson were co-conspirators and that the whole affair was 'a joke that went too far, not a malicious attempt to defraud'.

Gould bases his theory on Teilhard's writings and correspondence, including letters to Kenneth Oakley, but these letters are, in our view, no evidence of conspiracy and complicity. They are the letters of an old man who was trying to remember what really happened in Sussex that long ago, and had had for years his suspicions of what had been going on. After the exposure of the fraud Oakley wrote to him, 'You were hoodwinked about the whole affair', and Teilhard replied, 'No one thinks of suspecting Smith-Woodward. I knew Dawson pretty well – a methodical and enthusiastic character. When we were in the field I never noticed anything suspicious in his behaviour. The only thing that puzzled me, one day, was when I saw him picking up two large fragments of skull out of a sort of rubble in a corner of the pit . . . When I found the canine, it was so inconspicuous among the gravels that had been spread on the ground for sifting that it seems to me quite unlikely that the tooth would have been planted. I can even remember Sir Arthur congratulating me on the sharpness of my eyesight.'

Yet it *was* planted, and the question remains, by whom? Kenneth Oakley was insistent, in replying to Gould's criticism, that there was no proof of Teilhard's involvement and that until such happened he must be given the benefit of the doubt. Not only is this right, but we must study with care the life of this distinguished man, 'scientist and seer', as Charles Raven called him. The biographies by Claude Cuenot, Robert Speaight and Mary and Ellen Lukas leave no doubts in our mind that S. J. Gould is making a most unfortunate canard. We never met Teilhard, but knew him through Miles Burkitt, Dorothy Garrod, the Abbé Breuil and Mademoiselle de Saint-Mathurin, and they testify that he could never have taken part in the Piltdown hoax. By a fortunate chance, and through the good offices of

Dr Paul Bahn of the University of Liverpool, we have a remarkable document from Count Max Bégouën (one of the famous Trois Frères), which he has specially written for ANTIQUITY. Max Bégouën was one of Teilhard de Chardin's closest friends, and Teilhard wrote of him to Madame Haardt on 28 December 1934, 'There are few minds I know of so fine, so intelligent and so clear.' Here is the *témoignage* of this fine, intelligent, clear, mind:

La découverte fin 1912 de l'Homme Préhistorique de Piltdown (Angleterre) eut un grand retentissement dans le monde scientifique.

Mr Emile Cartailhac, chargé de l'enseignement de la Préhistoire à la Faculté des Lettres de Toulouse, où j'étais étudiant, parla longuement de cette découverte à un de ses cours de printemps 1913. Il était très exactement tenu au courant de toutes les nouvelles concernant la Préhistoire, par son compatriote et ami Mr Marcelin Boule, professeur au Musée et Directeur de l'Institut de Paléontologie Humaine.

Parmi les élèves de Marcelin Boule il y avait un jeune Jésuite, Paléontologue, le Père Teilhard de Chardin, qui, au mois d'août 1913 se rendit à Piltdown accompagné d'un des découvreurs du gisement, Mr Dawson. Et le Père Teilhard mit à jour une canine étrange qui vint aggraver les contestations dont étaient déjà l'objet les divers fragments fossiles de crâne humain précédemment découverts.

Revenant à Paris, en automne, le Père Teilhard fit la connaissance de mon père dans une réunion où se trouvaient l'abbé Breuil, Salomon Reinach, et, je crois, aussi Mr Boule.

Bien entendu, l'histoire de Piltdown prit donc dans mon esprit de jeune étudiant en préhistoire un relief tout particulier.

Survint la guerre. Le 1er Août 1914, mon frère cadet et moi sommes incorporés dans un régiment d'infanterie coloniale qui se trouva former brigade avec un régiment de zouaves tirailleurs.

J'ai raconté par ailleurs comment un certain après midi de Juin 1915, sur le front de Belgique, au village de Killem je fus interpellé par un caporal de tirailleur, alors, qu'agenouillé au bord d'une mare, je lavais mon linge . . . quand il se présenta: 'Teilhard', je me dressai d'un bond et m'écriai. 'C'est donc vous l'homme de la dent de Piltdown!'. C'est que, pour moi, alors, le nom de Teilhard était indissolublement lié à ce fameux vestige humain préhistorique.

Bien entendu, nous demandâmes au Père de nous faire le récit de sa découverte. Ce récit fut d'une parfaite simplicité. Teilhard avait été conduit par son ami Dawson sur le champ de graviers dans lequel avaient été trouvés quelques morceaux d'un crâne humain fossile, et il avait recueilli, en creusant dans les galets, la dent dont on devait tant parler – c'est tout.

Blessé quelque temps après, et évacué, je ne retrouvai le Père Teilhard qu'en 1920. J'allais alors assez souvent au Muséum d'Histoire Naturelle ou Marcelin Boule m'accueillait avec beaucoup de bonté. Une fois seulement, je crois, j'entendis Boule et Teilhard parler de Piltdown, et c'est pour entendre émettre des doutes sur l'âge des ossements.

Les années passèrent. Choukoutien supplanta Piltdown.

La deuxième guerre mondiale écrasa le monde pendant cinq ans.

Puis éclata le scandale: la fameuse dent de Piltdown était un faux. La nouvelle me choqua et me peina profondément, car je ressentais le choc que cette nouvelle donnerait au Père.

D'abord, et avant tout, il connut la déception cruelle d'avoir été trompé par un ami en qui il avait pleine confiance, et, ensuite, la mortification de s'être laissé duper. Il avouait qu'il manquait alors d'expérience 'du terrain'. S'il avait eu des doutes sur l'authenticité de sa trouvaille, il les aurait sûrement formulés. Mais il était aveuglé par la confiance.

Quand je revis le Père Teilhard à Paris et que je lui parlai de Piltdown, il me dit: 'Je ne puis encore imaginer que Dawson ait voulu me tromper et qu'il se soit servi de moi pour couvrir une pareille fraude. En tout cas il est réconfortant de savoir que la Science a atteint un degré de finesse tel qu'elle est en mesure de dévoiler les fraudes les mieux élaborées.'

Je suis persuadé que jusqu'au bout, le Père Teilhard essaya de sauvegarder l'honneur de son ancien ami. Il était d'une trop haute valeur morale pour se venger. Il est impensable que le Père Teilhard ait pu être complice d'un trucage en face d'un maître qu'il respectait, qu'il estimait, qu'il aimait: Marcelin Boule.

The accompanying letter to Dr Paul Bahn from Count Bégouën, dated 8 November, is also of interest:

J'ai eu du mal a exprimer ma pensée sur 'la dent du Piltdown' et le rôle de Teilhard, car je n'ai aucun argument scientifique à apporter dans la discussion.

Ma conviction intime, absolue, est que le Père Teilhard a été 'roulé' – une fois de plus – car il ne voyait pas le mal. Il était d'une candeur désarmante, et il redoutait par dessus tout de faire de la peine à un ami.

Il est *impensable* que le Père ait pu se tremper dans une machination dans laquelle la réputation scientifique du laboratoire de son maître Marcelin Boule pouvait être indirectement atteinte.

Le témoignage que je donne est celui de 40 ans d'amitié avec le Père Teilhard – 40 ans au cours desquels j'ai, maintes fois, été à même d'éprouver et de constater les qualitiés de *loyauté* et de dévouement du Père en de nombreux cas.

Que de fois n'a-t-on pas – sur des plans divers! – abusé de sa candeur et de sa trop grande indulgence. Il était très bon . . . Teilhard avait grande peine à croire à l'existence du mal.

We are well aware we may be told that this is subjective character assessment, not evidence as to the facts of what did, or did not, occur. True. But we are immovable in our view that this kind of first-hand *témoignage* is of great value – even that it would be considered so in a court of law. And of course we do not forget the statement made by a woman from Lewes when it was suggested that Charles Dawson had done dubious things, including Piltdown: 'Impossible! He is a gentleman – I played golf with him.'

July 1981

❦ Cave 5615 in the Wye Valley in the cliffs above Symond's Yat East, on the English side of the Wye a few miles above Monmouth, is where, it is claimed by Tom Rogers, Andrew Pinder and Rodney C. Russell, they have discovered two examples of representational Stone Age cave art, the first to be found in Britain (*The Illustrated London News*, 18 January 1981).

Let us deal with the Symond's Yat cave first: and let us say at once that, tolerably aware as we are of the main workers in most fields in British archaeology, we had not heard of these three authors before. We now learn that Rodney Russell, aged 39, is attached to the Bureau of Archaeology at Zurich. Andrew Pinder, aged 25, is a Research Student in the Institute of Archaeology of the University of London but now, in a letter to the Editor, dissociates himself from the affair. Mr Rogers is described as a 48-year-old archaeologist born in Canada: on his writing paper he lists himself as 'Thomas Rogers B.A., Ph.D. Director of the Stone Age Studies Research Association (Canada)', of which institution the Editor of ANTIQUITY, in his abysmal ignorance, had been hitherto unaware. Martin Walker, of *The Guardian*, has been checking the bona fides of Rogers, who claims he was an undergraduate of Dalhousie in Canada and a Ph.D of the Pittsburgh University School of Anthropology. Walker discovered that Dalhousie did not award him a degree: Pittsburgh admitted that they did receive from Rogers 'a copy of his so-called thesis, which he had printed himself', and described it as 'a tissue of all kinds of strange things.... We just discarded it.' The dissertation is apparently called *Moon, Magic and Megalith* and we have asked Rogers if we can read it. Rogers said that he believed Pittsburgh had accepted his Ph.D thesis but would now remove the title Dr from his notepaper and not refer to himself as Dr Rogers any more. 'They give away degrees as if they are confetti in the U.S.A.', he said. 'It will be quite a relief to be plain Mr again. But the important things are the finds themselves' (*The Guardian*, 24 January 1981).

All this, not unnaturally, predisposes one to regard the Symond's Yat finds with caution, and this cautious approach is strengthened by the fact that we cannot see any palaeolithic engravings in the exclusive pictures published by the *ILN*, while readily admitting that it is very difficult to photograph palaeolithic engravings. What is strange is that the authors have resuscitated the sad affair of the Bacon Hole in the Gower peninsula, where they claim there is an abstract example of palaeolithic art! Don't they read the literature and study the history of their subject? The Bacon Hole 'palaeolithic' paintings were made in AD 1896: it was sad that Breuil and

Sollas fell for them in 1912. They were soon discredited and relegated to books on frauds, fakes, forgeries and follies in archaeology.

The Symond's Yat site belongs to the Forestry Commission and that body invited the British Museum, which advises them on various matters, to visit the site. Gale and Ann Sieveking, Dr Geoffrey Wainwright and Dr Mark Newcomer visited the site on 12 February and we are allowed to publish Mr Sieveking's report. It should be read with care and compared with the original *ILN* article; it concludes with these words: 'the claim for palaeolithic engravings at Symond's Yat cannot be substantiated'.

❧ Many of us, though not the writer of these words, will be wending our way to Mexico, in October, for the Congress of Prehistoric and Protohistoric Sciences. This is the first meeting of the Congress to happen in the New World and we wish it well. We hope the next Congress in 1986 may be in London. But we repeat what we have said many times before: this Congress needs rethinking. Nice showed it was too big; and should the members be allowed to bring as associates their wives, mistresses, children, catamites – what have you? All this means that no reasonable, serious archaeological excursions are possible.

What we need are smaller and more specialized conferences. The symposium on archaeo-astronomy, sponsored by the International Astronomical Union and the International Union for History and Philosophy of Science, will be held in Queen's College, Oxford, from 4 to 9 September 1981. How wise to fix a small-scale conference, and how more than wise that the membership is by invitation! Otherwise the meetings would be filled with crackpots and Phuddy-Duddies spewing up and down the High. We hope this conference will mark an important stage in the writings about astro-archaeology or archaeo-astronomy or whatever you like to call it. We feel that the era of uncritical acceptance of the theories of Hawkins and Thom is coming to an end. We have never had anything but the greatest admiration for the survey work of Alexander Thom and his devoted team of skilled surveyors, but none for the observer-imposed theories which have been set down as facts from these surveys. These theories are gradually being attacked in articles in ANTIQUITY and elsewhere. Can anyone who has read the Moir, Ruggles and Norris article in our March 1980 issue, or the even more devastating article by Evan Hadingham in March 1981, really believe any longer the Thom theories? We do not share the cruel dismissal of all this as Thomfoolery, but we remember the words of Elliot Smith in his 1928 Huxley Memorial Lecture when he said: 'The set attitude of mind of a scholar may become almost indistinguishable from a delusion', and this is our sad view of those who make our megaliths into observatories. They are deluded men (as, let us not forget, was Elliot Smith himself with his Egyptocentric fantasies). Of course there was a general orientation of many monuments, and Stonehenge and Newgrange demonstrate exact orientations: the fortunate invitees to the Oxford conference should read and reread Aubrey Burl's article, 'Science or symbolism: problems of archaeo-astronomy' (1980).

It was the Editor of ANTIQUITY, together with the late Paul Johnstone, who first introduced Alexander Thom to the megaliths of south Brittany many years ago. He was reluctant to cross the Channel. Would it be hot? He found it hot in Oxford after travelling south from the coolth of Dunlop in Ayrshire. Would not the food be horrible? He took elaborate precautions about food and brought with him large canisters of porridge oats. But gradually we weaned him away from the idea that the French ate nothing but snails and frogs' legs, and he took to *langoustines* in a big way and also to pancakes, though he would make no compromise with the language, and coming away from a *crêperie* once said, disarmingly, 'Daniel, I'm getting very fond of these creeps.'

❧ May we, on behalf of all our readers, send our warm congratulations to one of our most avid readers, His Royal Highness The Prince of Wales, on the news of his engagement to be married. We felt particularly honoured and touched that on 25 June he was able to find time to attend the party given in Stationers' Hall, by Thames and Hudson, to celebrate the 100th volume in the 'Ancient Peoples and Places' series, and to present to the Editor the *Festschrift* organized and edited by John D. Evans, Barry Cunliffe and Colin Renfrew, for which he contributed a foreword.

Many years ago when Prince Charles was an undergraduate in Cambridge, with John Coles we took him on a short tour of the Dordogne caves and the Morbihan megaliths, and there are now rooms in the Hotel Les Glycines at Les Eyzies and the Hotel Le Rouzic at La Trinité saying, 'Prince Charles slept here'. But in Les Eyzies he is described as 'Prince d'Angleterre'. Is this error a memory of the Hundred Years War? We think it is. Forty years ago when we had discovered in the Lukis Manuscripts in Guernsey plans and drawings of chambered long barrows in Aveyron, and set off hot foot to Rodez to see them, we were told, in the little village of Salles-la-Source, 'Eh bien, monsieur, vous cherchez les tombeaux des Anglais?' It was a curious question, as even at that time the megaliths of the Aveyron were at least 2,000 years earlier than any Englishman had appeared in the Rouergue. But in a way it was true: all of us archaeologists are searching for the tombs, temples, houses of our ancestors whether they be English, Welsh, Goths, Greeks or Olmecs.

☙ *Postscript:* As we go to press *The Illustrated London News* for May prints a note entitled, 'Back to Symond's Yat'. We quote part of what they say:

Since the publication in our January issue of the finding by Tom Rogers of markings on the rock face in caves above Symond's Yat in the Wye Valley, that green and wooded spot...has become the centre of rather concentrated archaeological attention.... His conclusion ... was that at least some of the lines on the rock shapes had been made by the same palaeolithic man who had left his flints and other debris in the area some 10,000 years or more ago. Few archaeologists who have seen the site so far are prepared to accept this interpretation, and a party of archaeological heavyweights, who hauled themselves up the precipitous slope of the valley recently, have now pronounced that the markings on the rocks are not the work of palaeolithic man but of nature.... Failing further evidence, which Mr Rogers has not been able to provide, their conclusion can hardly be challenged. Experts can be wrong...and not all the great discoveries have been made by experts. But in this case clearly more proof is needed if Symond's Yat is to be generally accepted as a site of palaeolithic engraving. Perhaps continued excavation will reveal more.

What an ungenerous piece of reporting, unworthy of the high traditions of the *ILN*'s archaeological writing! As the Editor and the Archaeology Editor of *The Illustrated London News* scrape the egg off their faces, we ask them why, when Rogers reported this alleged discovery to them, did they not invite a party of what they churlishly describe as 'archaeological heavyweights' to visit the site *before* rushing into publication?

November 1981

☙ Thames and Hudson gave a special party in Stationers' Hall on 25 June attended by HRH The Prince of Wales. Happily our forward-looking reportage proved correct and it was, indeed, a very happy occasion, attended by some 300 people, including over half the 100 authors of the 'Ancient Peoples and Places' series. Our readers may like to hear a little more about this splendid happening. It was first to celebrate the publication of the 100th volume of AP&P: this had been commanded by Eva and Thomas Neurath to be written by the Editor. We hope for a review in these pages by Professor Brian Fagan which discusses the series as a whole and the contribution it made over the last quarter of a century to archaeological writing. The second reason was to announce the publication of *Towards a history of archaeology*, being the papers of the Aarhus Conference on the History of Archaeology held in 1978: this book, reviewed by Dr David Wilson in this issue, was to have been edited by the two organizers of the

Aarhus Conference, namely the Editor of ANTIQUITY and Professor Ole Klindt-Jensen of Aarhus, but his untimely death made this impossible; the book is now edited by Daniel, and dedicated to Klindt-Jensen.

The third reason for the party was one of the nicest things that has ever happened to the Editor, namely the presentation to him of a *Festschrift*. The presentation was made by The Prince of Wales [Plate 14] who had written what Philip Howard in *The Times* agreeably described as 'a breezy and affectionate introduction'. We have never made any secret of the fact that we disapprove of *Festschriften*; and as an Editor find them the most difficult of books to get reviewed. But none of us, on every occasion, carries through principles and prejudices into practice, and when we were offered a *Festschrift* ourselves we were delighted, humbled and deeply grateful. When A. E. Housman was sent a privately printed list of his writings − no one had the temerity to offer him a *Festschrift*, a man who had already declined seven honorary degrees and the Order of Merit − he wrote, 'However deeply I may deplore the misdirection of such energy, it is impossible not to be touched and pleased by the proof of so much kindliness and friendliness.' What we said in replying to The Prince of Wales's charming and witty speech was how touched and pleased we were by so much kindliness and friendliness, and how much we welcomed the well-intentioned direction of such energy.

So you see, dear readers, it has been a remarkable summer for the Editor. Since the Editor and Production Editor were graciously summoned to, and happily assisted in the French sense at the Royal Wedding of the year, preceded by a glittering reception at Buckingham Palace, we like to feel that we were representing all those readers who were not so fortunate as to be present. To return to the subject of the personal appreciation of which the Editor has been the humble and grateful recipient, he would like to say openly, what all his friends and associates know to be true, that none of this would have been remotely possible without the efficient and caring support of his wife, Ruth, better known as your Production Editor.

It is a care that she mainly succours in the interests of all of you, for accuracy and meticulous attention to detail. Almost uncomplaining, she recasts and retypes bibliographies which are often submitted with little attention to our house style; or perhaps, more complainingly, long outmoded footnotes into Harvard-style bibliographies. (The correction of grammar and spelling, including the Editor's, she takes in her stride!)

❦ The sudden and untimely death of François Bordes in the United States of America at the end of April came as a shock to the world of archaeology. We are grateful to Mademoiselle de Saint-Mathurin and Dr Derek Roe for writing to us about him – we only knew him slightly – but wanted to say something ourselves about the man who came into our life when we were driving in the motorcade from Bordeaux to Les Eyzies with The Prince of Wales. We were all suddenly halted and the French Security and the British Embassy were in confusion: a suspicious American was following us. Did he have a gun? What was he doing? We, nervously, went back to inspect this person. It was François Bordes who was attached to us to show us the archaeology of Perigord which he did brilliantly. But it was true he had a string tie and was wearing a Stetson and insisted on speaking to the French police in a faded American accent. That perhaps encapsulates him: a brilliant archaeologist but a man who delighted in fighting against other archaeologists and parts of society.

Bordes was without question one of the dominant figures in twentieth-century palaeolithic archaeology and far beyond France. We quote from Derek Roe's letter to us:

Bordes undoubtedly throve on controversy, defending his views with colourful eloquence in French or English, as numerous papers of his testify, and doing it from intimate personal knowledge of the material concerned. In speaking English, he predictably developed a fine aggressive command of idiom. Many colleagues will remember delightful examples, like this majestic disposal of certain radiocarbon dates from the Haua Fteah cave, which he regarded as intolerably early: 'Yes, you tell me 'e 'as zese radiocarbon dates, but me, I ask you so what? You tell me Louis XV 'e ride a motorcycle. Maybe 'e did, maybe 'e didn't, but me, I do not believe it.'

March 1982

☙ What is now known as the Elgin Marbles syndrome keeps coming up in newspaper articles and in broadcasts. It was started up again in *The Times* for 18 October 1981 in an article by Richard Dowden entitled, 'Should we give back these treasures?' We quote his first paragraph:

The Elgin Marbles, the monuments of Egypt, and the Koh-i-Noor diamond, the Benin Bronzes and many other unique and perfect expressions of past civilizations now lie in western Museums. Are our museums therefore the preservers of the culture of mankind or the receivers of stolen property? An increasingly vocal lobby in those countries which have lost their art treasures are demanding their return, claiming that they were looted by imperialists.

We have had a number of letters about this important and interesting issue and we quote some of them. First a careful statement of policy from Dr

David Wilson, the Director of the British Museum, who has called for a
meeting of the major western European museums to discuss a common
approach to the whole question. Dr Wilson writes (4 November 1981):

The 'return of cultural property' problem has been around for some years now. It
was raised originally by the Secretary-General of UNESCO who is from West Africa.
It has been a rallying cry of emergent nationalism in Africa for a number of years
and the British Museum is in the middle of the argument. So far we have had a
number of requests for the return of individual items acquired during the years of
colonialism. In only one case – Sri Lanka – has a country formally asked for
everything to be returned, but requests from other countries do come in occasionally
and take an inordinate amount of our time.

There are many answers from the British Museum point of view. The legal
answer is the most convenient – we are not allowed to alienate objects by Act of
Parliament – but it is no use simply hiding behind that document. We must be
positive. Our main reply is that the British Museum is an important part of the
cultural heritage of the whole world and that if you start dismantling the Museum
you are doing irredeemable damage to world culture. The British Museum –
perhaps uniquely – is a universal museum; it is worth more than the sum of its
total parts. We have been in the business for 225 years and we have done rather
well for the world. If the British Museum had not been there, the material brought
back by Captain Cook would have been dispersed, classical sculpture would have
been further damaged by the elements or by the people, there would be nowhere
in the west where you could study Siberian costume, and so on.

In most countries it is possible to collect today (this is not universally true, but
it is none the less generally so). We are indeed still collecting throughout the world
with the full approval of governments and antiquities services. If you want to see
a pigmy hut, Papua-New Guinea sculptures, Mexican-Indian pottery collected from
contemporary societies, you can probably only see them in the British Museum
and certainly only see them together there.

We do not collect illegally exported material – although the temptation is
great – and by and large (and in the lights of the times in which the collections
were built up) we have always collected within the law – the Elgin marbles, the
Benin bronzes or what you will. We must go on collecting or we shall die. A non-
collecting museum is a dead museum. I deplore, as does UNESCO, the illegal traffic
in antiquities and will do anything I can to discourage it. If this could be stopped
by international agreement I would jump for joy. But the international community
of dealers has so far successfully stopped the major governments from signing a
concordat on this subject. There is too much involved and some of the countries
from which material is now seeping are too difficult to police and have so much
material that the authorities are not terribly interested in the problem. If the
countries involved would buy or dig, most could (like Nigeria) build up reasonable
national collections.

We will lend material (so long as it is fit to travel), but will never give away
to other countries material from our collections.

A forthright and important statement by the head of one of the two or three most important museums in the world. Incidentally, it was in 1960 that Sri Lanka lodged a list with UNESCO of some hundred items, taken from that country between 1505 and 1948, which are now in twenty-one museums in Europe and the United States. Of these, thirty-five objects, ranging from elephant armour to gold-leaf manuscripts, are in British collections. We are told that the British Government has not yet replied to this request – but surely it has replied and said that the whole affair is under consideration? And what is the truth about Belgium and Zaire? In 1970 Belgium returned objects to Zaire in the way UNESCO recommends that restitution should be made to de-colonialized independent states. We are told – is this true? – that the returned objects have recently appeared on the international commercial art market.

Dr David Wilson's views were solicited by us and we were very happy that he readily agreed to have his letter published. Meanwhile an unsolicited letter came from Nicholas Thomas, Director of the City Museums of Bristol, and we quote it:

I fully appreciate the reasons why emergent countries feel that much of their heritage has been removed but I feel extremely strongly that it would be disastrous at the present time if the West were to consider returning such material on grounds which would mainly, presumably, be political. These days I believe that Western museums are far more accessible to visitors, who come to them in enormous numbers, than museums in Third World countries and I also fear that, however stable such countries may appear to be, you cannot guarantee stability anywhere outside the West, and that the return of material could be very likely to result in its destruction or in its use by those countries for political purposes which may not be in the best interests of the objects. The principal task of a museum, surely, is at all costs to protect and preserve its collections, and I do not believe that any museum professional at the present time thinks returning an object of art to a Third World country, with assurance in his heart, that he is doing the best thing for the object. Once such a process of return starts, it could snowball with disastrous consequences to world culture and I most sincerely hope that we can all resist the current trend.

These are statements from two museum directors. We asked Professor Thurstan Shaw, with his very extensive knowledge of these matters as they relate to West Africa, to give us his views. He writes (5 November 1981):

There are five points to take into account:

1.   Each case has to be considered on its merits, especially the circumstances of removal from the country of origin: one cannot generalize.
2.   Cultural material should not be removed from good security to bad.
3.   Cultural material should be freely available for study by international scholars. This means that it, and its documentation, should be easily accessible to all bona fide scholars, but 'accessibility' does not mean that something should be in London,

Paris, Moscow or New York simply because those places are easier for western and northern scholars to get to than Lagos or Port Moresby.

4. In spite of the foregoing considerations, in a great many cases it would be morally right for the holding country to return cultural material to the country of origin. Where things were obtained 'by right of conquest' at a time when the country of origin was weak (e.g. Benin bronzes, Ashanti gold, Burmese treasure, much from India in the Army Museum, etc.) the ex-imperial country, if it hangs on to these things, is denying the country of origin part of the 'independence' which was 'granted' with such self-righteous fanfare some years ago; retention is a neo-colonialist policy.

5. People in western and northern countries do not realize how passionately people in the countries of origin feel that they are being cheated of their rightful heritage. This is one of the reasons why, however desirable it might be, this question cannot be 'kept out of politics' – any more than sport can be. Academics who disregard this are living in an ivory tower. It is totally unrealistic to exclude considerations of 'national pride'. Do we not, as a nation, take pride in Shakespeare, in Constable and Turner, in Henry Moore and Barbara Hepworth? How should *we* feel if, invading Nazis having removed all our Constables and Turners and the rest of the contents of our museums and art galleries, a 'reformed Germany, having restored our political freedom [Would that have happened? – *Ed.*], nevertheless refused to restore our works of art?'

Here in these letters is enough material for discussion, and the writers of the three letters are wiser in these matters than the Editor. We would make only three comments: first that Dr Wilson's firm white-washing of the collecting activities of the British Museum will hardly live up to the facts of early nineteenth-century BM activities. He should remember Belzoni and Rassam, delicious scoundrels and tomb-robbers whose unprincipled looting of Egypt and Mesopotamia have enormously enriched the British Museum collections. Secondly, there is already an important change and those people who want to see the most ancient remains of man unearthed in East Africa will, very properly, have to go to Kenya. In a recent review-article in *Nature* (1981) Professor Desmond Clark, looking back at the history and development of archaeology, and recollecting that it had indeed been, at first, a product of Western European civilization, said, 'But the focus has now shifted to the Third World and other countries since it is here that we are learning what it was that made us human. It is here also that archaeology has a greater role to play than in the Western world since, for many nations, it is the most important source of knowledge of their past. Even though this may be regarded as only small beer and lentils, the record is as good as or surpasses that which has gone before.'

This is a very true and important comment and we shall look for new national museums throughout the Third World. But in our view they should own *some* of the objects in the national museums of the West. Is there any good reason why *some*, and we deliberately say *some*, of the Benin bronzes should not go back to Africa? Is there any good reason why the Rosetta Stone should be in Bloomsbury rather than Cairo? It came to us as the spoils of war, and indeed if Nelson had not defeated Napoleon would be in the Louvre, for which museum it was intended. It has served its purpose: Champollion is dead and Egyptian hieroglyphics have been deciphered. One museum certainly deserves credit for returning cultural material; the rather special objects relating to the Kabaka of Buganda were returned by the Museum of Archaeology and Ethnology at Cambridge when Uganda became independent.

☫ In the fifties the BBC were running a programme called *Animal, Vegetable, Mineral?* of which the present Editor of ANTIQUITY was, for most of the time, chairman. We well remember the contest with the Prague Museum and Jiri Neustupny's cheerful appearance, and the famous Sir Mortimer Wheeler session about Brigadiers with moustaches in Cheltenham which Jiri enormously enjoyed. We remember that occasion because it was one of the many when Gordon Childe, who read all European languages, thought he could also speak them. After a period of anomalous esperanto-ish gibberish, Childe and Neustupny talked together agreeably in English and French.

Hugh Hencken and Kenneth Oakley were close friends of ANTIQUITY and the Editor, and their deaths are a special sadness. The Editor first heard of Hugh Hencken (who died on 31 August 1981 at the age of seventy-nine) when he was discussing with H. M. Chadwick his plans to read for a Ph.D. on the prehistoric megalithic chambers of England and Wales. 'Oh, don't you know Henck the Yank?' said Chadders, 'he's a great man and a great archaeologist.' What a very true judgement!

July 1982

☫ And now we come to Judge William Overton who, in an historic decision, ruled that the Arkansas law which attempted to force schools to give equal weight to the Biblical creation theory and the science of evolution, violated the constitutional ban on religious teaching in schools. To teach religion in state schools would be quite contrary to the constitution drawn up by people fleeing from religious persecution. Judge Overton said: 'No group, no matter how large or small, may use the organs of government, of which the public schools are the most conspicuous and influential, to force its religious beliefs on others. The evidence is overwhelming that Act 590 is the advancement of religion in the public schools ... [it is] an extension of the fundamentalists' view that one must either accept the literal interpretation of Genesis or else believe in the god-less system of evolution.'

Creation science was 'simply not science', he said, and he thought teaching creation-science would 'have serious and untoward consequences for students, particularly those planning to attend college'. He quoted former Supreme Court Justice Felix Frankfurter who said, 'We renew our conviction that we have staked the very existence of our country on the faith that complete separation between the state and religion is best for the state and best for religion.'

Arkansas Law 590, known as the Balance Treatment for Creation-Science and Evolution-Science Act, was approved with little debate during the final days of the 1981 legislative session, apparently in a fit of absent-mindedness, and Governor Frank White now admits that he signed it without reading it! It would perhaps be unfair to the Governor and the Arkansas legislative assembly to say that they were suffering from paraphrosyne or at least paraphronesis, but Act 590, signed in ignorance, and promulgated at least in absent-mindedness, was due to take effect last September. The American Civil Liberties Union filed a suit against the law. Judge Overton's wise, firm and, in our view, correct decision is not only important specifically for Arkansas, and generally for the world, but also because similar legislation was being prepared for enactment in sixteen other states: and a similar law had already been passed in Louisiana.

Judge Overton was right: there is no such thing as creation-science. There is only a passionately held belief in the literal interpretation of the Bible, and the conclusion that the genealogies in Genesis show that the world and man were created in 4004 BC. It has always puzzled us how fundamentalists can manage to live in a world which has television sets in their salons, radar to direct the landing of their ships and aircraft, and space-ships which go to the moon. They must accept some aspects of science, yet why do they deny the scientifically established C14 dates which show that some of the megalithic monuments of Malta and Britain and the cave paintings of Altamira and Lascaux are before 4004 BC? You can't have it both ways: the fundamentalists are schizophrenics, accepting the Jekyll of science when it gives them TV, laser beams and men on the moon, but rejecting the Hyde of C14 and potassium-argon dating. The boys in the Bible Belt ought to take up a hammer and hack their TV sets to pieces: their construction is based on scientific knowledge which is fundamentally opposed to fundamentalism.

The Little Rock trial brought out some strange pieces of writing. Sir

Fred Hoyle wrote in *The Times* on 7 September 1981, under the heading 'Will Darwin bite the dust in Little Rock?', a curious piece which said of the court hearing 'it is Darwin's theories which are likely to be debunked'. He said, 'My own recent work has caused me to doubt, not that evolution takes place, but that it takes place according to the usual theory of natural selection operating on randomly generated mutations', and he even went so far as to say that his concern was 'that what the American Civil Liberties Union is seeking to impose on the state of Arkansas may be scientifically wrong'. This statement could not have helped those who wanted modern biological theory properly taught in schools and did not want religious mythology substituted as a legitimate state-approved view of history.

It was a startling, and at first and second sight an irresponsible thing for a distinguished scientist to say. But then Hoyle and his collaborator Chandra Wickramasinghe, Professor of Applied Mathematics and Astronomy at University College, Cardiff (and a witness at the Arkansas trial), are rooting for their own creationist theory, namely that man's ancestor was a spore from outer space. The life-from-space theory (and this should be firmly distinguished from the man from outer space of the Van Dänikens and Co.) dates back to the sixties in Cambridge when Hoyle and Wickramasinghe were trying to explain the fogging of starlight by interstellar grains. In 1977, as Bryan Silcock, the Science Correspondent of *The Sunday Times* put it in his clear, cogent and brilliantly titled article 'Hoyle's lore' (17 January 1982), Hoyle and Wickramasinghe 'stepped across the boundary between the unorthodox and the wayout. They proposed that the grains not only contained complex organic molecules but were living bacteria-like organisms.' They argue that huge numbers of cosmic micro-organisms were frozen into comets and reach the earth in cometary debris.

And now Professor Francis Crick, who shared a Nobel Prize in 1962 for what another Nobel Prize-winner has called 'the greatest achievement in science of the twentieth century', has come up with another cosmological theory which prompted *The Observer* (28 February 1982) to print an article entitled, alarmingly and apparently way out on the lunatic fringe to begin with, 'Did Noah's Ark bring first life to Earth?' Crick (then a Cambridge don, now a Professor in California), with the American James Watson, worked out a structure of the genetic material DNA and so discovered the key to the reproduction of all living things. In his book *Life itself: its origin and nature* (London, 1981) he joins the bandwagon which suggests that life on earth came here from outer space. He believes that organic soups may have formed on a million planets in our galaxy alone, and that on another planet, with more favourable conditions than on ours, life itself began. He thinks that life on another planet would have been able to generate an advanced civilization which could have sent out bacteria by guided rockets to the infant Earth. Billions of them could be fitted into a space-ship and would be deep frozen for the 10,000 years the journey would take. Professor Crick said he was floating this theory as a hypothesis but was by no means committed to it: it was a theory 'put in a bottom drawer to see how the evidence goes'. It is in fact a creation cosmological model.

All societies have creation myths or models: and there is no reason why a scientifically based society like ours should not have scientific creation myths and cosmological models. We think that children in schools, not only in Arkansas and Louisiana, but all over the world, should be taught about the various ideas that societies have had about the origins and nature of man and the world, but this would be comparative anthropology. But then we think that a little anthropology and archaeology should be taught to every schoolboy and girl. There is only one way to a good liberal education and that is the comparative and impartial study of human societies; even if it leads some, like ourselves, to the Buddhist doctrine that much of what we want to know is unknowable and thus, to put it as Alan Ryan did recently so succinctly, 'despairing completely, we may decide the world's a mystery and nescience the proper condition of the mortal mind' (*The Listener*, 25 February 1982).

The headlines in the Little Rock trial were amusing. 'A win for Darwin in the second Monkey trial' said *The Daily Telegraph* (6 January 1982); and the case became known as the Scopes II Trial, after the 1925 Monkey Trial in Tennessee when a schoolteacher called John Scopes was convicted of violating a state law forbidding the teaching of Darwin's theory of evolution. This trial aroused world-wide interest. His conviction was overturned by the State Supreme Court on a technicality.

But why should Hoyle say that the teaching of the Darwinian theory of evolution in Arkansas or elsewhere may be scientifically wrong? It is because it is becoming fashionable to say that while evolution existed, Darwin's theory depended on random mutations and that intermediate forms between species, allegedly in an evolutionary sequence, are missing.

What critics of the Darwinian theory of evolution forget is that man by selective breeding has produced new species. Professors D. S. Falconer and Alan Robertson of the Department of Genetics in the University of Edinburgh have very properly reminded us of the dogs. 'If the present breeds of dogs were found as fossils,' they write (*The Times*, 9 December 1981), 'the palaeontologists would without doubt classify them as different species or even different genera. Furthermore, their evolution has taken place so quickly that it would appear from the fossil record to be instantaneous, without intermediate stages.'

March 1983

❧ We have never had a formal rejection slip or letter to send out week after week to the many contributors who kindly send in notes or articles for consideration, and for whose work we sadly cannot or gladly do not want to find space, but we are encouraged to draft one, inspired by that used by the editors of a Chinese economics journal, and referred to in *The Times* Diary, 9 July 1982:

We have read your manuscript with boundless delight. If we were to publish your paper it would be impossible for us to publish any work of a lower standard. As it is unthinkable that, in the next thousand years, we shall see its equal, we are, to our regret, compelled to return your divine composition, and to beg you a thousand times to overlook our short sight and timidity.

July 1983

❧ It is surprising that though the first archaeological air photograph was taken from a balloon in 1906, and *Wessex from the air* was published in 1928, no general handbook for archaeologists telling them how to interpret air photographs has existed until now. *Air photo interpretation for archaeologists* by D. R. Wilson (London, 1982) fills this need and does so admirably.

In this manual Wilson takes us through the techniques of air photography and of interpretation and it is healthy to find him insisting that one must see the ground and look at photographs with the shadows falling towards one. A brilliant example of this is shown in the pair of photographs of Walton Hall, Warwickshire. Wilson is very good in discussing the pitfalls of interpretation, namely natural features and recent man-made features. Among natural features he has good photographs of ice wedge polygons, parchmarks, jointing in limestone, collapsed frost mounds and frost cracks, and limestone solution holes. His examples of modern features including spoil heaps from coalmining near Tankerlet, the site of a fête at Orsett Heath, the riding school at Wramplingham, and emplacements of the 1939–45 war. The appreciation of the fact that everything on an air photograph is not made by prehistoric man is a very important lesson to be learnt by interpreters in peacetime, just as in war it was important that interpreters did not mistake normal features of the cultural landscape for military targets. Generations of archaeological undergraduates shown the Yarnbury photograph in *Wessex from the air* could never condition themselves to think of sheep-pens and fairs; everything had to be very old.

And we recall, wryly, being excited by discovering in 1941 on air photographs of occupied France what we thought were clear traces of prehistoric villages at low water in many places on the Norman and Breton coasts. Stuart Piggott and Terence Powell shared our excited discovery and we began to think that perhaps archaeologists serving as military interpreters in the war might pick up all sorts of discoveries, as the late lamented John Bradford most certainly did in southern Italy. But our prehistoric villages did not exist. We showed the pictures to that omniscient man, Charles Phillips (who once said to a photographic interpreter wrestling with pictures of a Hungarian city, 'If there was a second railway station there, I would have known about it'), and he looked at us all with that kind and sympathetic glance which always meant that he was dealing with ignoramuses, 'Good heavens,' he said, 'I'll excuse Stuart and Terence but not you. You've been to Brittany so often. Oyster beds, my boy. Oyster beds.' And of course that is what they were.

❦ We had hoped that Professor Barry Fell had shot his bolt with *America BC* and *Saga America*, but, alas, not so. Here comes *Bronze Age America*, the third, and please God the last, of these bizarre accounts of his invented past of America before Leif Erikson and Christopher Columbus: his trilogy of fairy stories for foolish fabulists. In *America BC* (1976) he described roving Celtic mariners crossing the Atlantic from Iberia, establishing settlements in New England and Oklahoma, followed or accompanied by other colonists from Europe and North Africa speaking Basque, Phoenician and Libyan. Latin numerals, calendar systems, and ancient Greek astronomical knowledge were, he told us, brought to America then. This tarradiddle of rubbish sold like the hot cakes of apostasy, and in 1980 there appeared *Saga America* in which we are told that pre-Columbian Europeans and North Africans crossed the Indian and Pacific oceans as well as the Atlantic and settled in California and Nevada from the third century BC, and that there is rich evidence of a Chinese presence, and an early Arabic presence, including (yes, believe it or not) the decorative signature of the Prophet Mohammed. The name America, according to the deluded Dr Fell, is nothing to do with Amerigo Vespucci, but comes from a Libyan word meaning 'land across the ocean'.

So far, so bad – twice round the bend and well up to winning the lunatic stakes and the Von Däniken Cup. What fresh follies and fantasies were we to be subjected to, we wondered, as we opened the pages of *Bronze Age America* (Boston, 1982). Had the emeritus Professor of Biology at Harvard made it? Yes, he has. This beats all the other runners from Elliot Smith to Mrs Maltwood, John Michell, C. E. Joel, Alfred Watkins, Uncle

Tom Cobbleigh and all. Here we are told that seventeen centuries BC a Nordic king called Wodenlithi sailed across the Atlantic, reaching the neighbourhood of Toronto, and established a trading colony with a religious and commercial centre at what is now Peterborough, leaving behind an inscription recording his visit, his religious beliefs, a standard of measures for cloth and cordage and an astronomical observatory for determining the Nordic Calendar Year. 'Flotillas of ancient Norse, Baltic and Celtic ships', he tells us, 'each summer set their prows to the north-west, to cross the Atlantic, to return later in the season with cargoes of raw materials furnished by the Algonquins with whom they traded.'

When I am next in the Blue Bar of the Algonquin Hotel on West 44th Street in New York I will lift a glass in desperation and despair to learned professors from Elliot Smith to Barry Fell and van Sertima who degrade scholarship and besmirch good sound learning by their opinionated and ignorant oddities. Elliot Smith, himself with Perry a prominent pedlar of pernicious and private prehistories, once said (and we say yet again), 'The set attitude of mind of a scholar may become almost indistinguishable from a delusion.' Fell is a sadly, badly, unhappily deluded man. Most readers of this journal will, fortunately, not share his delusions, or accept his flotillas of fantasies, but the commuters crowding round the bookstalls at Grand Central Station and Harvard Square will be tempted to buy the book. The title is good and a catch-dollar, but it is outrageous that his publishers in England demand £10 for this fumbling farraginous charade.

☙ We are sometimes accused of paying too much attention in the Editorials of ANTIQUITY to the lunatic fringes of our subject, but we quote again with warm approval the words of Professor Jeremy A. Sabloff which we quoted in our November 1982 issue: 'It is the responsibility of archaeologists to correct the misinformed perspectives of the discipline of archaeology that many members of the popular media and the general public seem to have.' This was not the view of an earlier generation of archaeologists: Mortimer Wheeler was of the view that bad books and cranky books should not be reviewed, and Crawford was also against bothering about crackpots and cranks except for refusing to print advertisements for Watkins's *The old straight track*. In 1935 Gordon Childe surprisingly ended his Presidential Address to the Prehistoric Society with these words: 'It is the peculiarly British practice to ignore in scientific discussions the groundless hypotheses of amateurs and cranks, however much publicity these may have in the provincial press. Whether that results from laziness, snobbishness, the law of libel or a sound historical tradition I do not know. My references to unacceptable theories of diffusion will emphasize my silence on the much advertised drivellings of charlatans' (*PPS*, 1935). We therefore welcome and warmly applaud the courage of the editors of *Popular Archaeology* in devoting much of their February 1983 number to a discussion of some widely held crankeries such as the Glastonbury zodiac, dowsing (with the good results that can come from it), and particularly ley-lines: indeed the issue is called 'The Great Debate: living leys or laying lies', and devotes six pages to a lively debate on leys between Aubrey Burl and John Michell. It all makes very good reading, and is gutsy stuff.

March 1984

❦ Our Plates 12 and 13 record some aspects of a visit to the United States in September 1983 to study some of the alleged antiquities which many now claim to prove that America was not discovered by Columbus in 1492 but that, long before, it had been visited and perhaps colonized by Vikings, Irish, Welsh, Phoenicians, Etruscans, some of the lost tribes of Israel, Egyptians, Libyans, Berbers. To these may be added the inhabitants of lost continents, such as Atlantis or Mu, or visitors from outer space on package tours by von Däniken Travel Unlimited – you take your choice, we will provide you with appropriate inscriptions decipherable only by the aficionados of these uncertain immigrants, and some tendentious literature by non-scholars, woefully ignorant of the prehistory and protohistory of Europe and America, such as Elliot Smith, Cyrus Gordon, Barry Fell, and Ivan Van Sertima.

Our steps took us to Minnesota and we drove through the lovely Middle West of America from Minneapolis to Alexandria, passing some of the many lakes which have given Minnesota the name 'state of 10,000 lakes'. Alexandria is 93 miles (150 km) NW of Minneapolis: in 1898, shortly after New Year's Day, the University of Minnesota was informed that a stone, containing a long inscription in unknown characters, had been found by a farmer called Olaf Olsen near Kensington, Douglas County.

This stone now occupies a place of honour in the Runestone Museum, in the Chamber of Commerce Building at Alexandria, Minnesota, which now proudly, but dottily, proclaims itself *The Birthplace of America*. Outside the museum (itself an excellent example of what a provincial museum should be, with everything from local birds and beasts to early twentieth-century typewriters and dentists' chairs), is a 20ft-high statue of a Viking – 'Big Ole' – bearing mistakenly on his shield the rubric *Birthplace of America* [Plate 13]. On the outskirts of this quiet, undistinguished, but self-deluded town is Runestone Park, with a very large replica of the Kensington Stone and one of the so-called Viking mooring stones: Plate 12 shows the Editor and Production Editor gazing spellbound at this bogus artifact.

Let us make no mistake here: the Vikings got to America and have left archaeological proof of their presence, notably at L'Anse-aux-Meadows in Newfoundland and on Ellesmere Island, and in the shell-midden in Penobscot Bay (ANTIQUITY, 1980). But they didn't get to Minnesota or leave any runic inscriptions anywhere (we suspect that there is a factory somewhere in America making runic inscriptions!). Of course there are many people, in and out of the Chamber of Commerce at Alexandria, who firmly believe in the authenticity of the Kensington Stone, but the weight of informed archaeological and linguistic opinion has no doubts but that it is a crude fake. Yet it was exhibited in the Smithsonian Institution, Washington DC, in 1948–9, and Dr M. W. Stirling, Director of the Bureau of American Ethnology in that great institution, declared that it was 'probably the most important archaeological object yet found in N. America'. It is, in our view, probably one of the most important archaeological frauds found in North America.

One of the most consistent and continuing advocates of its authenticity was the late Hjalmar R. Holand, and the last of his many books, *A Holy Mission to Minnesota 600 years ago*, is for sale in the Runestone Museum. This should be read in conjunction with Professor Erik Wahlgren's *The Kensington Stone: a mystery solved* (Madison, Wisc., 1958). In 1982 an eminent Italianist and Professor Emeritus of Linguistics at Cornell, Robert A. Hall, published his book *The Kensington Rune-Stone is genuine*, in which he proclaims a '98 per cent certainty' that the inscription is authentic: his book was reviewed by Erik Wahlgren in our July 1983 issue, and found wanting.

But the battle goes on, and if anyone wants to see the faith and fury of the Viking protagonists in the post-Holand period they should read the May–June 1975 issue of the American magazine *Popular Archaeology*. All the old Viking follies are set out here – runestones, mooring stones, the Newport Tower, the Vinland map, the Spirit Pond Stones (described as to be 'counted among the most important relics of American history'!). The treatment of the Yale Vinland map by the Viking protagonists is a fascinating example of chicanery, trickery, sophistry, subterfuge, and deception. 'Of course,' they say, and this was said to us on several occasions in September 1983 in America, 'the Yale Vinland map is a forgery. The critical ink ingredient of titanium dioxide could not have been used before 1900. The map is a copy of an original map kept in the secret archives of the Vatican which is extremely reluctant to permit pre-Columbian research.' To quote W. R. Anderson, 'The Catholic Church is between a rock and a hard place, to use an expression common in the south. It must take care not to offend the powerful Knights of Columbus, yet acknowledge that Leif Ericson was, indeed, the first Catholic missionary to the New World.'

Those who want to hear what seems to us the real story of the Spirit Pond affair should read Erik Wahlgren's admirable article 'American Runes: from Kensington to Spirit Pond' in the *Journal of English and Germanic Philology* (1982). This periodical is published quarterly by the University of Illinois Press, and for those of our readers who have no easy access to *JEGP* we quote Professor Wahlgren's conclusions:

The Spirit Pond 'cryptogram' may well have been a fraternity house joke that managed to stir up ripples in the adult world. Conceived and carried out with spontaneity and humor rather than with wrinkled brow and importful intent, it could not hope to re-write history or philology...the petroglyphs are in the aggregate a witty commentary on the perennial struggle between reason and credulity, between our respect for evidence and our desire to shape a flattering past.... Meanwhile would the real Jack Runemaster care to stand up?

It is good to know that Professor Wahlgren, in his retirement, is planning to write a book on *The Vikings in America* in which he will, with his usual scholarship, impartiality, and great sense of humour and appreciation of the ridiculous, put this whole controversy in its proper perspective.

The reason for our own holy (?) mission to Minnesota was to film this notorious runestone as part of a TV programme provisionally entitled *Myth America*, directed by Paul Jordan, archaeological and historical programme producer of Anglia Television, which will be shown by the British Channel 4 in the first half of 1984, and later in America. We visited and filmed many other pseudo-artifacts of alleged antiquity: the Newport Tower in Rhode Island, the many strangely placed glacial rocks which superficially resemble European megalithic chambers, and of course Mystery Hill, North Salem, New Hampshire, which has now been proudly, pompously, and wickedly called *America's Stonehenge*. The green state signposts point unquestionably to Stonehenge:

> AMERICA'S STONEHENGE 1 mile from Route 111, N. Salem. Open April 1–Dec. 1, wknds in Apr. and Nov., weather permitting. Hours 10:30–4:00 p.m. spring and fall 9:30–5:00 p.m. summer. Largest site of its kind in N. America, built and used by ancient culture 4,000 years ago. Research continuing, 3 B.C. carbon dates obtained; ancient inscription of Iberians and Celts deciphered. Trails to astronomical stones, sighting platforms, viewing ramp. Snack bar, gift shop, museum. Adm: $4.00 adults, $3.00 students and sr. cits., $1.25 children 6–12. Tel: 893–8300.

Mr Colin McFadyean has sent me this advertisement from *Summer Week*, a New Hampshire paper, for 22 September 1983. So travellers in search of the American past, as you drive north on Interstate 93 about 10 miles across the boundary between Massachusetts and New Hampshire, take Exit 3 on to Route 111, and soon you will find signs to *America's Stonehenge*. But when you get there you will find a collection of curious colonial buildings of the seventeenth and eighteenth centuries claiming to be 'a giant megalithic astronomical complex built over 4,000 years ago'!

The extravagant claims made for pre-Columbian invaders continue to mount in improbability, although we felt that in New York the bookstalls in Grand Central Station and the bookshops on Fifth Avenue (alas, Brentano's no more!) were not displaying so many dotty books of the Fell/von Däniken genre as they did a few years ago; but there were still plenty of them!

And the interpretation of alleged inscriptions carries on apace. We have just been sent the March 1983 issue of the magazine *Wonderful West Virginia*; its cover has a colour photograph captioned, 'Shortly after sunrise on 22 December 1982, the sun illuminated the entire Wyoming Country Petroglyph', which looks to an impartial observer (that's the Editor) like natural and/or native American Indian scribings. Professor Barry Fell has, to our continuing astonishment, deciphered these rock-marks and finds that there are, surprisingly, *three* languages represented. The main inscription is in Ogam which, Fell claims, says: 'At the time of sunrise a ray grazes the notch on the left side on Christmas Day. A Feast-day of the Church, the first season of the year. The season of the Blessed Advent of the Saviour Lord Christ. Behold, he is born of Mary, a woman.'

This is indeed, as Ida Jane Gallagher says, an 'astounding message' to find on a rock surface in West Virginia. Fell also found, near by, an inscription in Algonquian saying, 'Glad Tidings', and an inscription in a third script which says, 'Information for regulating the calendar by observing the reversal of the sun's course.' This, he tells us, is in Tifinag, 'a Scandinavian Bronze Age script that linguists have identified in Canada, Great Britain, Libya and North Africa'.

All my eye and Betty Martin: but worse is to come. The *Publications* of the Epigraphic Society of America have now come our way and include an astonishing decipherment of the Glozel inscriptions – astonishing or even astounding. Donald Buchanan of Vienna, Virginia, finds some of the inscriptions to deal with problems of sexual potency. We will return to the archaeo-pornography of Glozel in the next issue, when we may also have news of the excavations which Dr Flouest conducted in a Glozelian site last summer.

How can we as serious dedicated archaeologists cope with this insidious nonsense? Two ways are by writing books and teaching. For the last few years Professor Stephen Williams has been running a course of lectures at Harvard called 'Fantastic Archaeology' – his class this year is 180, and Cazeau and Scott have been running a comparable course in Buffalo.

This is all admirable, but if we sometimes despair that our efforts in lecturing, writing, broadcasting are not succeeding, what can we do? Take to drink? But what drink? Perhaps the Viking Vodka whose advertisement we print here, free, and untasted.

July 1984

❧ A highly recommended book is *The invention of tradition* edited by Eric Hobsbawm and Terence Ranger (Cambridge, 1983). The most hilariously funny story in the book is Trevor-Roper's account of the origins of the Scottish kilt, regarded by many as one of the ancient traditions of Scotland, but invented by Thomas Rawlinson, an ironmaster of Furness in Lancashire who built a furnace and cut down forests at Invergarry near Inverness in the years 1727–34. 'The kilt', Trevor-Roper writes, 'is a purely modern costume, first designed, and first worn, by an English Quaker industrialist... bestowed by him on the Highlanders in order not to preserve their traditional way of life but to ease its transformation: to bring them out of the heather and into the factory.... When the great rebellion of 1745 broke out, the kilt, as we know it, was a recent English invention, and "clan" tartans did not exist.'

❧ We said in our last issue that we had some curious things to reveal about the alleged decipherment of the Glozel tablets: suggesting that Glozel was a prehistoric sex-shop, which far exceeds the imaginary decipherments of Barry Fell and others, who have, so far as we and our research associates know, confined their invented readings of bogus runes and natural rock-scribings to decent matters. Not so Donald Buchanan.

The occasional *Publications* of the Epigraphic Society of America have now come our way: founded in Harvard in 1974, the Society is now run by the Editor, Professor Barry Fell, who, retired from Harvard, lives in California; and is described as 'a major international vehicle for reporting the discovery and decipherment of ancient inscriptions, especially those of the Americas'.

That most archaeologists and readers of ANTIQUITY think there are no ancient inscriptions in N. America is hardly worth repeating: and it comes as no surprise that Volume 10 (1982) of the Society's *Publications* contains an article by Fell himself on 'Punic and Ogam inscriptions in Pennsylvania and Texas'. What does come as a surprise to us, case-hardened as we are and cynically prepared for the junk archaeology that daily rattles through our letter-box, is an article by Donald Buchanan, of Vienna, Virginia, entitled 'A preliminary decipherment of the Glozel inscriptions'. Buchanan complains that Dr Morlet (whom God preserve together with Dr Strabismus!) even published some of the inscriptions upsidedown (but does it matter which way you look at these 1924–7 forgeries?). He concludes that Glozel 'was some sort of bazaar, whether seasonal or permanent is not known. Since the language was Semitic and the script Iberic, it would appear that Iberian Punic merchants were operating a trading centre and dealing with a predominantly Celtic population. The bazaar dealt in livestock, devices to ensure sexual potency [!! Ed.], various salves and ointments, curative charms and amulets, and primitive tools suitable for customers engaged primarily in agriculture and animal husbandry.'

With this bland and entirely invented account of Glozel we turned with eagerness to Buchanan's decipherment of these bogus inscriptions. It is almost unbelievable what this man has made of the Fradin-Morlet forgeries and we must quote his fantasies verbatim:

Four artifacts which are…rings of relatively soft schist. Their size is not given, but it is believed that they are too small to be bracelets and too large to be finger-rings. In fact as the decipherments clearly show, they are primitive erection rings [*sic*!]. The first three inscriptions read from left to right: the last from right to left. [What does it matter? We thought they were upsidedown anyhow. – Ed.]

49/2. To make hard the lance of love.
50/1. To assist in approaching erection.
50/2. To restore potency to drooping desire.
51/3. To prolong arousal so that a scrawny penis can grow.

But this is porno-archaeology, not merely pseudo-archaeology. What lies behind the mental structure of men like Fell and Buchanan who can find the name of the Saviour Jesus Christ in natural marks in Virginia and flaccid pricks on upsidedown Glozelian inscriptions? If Buchanan is to be believed, and we believe nothing of his article, Glozel must really have been a bizarre bazaar.

Lionel H. Atkinson of Yorkshire tells us that he is the English representative of the Epigraphic Society of America and says 'over the past few months Barry Fell has deciphered many of the Cup and Ring marked rocks situated on Ilkley Moor and from this work we intend to publish a joint paper'. We await with interest this paper as the possibly ultimate folly in this kind of bogus archaeology. Is Ilkley Moor to be an Iberian bazaar or a Libyan bawdy-house? And will the cup and ring marks be found to speak to us in Berbero-Celtic? Perhaps they will say: Ogam, Onan, Odam. But we are prepared to be told of a prehistoric sex-shop in a Berber bazaar on Ilkley Moor. Surely there must come a moment when these archaeological lunatic-fringers from California to Cornwall will look in their shaving-mirrors (to plagiarize the *Sunday Express* 'Crossbencher' column) and ask: 'Whom are we fooling? Can it be ourselves?'

November 1984

❦ The Greek Government has officially asked the British Government for the return of the Elgin Marbles and the present British Government has declined to do so. Mr Neil Kinnock, the present leader of Her Majesty's Opposition, says that when the Labour Party is in power it will immediately return the Marbles to Greece. We wonder: we do not rule out the probability of this happening one day.

We are always reminded that the 1963 British Museum Act expressly forbids the Trustees from disposing of objects in their care and that this is the principal stumbling-block which prevents the return of the Marbles. We do not think so: we think it is the Trustees' view of the principle of restoring cultural property. But the Trustees have recently changed their views on the return of foreign antiquities by agreeing to the permanent loan to Egypt of a 3,000-year-old stone fragment, part of the original beard of the Sphinx at Giza. The British Museum says that the beard fragment is being given to Egypt as part of a loan and exchange agreement and that the Museum is to have the body of a jackal from Thebes in exchange.

A spokesman for the Museums Association (*The Observer*, 13 May 1984) says, 'It is a change of nuance, a sort of bowing to the International Council of Museums and to UNESCO. Obviously it's a permanent loan: they are virtually giving it back.'

The discussions for the return of the Sphinx's beard have gone on for two years and have been closely followed by other countries, such as Nigeria, who want the return of a priceless Benin bronze mask, and Ghana, who want back the Ashanti royal regalia. Other countries in Europe have agreed to return antiquities: France in 1980 returned to Iraq fragments of Babylonian codes, and Holland in 1978 returned Hindu and Buddhist sculptures to Indonesia.

Mr Salah Stetie, Lebanese Chairman of UNESCO's committee for the return of cultural property, argues for the return of special and selected objects which have 'a fundamental significance to a country's cultural tradition', and says that from all the museums in Europe and America these would only number a few among their hundreds of thousands of objects. This seems to us a very good argument and may prevail. We hope so.

☏ Lascaux, discovered by accident in September 1940, and opened to the public in 1948, was justly one of the great tourist attractions of Western Europe for many years. In the early sixties 2,000 visitors a day went to see these unbelievably beautiful and moving prehistoric paintings made by Magdalenian artists 17,000 years ago. In 1963 the cave had to be closed to the public and will never again be reopened to them. The brilliant idea was thought up of making a replica: Lascaux II was created and opened to the public in the autumn of 1983.

We ourselves visited Lascaux II on 14 June this year. When we got there at 9.30 a.m. there were already between 30 and 40 people waiting to get in when the gates opened at 10. The entrance free is 22 francs which also includes admission to the centre of prehistoric art at Le Thot, 7 km away. The site is open from 10 to 12 and 2 to 5.30 each day (except Monday). Visits are in parties of 40 and the conducted tour, with French-speaking guide, lasts 40 minutes. Our ticket was no. 122,406.

Lascaux II is brilliantly done and everyone deserves the greatest praise for the work carried out, especially the main painter, Monique Peytral.

As we wrote elsewhere (*The Times*, 5 July 1984): 'Have we in England a lesson to learn from the successful creation of Lascaux II? Why not create a facsimile of Stonehenge, that other great wonder of prehistoric Europe? Stonehenge B could be built within sight of the original with a museum and information centre. The original would then be forever banned to the public – even those bogus midsummer druids. This is not a new idea but Lord Montagu's Heritage team should visit Montignac and see the happy crowds at Lascaux II.'

A few miles away from Lascaux I and II the crowds still pack into Rouffignac: and now we can all study its paintings and engravings at our leisure in the well-illustrated *L'Art pariétal de Rouffignac: la grotte aux cent mammouths* by Claude Barrière (Paris, 1982). This volume, which has a preface by Professor Nougier, is *Mémoire no. IV* of the Institut d'art préhistorique de Toulouse, published under the auspices of the Fondation Singer-Polignac.

As a record of what is at present on the walls of Rouffignac it is invaluable. As a critical analysis of the circumstances surrounding the discovery of this controversial site (and Nougier and Robert are now arguing publicly as to who should take the credit for the 1956 discovery), and the world's awareness of it in the previous sixty years, we are told practically nothing. A conspiracy of silence and deliberate misrepresentation disgracefully mars page 11 which purports to set out the history of the discovery of the site. We are told that the Guerre des Mammouths is over and that

Un débat scientifique sur place a lieu en septembre avec tous les grands noms de la Préhistoire, il conclut à l'authenticité des oeuvres pariétales de la grotte de Rouffignac.

We well remember that strange visit to Rouffignac on 12 September 1956. All the great names in prehistoric archaeology were certainly not there and some, great and small, left profoundly disquieted and declined to sign the document of authentication – which was however signed by many Spanish archaeological students who happened to be on a field trip to Dordogne at the time!

Barrière and Nougier triumphantly refer to the discovery of the site on 26 June 1956. They do not refer to the photograph printed by Bernard Pierret in his *Le Périgord souterrain* (1953) which was reproduced in Glyn Daniel, *The Hungry Archaeologist in France* (London, 1963) and shows him camped in front of the rhinoceros frieze taken more than two years before its 'discovery'! We are still waiting for an explanation of why Martel, the great French speleologist who knew Rouffignac well, the abbé Breuil, who visited it in 1915, and the abbé Glory, who visited the site in 1948 with Dr Koby of Bâle, made no mention of having seen any paintings or engravings.

Barrière pays no attention to the testimony of Colonel Arthur Walmesley-White who visited Rouffignac, with the Cambridge University Speleological Society in March 1939 – a group of keen, healthy, vigorous, sharp-eyed young men trained in geology and archaeology who had already spent a week visiting all the other painted and engraved caves in south-west France. He says, 'We never saw any drawings or paintings and . . . the owner didn't know of any' (*in lit.*, 27 September 1956). Barrière cannot, however, brush aside the testimony of Pierret and his colleagues. He writes:

Si certains ont 'vu' les dessins de Rouffignac, aucun de ceux-là n'a su et compris ce que cela représentait, même les spéléologues de Périgueux qui ont refait le plan de la grotte, longuement explorée alors de dizaines de visites.

But Pierret said many times that he didn't comment on them because he knew them to be of recent date; and Séverin Blanc, who made visits to Rouffignac every year, says how surprised he was to see these animals appear on walls that had previously been unpainted!

It is now nearly thirty years since the alleged 'discovery' at 15.00 hours on 26 June 1956. It is infamous that Nougier and Robert have not felt able, after all these years, to tell the real story of Rouffignac in the twenty years before 1956; and Barrière compounds this infamy, which enormously detracts from the value of his book. François Bordes once told us that maquisards sheltering in caves had almost certainly added to the prehistoric art in many sites, including Rouffignac. There is no suggestion in Barrière that any of Rouffignac is other than authentic, but anyone looking through his plates will wonder again and again and remember the remark of Mademoiselle G. Henri-Martin: 'There are two styles represented at Rouffignac – one is a pastiche copy of other palaeolithic art, the other is *Babar l'Eléphant*.' We believed her at the time but now think that there *may* have been some original authentic paintings and engravings improved and added to by maquisards. And yet, and yet, and this is the question we always come back to in discussion of Rouffignac with our French colleagues: if there were original authentic paintings why were they missed by Martel, Breuil, Glory, Koby and Séverin Blanc?

The 'Holiday Which' Guide to France (1982) says of Rouffignac, 'whose Magdalenian paintings were only recently discovered among fakes and multitudes of graffiti'. This is the disappointing and unsatisfactory nature of Barrière's book: it assumes the palaeolithic date of everything. But are Mammoths 107, 138 and 174, Bouquetin 104, and Bison 209 datable except on subjective grounds? The cave has been open for years and camped in for years. Surely Figs. 8 and 9 of Gallery G are the work of modern man?

March 1985

❦ The idea of a Stonehenge replica which was mentioned in these pages last year is being taken seriously by English Heritage, and has captured the imagination of columnists and cartoonists. The idea is not new: indeed in the twenties, when wiser counsels prevailed, those amusing lunatic bogus

Druids (who are now allowed by a misguided Home Office to cavort at Stonehenge at Midsummer) were about to be, rightly we think, banned from performing their far from ancient invented nineteenth-century rites in the 5,000-year-old monument, suggested the construction of a replica Stonehenge not far away. If Stonehenge B is constructed this would be an ideal place for Druidic junketings: replica Druids in a replica Stonehenge.

The Sunday Times reports (7 October 1984) that a study carried out recently by the construction firm, Wimpey, for a television programme, calculated that it would cost £332,640 to rebuild the monument, using thirty men. Why don't we have Stonehenge B on Salisbury Plain in time for the World Archaeological Congress in September 1986? Meanwhile we learn that engineers and astronomers at the University of Missouri have erected on the University's campus, at Rolla, a half-scale partial reconstruction of Stonehenge: it was dedicated on 20 June 1984, the date of the summer solstice [Plate 3].

Construction of the replica was begun in October 1983. It is built of 160 tonnes of granite but to the proper dimensions, 'by the university's waterjet equipment'. The monument incorporates, we are told, many of the features of the original, but includes two 'capabilities' the original did not possess. There is low-level lighting for night use: and the Rolla Stonehenge is provided with an aperture for an analemma. During the year, the noon sun shining through this opening describes a figure of eight on 'the horizontal and vertical stones at the base of the trilithon' (*Archaeology*, September 1984).

If we do have a replica Stonehenge it should be a copy of what the monument is at the moment, and full scale. We don't want any interference from those who think they know what it originally looked like or what it should have looked like, or what it ought to have been. Down with Hawkins and Hoyle: up with the firm of Atkinson, Piggott, Chippindale, Merlin, and Wimpey. There are over eighteen months between now and the opening of the World Archaeological Congress: enough time to build several Stonehenges. But one will do: we deplore Peter Simple's suggestion in *The Daily Telegraph* that we should build Stonehenges all over England to cut the tourist load on Salisbury Plain.

July 1985

❡ Evelyn Waugh's *Labels* has just been reissued in the Penguin Travel Library: it was first published in 1930 and recorded his views as he travelled about the Mediterranean, the Middle East, and North Africa. The art of

Ancient Egypt excited him and he wrote:

There seem to me few things more boring than the cult of mere antiquity. I would view with the utmost equanimity the obliteration of all those cromlechs and barrows and fosses of our remote ancestors which litter the English countryside: whenever I see Gothic lettering on the ordnance survey map I set my steps in a contrary direction. I wish all the rectors who spend their days in scratching up flint arrowheads and bits of pottery and horrible scraps of tessellated pavement would bury them again and go back to their prayers. But Egyptian antiquities are quite another matter. There is nothing here to evoke that patronising interest with which we arm ourselves in our surveys of ancient British remains.... How clever of Dr So-and-So to guess that that little splinter of bone in the glass case was not really a little splinter of bone but a Pictish needle – and how clever of the Picts all those years ago to think of making a needle out of a little splinter of bone.... There is nothing of that in our appreciation of Egyptian remains, particularly the incomparable collection recently unearthed in the tomb of Tutankhamen. Here we are in touch with a civilization of splendour and refinement, of very good sculpture, superb architecture, opulent and discreet ornament, and, so far as one can judge, of cultured and temperate social life.

An interesting passage: Evelyn Waugh was always deliciously opinionated and often disgracefully ignorant. Lancing and Oxford had not taken him to the Alfred Jewel in the Ashmolean or to the remarkable treasures of the pre-Roman barbarians in the British Museum, Saint-Germain-en-Laye, and the Musée Borely: he thought, as many people do, of our pre-Roman ancestors as groove-and-splinter men, forgetting Lascaux, Gavrinis, and the Trawsfynydd tankard, human beings and artists described in our current number by Stuart Piggott in a memorable phrase as 'stinking likeable witless intelligent incalculable real awful *people*'.

November 1985

ꙮ Stonehenge stole the headlines for days between 1 June and Midsummer this year. English Heritage announced that the pop festival which had disfigured and disgraced Stonehenge for the last ten summers would not be allowed this year or in future years. In 1984 during the pop festival trees were hacked down, cars burned out and Portakabins petrol-bombed; holes were dug through barrows and motor-cycle tracks scored across them, ritual and funerary sites disturbed as described by Professor Barry Cunliffe in a letter to *The Guardian* (19 June) where he writes of the Stonehenge area as 'probably the richest archaeological landscape in Europe' and Stonehenge 'a monument of international importance'.

Writing in these pages recently Christopher Chippindale said: 'A show of determined force is, regrettably, probably the only way to see the festival off. . . . Given the very public violence in the recent British mining strike, and the ugly mood the festival has shown in the past, a spectacular punch-up at Stonehenge is a very real possibility.' How true a prophecy that, sadly, was!

Late in May notices like this one were stuck to posters all over Britain:

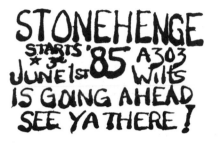

The Wiltshire police dealt firmly with the invaders, and the so-called Battle of Stonehenge, in all its violence, was seen on British television. The pop festival desecrators were routed and the Midsummer Solstice passed off without any undue incident. It was raining, which helped to dampen insurrectional enthusiasm. The *Times* reporter, Tim Jones, gave an amusing account of the goings-on (22 June):

As dawn broke on the longest day of the year, the hippies who had threatened to invade Stonehenge remained huddled at their sodden encampment 20 miles away. . . . The beginning of the solstice was celebrated near the monument by about 50 members of the Pagans for Peace movement who, after marching from London, were allowed to stand behind barbed wire protecting the stones. Shivering beneath their protective blankets they held hands and chanted 'I am at one with the infinite sun'. The object of their worship remained hidden behind the cloud which dispensed unremitting rain. Police made one arrest when a lone pagan attempted to gain access by trying to cut his way through the wire. . . . Mr Sid Rawle, the unofficial spokesman for the hippies . . . said that 'English Heritage . . . was responsible by its action for the terrible weather'!

Powerful though the National Trust, English Heritage, and the Wiltshire police are, it is a mistake to suppose they have supernatural rainmaking powers. Nevertheless, we are grateful to them for their wisdom and resolution in maintaining law and order at Stonehenge which is a sort of prehistoric Westminster Abbey, Westminster Cathedral and St Paul's all rolled into one. No one would dream of allowing hippies to camp around these London Christian temples or permit neo-Druids to perform their rites of worship in them. Remembering the police presence that was necesssary this summer we print a delightful photograph by Mike Wells taken in 1976, before the present troubles [Plate 4].

July 1986

❧ We begin as, alas, we must do if ANTIQUITY is to be a record of and comment on the current world of archaeology, with the regrettably sad affair of what an Australian colleague calls 'the shameful scandalous shambles of the Southampton World [*sic*] Archaeological Congress'. Things were on the boil as we were passing the final proofs of the March number in mid-February: we hastily printed an insert notice which we now reprint for the textual record:

We drew attention (ANTIQUITY, 1985, 4) to the second announcement of the XIth Congress of the International Union of Prehistoric and Protohistoric Sciences to be held in Southampton and London from 1–7 September 1986. The third and final announcement was sent out in October of last year and stated that the UK Executive Committee had decided that it could not accept South African participation, and this decision was ratified by the UK National Committee. The Executive of the IUPPS, at its meeting in Paris on 17 January, insisted that its rules precluded any ban on any country, declined to give the Southampton Congress its blessing, and transferred the XIth Congress to Germany where it will meet in Mainz under the Presidency of Professor K. Böhner and the Secretaryship of Professor K. Weidemann.

Following a meeting in London on 8 February of the UK National Executive, Professor Ucko announced that a Congress will, nevertheless, be held in Southampton from 1–7 September. As we go to press (15 February) it would appear that there may be two conferences – one in Southampton and London, the other in Mainz, but not, we hope, at the same time. This is a curious state of affairs and we hope to give more detailed news in our July issue.

The sad saga is not a complicated or disputed story. It was when the original British XIth Congress was well under way, and the third announcement shows how efficiently it has been organized with such detailed care and imagination, that four groups in Southampton – the Association of University Teachers, the students, the local anti-apartheid group, and the City Council – declared they would oppose the Congress if scholars from South Africa and Namibia were allowed to attend. The Executive Committee – six good men and true – with the greatest heart-searching and unhappiness, allowed themselves to be blackmailed and, under duress, imposed a ban on South African participation. This was the *trahison des clercs*. How they expected to get away with this it is difficult to understand. Paragraph 3 of the statutes of the IUPPS states, uncompromisingly, that its aim is 'la collaboration de savants de tous les pays à des entreprises pouvant contribuer à l'avancement des sciences préhistoriques et protohistoriques'; and the explicit instructions from the IUPPS for the 1986 Congress stated, again uncompromisingly, that Britain must accept 'all *bona fide* scientists at its venue, irrespective of nationality, philosophical conviction or religious faith'.

In a letter to Professor P. J. Ucko, the British National Secretary, on 28 October 1985, Professor Desmond Clark wrote:

It is both surprising and disturbing that the National Executive Committee, a group of distinguished academics, should have been persuaded to discriminate against scientists from South Africa because of the apartheid policies of the Government under which they have to live and work. Surely it must be repugnant to all true academics that workers who would participate in a conference in their personal capacity, and in no way as official representatives of their governments, should be excluded from the international community of science on the sole grounds of the political policies of those governments. On those grounds why not also exclude most Eastern Europeans? ... The Executive Committee's decision amounts to a slur on the hitherto enviable reputation of Britain which has always stood out for full and free exchange of ideas between scientists, irrespective of the policies of their governments.

The British National Executive were slow to realize what a disastrous boob they had made. They were supported in their wrong-headed views by the British National Committee but this availed them nothing. The Paris meeting of the Executive of IUPPS on 17 January removed its *imprimatur* from the British Congress and this was overwhelmingly confirmed by the 200 members of the Permanent Council: only eight approved the ban, eight abstained (there were three who said they could not understand what it was all about!). The XIth Congress will now be in Mainz in 1987 (probably September).

The mistake lay in knuckling under to the blackmailing organizations in Southampton. The British National Executive should have had the courage either to cancel or postpone the Congress, or to transfer it to some more liberal venue such as Oxford, Cambridge, or London. But they are not the villains: the villains are the students, the Southampton branch of the AUT and the Southampton City Council. For years Southampton has had a high name in the world of archaeology: it was the city of O. G. S. Crawford and its new Department of Archaeology was soon made internationally famous by its first two distinguished Professors, Barry Cunliffe and Colin Renfrew. In order to get our facts right we wrote to all the organizations in Southampton concerned with imposing the South

African ban. No replies from any official of the Southampton City Council, to their eternal disgrace. Replies came from the Southampton Association of University Teachers and from the Students Union of a confused and misinformed nature showing that not only were their hearts in the wrong place but their heads buried in the sands of irresponsible obscurantism. The Vice-Chancellor of the University of Southampton, while himself personally agreeing with the ban, pointed out that his University was not itself committed in any way. He had written to *The Times* to explain this but his letter had not been published: the 'Thunderer' has been slow to develop these interesting academic issues since it went down river to Wapping!

Nature and *Science* have carefully followed the Southampton dispute with both comment and correspondence. Barbara Bender and others, mainly from University College London, wrote a curious and unconvincing letter (*Nature*, 319, 532, 1986) supporting the banning of South African scholars from Southampton and asking, 'What is it that you are asking us to tolerate?' In a sharp reply Mandelstam, Harrison, and Hall say: 'The answer is simple: the presence of about two dozen archaeologists most of whom oppose apartheid. What is more they do so in South Africa where – unlike University College London – it takes courage.'

And so it goes on and will go on for a very long while. British archaeologists are divided into two camps and the name of British archaeology is not good at present in most European, American, Asian, and Australian contacts that we have or hear about. The 1985–6 Southampton crisis will eventually become a matter of sad history. Professor Ucko, formerly Secretary of the British XIth International Congress, is pressing ahead with a Southampton Congress in September 1986, excommunicate and in international disrepute. The new Executive consists of Professor Michael Day (Chairman), Derek Hayes (Treasurer), Professor Peter Ucko (Secretary), Dr Timothy Champion, Dr Juliet Clutton-Brock, Dr Andrew Fleming, Professor David Harris, Dr Ian Hodder, Dr Michael Rowlands, Professor Thurstan Shaw, and Dr Stephen Shennan – a highly respected and respectable group of scholars, though perhaps not as star-studded with world archaeologists as the President, Vice-Presidents, and members of the British Executive who have already resigned.

We wish the rebel Southampton Congress success, although as the present Editor of a journal committed to the free and liberal exchange of ideas by archaeologists of any persuasion and from any political regime, it would be indelicate to the point of impropriety to take part. But so much good work has gone into the planning of the Southampton meeting that some good is bound to come out of it; and those of us whose principles prevent us from being there will read the printed proceedings with excitement and interest.

Meanwhile we cannot disguise the fact that, alas, Southampton is at the moment a dirty word in the world of archaeology, and a distinguished Danish colleague said to us recently, 'I hope we will not have another Southampton at Mainz or Madrid.' That is the real issue behind the Southampton *pagaille*: can we be sure that we can, in future, organize international congresses in Britain, Germany, Spain or elsewhere where scholars from all countries can attend? We ought to remind ourselves of the saying attributed to Voltaire: 'I disapprove of what you say but I will defend to the death your right to say it.' We disapprove of the political regimes of South Africa, Russia, Libya, Poland and many Latin American countries, but will defend to the death the right of scholars from these countries to associate freely with the rest of the world.

Enough – or probably more than enough – about all this. And yet the rights and wrongs of *l'affaire Southampton* will be debated hotly all this year and for some while to come. We have set out our account and our views. Our successor as Editor may well have different views. Looking back on it all from the early summer of this year as we write, we concur with Georges Bernano's sentence in *Les Grands Cimetières sous la Lune*: 'La colère des imbéciles remplit le monde' (today the air is filled with the impatience of the ignorant). We offer an English translation for the benefit of some of the members of the four Southampton organizations who wrecked the British XIth Congress which we had been looking forward to with such enthusiasm and excitement since it was first planned by the late Professor Ole Klindt-Jensen and ourselves over dinner in Aarhus twelve years ago.

But some good has come out of the Southampton schemozzle. The British Academy have declared that all Academy conference grants in future would be on condition that members from any country world-wide would be welcome, and the Society of Antiquaries of London on 12 December 1985 passed the following resolution:

The Council of the Society of Antiquaries of London deplores the exclusion of South African participants from the World Archaeological Congress 1986, since this contravenes the principle of the free interchange of ideas. Although it accepts that this action of the Executive Committee of the Congress was taken unwillingly and under duress, and solely in order to avoid the cancellation of the Congress, it has decided to withdraw the Society's name from the list of sponsors for the Congress and to make no further financial contributions. The Society's future support of such international events will be conditional upon an undertaking by the organizers that the principle of the free interchange of ideas will not be contravened.

So we all know where we stand if and when we are asked to run another international conference. And perhaps by 1991 and, please God, long before, the hateful apartheid regime will have ceased to divide South Africa, the world, and archaeology.

November 1986

❦ Endless books pour from our presses introducing archaeology, describing sites, misrepresenting the past: we have often thought that there should be a special prize for the Worst Archaeological Book of the Year – the WABY prize (nothing to do with that elegant and distinguished Danish lady, Hofdame Kontesse Waby Armfelt, FSA). A high contender for this low award this year would be Gaynor Francis's *The First Stonehenge* for which the publishers, Christopher Davies of Sketty, Swansea, have the effrontery to charge £9.95. While all these dotty, ill-informed and badly researched books are appearing, why does no one have the good sense and humour to publish a book of archaeological jokes? Dr Warwick Bray wrote a fine article entitled 'Archaeological Humour: the Private Joke and the Public Image' in (ed.) J. D. Evans, B. Cunliffe and C. Renfrew, *Antiquity and Man* (London, 1981). This should be expanded into a book ideal for a Christmas archaeological stocking. A book of funny drawings would not only be an amusing exercise in itself, but a reminder that archaeologists, despite their talk of process, status, chieftains, territorial markers, leys and lines to the moon, are as human and fallible and funny as Asterix.

❦ And now, no more Editorial rumblings and bumblings from us. With this issue we, Editor and Production Editor, leave the scene, pursued by bears, probably the angry ghosts of Crawford and Wheeler. The curtain goes up on 1 March 1987 with a new Producer/Director/Editor all rolled into the one highly competent young energetic person of Christopher Chippindale. We wish him and the future of ANTIQUITY well. What ANTIQUITY needs in these difficult days of rising costs, necessarily increasing subscriptions and declining subscribers is one or two individuals or public bodies who would give money to our Trustees so that ANTIQUITY can go on as a totally independent prestige journal, and survey archaeology and archaeologists in a personal but responsible way without fear or favour.

Crawford was fortunate to die *en poste*. We, still alive, have had our obituary written by Philip Howard in *The Times*, 17 May of this year, in an article entitled 'Digging up the Future'. We quote from it:

Glyn Daniel...is about to retire as editor of *Antiquity*, the archaeological journal that is caviar to the field of learned publications. It was founded as a private venture by O. G. S. Crawford 60 years ago. For the 30 years since he died it has been edited by Professor Daniel and his wife, Ruth, as essential reading not just for archaeologists and historians, but for everybody with any interest in the past...*Antiquity* is remarkable for its scholarly sprightliness. The book reviews are notoriously honest, in contrast with the log-rolling in most academic journals where, ladling butter from alternate tubs, Stubbs butters Freeman, Freeman butters Stubbs...Its style and authority have always attracted the best writers. Charles Lamb was ahead of his time in a letter to B. W. Proctor on 22 January 1829: 'When my sonnet was rejected, I exclaimed, "Damn the age; I will write for Antiquity!"'

Philip Howard goes on to say succinctly in his inimitable style something which encapsulates what Crawford and the present Editor feel about the past and the necessity of a journal like ANTIQUITY: 'The past is a prologue to our world today', he writes.

Those who say that the past is a bucket of ashes, and that history is bunk, are not fully human. We cannot make a success of our world, which we have on a rent for a brief lease, unless we try to understand it, and ourselves, and what makes us tick. That is why archaeology is not just fascinating, but also useful, quite as relevant as computer studies or supply-side economics. Neophiliacs who do not reverence age do not take Hobbes's point that our present is the oldest age.

The essence of that paragraph could have been in Crawford's *Man and His Past* or for that matter Sir Thomas Browne's *Religio Medici*.

The world knows only too well what a special debt the present Editor owes to the Production Editor: indeed ANTIQUITY would not be what it now is without her devoted and unremitting care and relentless attention to detail. But for her a new Editor would have had to be appointed long ago.

Our thanks to all those in our printers and publishers, Heffers, who have helped, cared and cherished us for so long – and particularly Frank Collieson, that kind, wise *éminence grise* behind so many Cambridge authors and editors.

And now, *ave atque vale*: to parody Donne, 'Send not to know for whom the telephone bell in the ANTIQUITY office rings: it no longer rings for thee.'

Postscript (March 1960)

✿ A friend who has kindly read through the proofs of the present number of ANTIQUITY thinks that Dr Calvin Wells's *Study of Cremation* is rather strong meat – if that in itself is not an ill-considered phrase in this context – for most readers, and should be prefaced by the same sort of warning as, we are informed, appears before some television programmes, namely, 'Not suitable for children or adults of nervous disposition.' At first we did not think so, and yet, writing these words in a warm café in Amiens and watching the snow flaking past the window panes, we begin to wonder. Is it really a comforting thought for an Editor, who could be described in Dr Wells's objective terms as 'male, middle-aged, with a tendency to corpulency and a full head of hair' to realize that he will (*a*) burn rapidly, and (*b*) perhaps leave behind a large but curious Illington-type clinker of transformed keratin? With rich flames and hired tears they may solemnize our obsequies: but, Sir Thomas Browne, did you ever see those rich flames as gas-jets? We may, Sir Thomas, be carried out of the world with our feet forward, but how are we laid on the cremation bench? Is the cadaver (admirably objective word for use by all students of death and detection) laid prone or supine? Dr Wells will tell us, assisted as he was by the authorities of two modern crematoria 'with great courtesy and enthusiasm'. There is a marked lack of enthusiasm inside the café and the cold of the snow seems to be creeping in. *Garçon, un verre de Calvados, s'il vous plaît.* Shall I rather be pompous in the grave or splendid in ashes? Is cold clay to be preferred to the heat of those gas-jets? Let us settle on a collective tomb and the comfort that when my grave is broke up again, it will be for some second guest to entertain. Yes, good old John Donne is more comforting than Dr Wells's gas-jets and Sir Thomas Browne's urns. And yet, it is but cold comfort. *Garçon, encore un verre . . .*

SOURCES OF PLATES

1 Irwin Scollar
2 British Library, London
3 University of Missouri-Rolla
4 Mike Wells
5 *The Times* (Brian Harris)
6 Roger-Viollet, Paris
7 Roger-Viollet, Paris
8 Metropolitan Museum of Art, New York
9 Metropolitan Museum of Art, New York
10 Anglia Television
11 Peggy Guido
12 Paul Jordan (Anglia Television)
13 Runestone Museum, Alexandria, Minnesota
14 Thames & Hudson
15 Gwil Owen

INDEX